NATURAL ATHEISM

NATURAL ATHEISM

David Eller

2004

American Atheist Press
Cranford, New Jersey

American Atheist Press
P. O. Box 5733
Parsippany, NJ 07054-6733

www.atheists.org

Front cover photograph courtesy of Freestockphotos.com
Back cover portrait of author, photograph by Anita Otey

Library of Congress Cataloging-in-Publication Data

Eller, David, 1959-
Natural atheism / David Eller.
p. cm.
Includes bibliographical references.
ISBN 1-57884-920-9
1. Atheism. I. Title.

BL2747.3.E55 2004
211'.8—dc22
2004005574

To the freethinkers who came before me,
and to the thinkers of the future, who will be truly free.

CONTENTS

PART III *The Applications*

INTRODUCTION

A Natural Atheist

I was born an Atheist. All humans are born Atheists. No baby born into the world arrives with specific religious beliefs or knowledge. Such beliefs and knowledge must be acquired, which means that they must first exist before and apart from the new life and that they must be presented to and impressed on the new suggestible mind — one that has no critical apparatus and no alternative views of its own. Human infants are like sponges, soaking up (not completely uncritically, but eagerly and effectively) whatever is there to be soaked up from their social environment. Small children in particular instinctively imitate the models that they observe in their childhood. Certainly, there was religion in the environment of my childhood, but I was not compelled to attend or practice any particular religion, and as I grew I never saw any reason to 'convert' to any particular religion. I have thus been an Atheist all my life. I am a natural Atheist.

Some people — Theists mostly — doubt whether one can be a natural Atheist. They claim that Atheism requires an active rejection of religious belief, which cannot occur without prior exposure or even commitment to religion. So a newborn is not yet an 'Atheist' but something other than an Atheist or Theist, they maintain — a 'pre-Theist' maybe. Atheism must be a choice. I see this argument as spurious and actually negatively motivated: Theists do not want to admit that they were once Atheists too and that they gave it up not by any choice they made but by the forces imposed on them by a religious world.

Not all adult Atheists are natural Atheists, and I claim no moral or intellectual superiority for being one. In fact, I have probably missed some of the powerful and acute experiences and issues of Atheism by not having gone through the 'conversion' to Theism and subsequent 'deconversion' back to Atheism. And conversion it is — there is a distinct process of instilling in the mind of the child a religious system and thereby transforming that child from a natural question-poser to a socialized question-rejecter. The entire process of religious conversion is one of accepting a set of answers and an associated community and worldview in which further questions are not necessary and may even be actively discouraged. In the worst cases, this community and worldview entail a disparagement of the human mind and its capacity to ask and know altogether; asking questions, especially tough questions 'outside the box' — ones that question whether this is the right box or whether there is a box at all — may be anathema to the whole conversion process and outcome.

Although there are no hard numbers that I have ever seen, it is presumable that most Atheists are not natural Atheists but 'born-again' Atheists — people who have been through the conversion experience and who have 'deconverted' or 'reconverted' back to their original Atheism. However, born-again Atheism must be different from natural Atheism because of the experiences that have transpired in the life of the recovered Atheist. Above all, the recovered Atheist is a former Theist, so he or she has lived that life, believed those beliefs, been part of that community and that world. I can honestly say that I do not know what that is like. But I know from my friendships with (and in one case, marriage to) former Theists that the experience was not always pleasant and that the transition back to Atheism, although not always sudden and traumatic, was often painful and difficult but ultimately liberating. Born-again Atheists possess an intimate knowledge of religion from the inside, but the price of that knowledge is often an anger or bitterness toward those who indoctrinated them and the doctrines they were coerced to conform to. But almost universally, the benefit of deconversion is an experience — sometimes for the first time — of liberation and of the right to claim one's mind for oneself.

I am at once happy and sad that I have not had that profound deconversion experience for myself.

What is Atheism?

At first, it would seem transparently obvious what Atheism is. Atheism is the lack of belief in any god(s). Not just the lack of belief in the Christians' god; this is the 'dominant god' or 'majority god' in the American scene, but it is not the first or only god that has been claimed by a group of believers. In fact, through history and around the world, thousands upon thousands of gods have been worshipped and forgotten (see for example Jordan 1993), and each god was believed in equally fervently by somebody. And each god appeared to do practical and miraculous things before the believers, supposedly confirming that god's reality and power.

Atheists do not believe in the Christian god or any other of these past or present gods. It would perhaps be whimsical to argue that Christians do not believe in any of these other past or present gods either. That does not make them Atheists, exactly, but it should perhaps make them pause for a moment and reflect on why they discount or reject all of the world's religions but one. If they thought hard and honestly about why they dismiss those religions, they would understand why we dismiss theirs. We only disbelieve in one more god than they do. And at the same time, it is not whimsical at all to point out that they disbelieve all the other religions, for, from the perspective of those religions, they *are* Atheists. Muslims and devotees of other religions have occasionally labeled Christians Atheists, and vice versa. Christians have even labeled each other — heretical groups and splinter sects — Atheists; at one time or another, Catholics called Protestants Atheists, Protestants called Catholics Atheists, Protestant groups called each other Atheists, and everyone called Unitarians and Quakers Atheists. An Atheist, in one sense, is anyone who does not believe what you believe. It often does not mean 'believing in no god' but 'believing in the wrong god.' Or, since all other gods but yours are false, then that is saying the same thing — believing in any other god is believing in no god, in a non-god.

But this is not what we Atheists do, and this is not what we want Atheism to be. Yet, while it would seem like Atheism is the most straightforward thing in the world, it is actually a fairly contentious concept. There are those, for instance, who maintain that Atheism is a belief system too or even a religion.

Atheism is not a belief system, though, because it is not a system at all; there is nothing 'systematic' about it. A system is a structure with multiple parts in co-relation and cooperation. But Atheism does not even have multiple parts; it has one part — lack of belief in god(s). That a 'lack of belief' could be a belief too is preposterous and, as I maintain throughout this book, Atheists do not 'believe' there is no god, they conclude on the basis of fact and logic that there is none. This has nothing to do with belief whatsoever.

Still, some critics, and even some Atheists, say that Atheism is a religion and/or that Atheists are religious. That depends on your definition of religion, I suppose. I know people — even intelligent, liberal people — who define religion as anything you feel strongly about. In that case, money can be a religion to some folks, sex a religion to others, and football a religion to yet others. This is, of course, silly. A slightly more sensible claim is that a religion is any statement about god(s). Then, since Atheism holds that there are no gods, it is talking about gods and is therefore a religion. But that is frivolous too. Religion is not just any old statement about god(s), and if there is a god, I am sure that he/she/it/they will not take kindly to such an attitude. A religion is specifically *a system of beliefs and 'knowledge' about what are accepted to be really existing supernatural, spiritual forces and / or beings and the associated rules, rituals, stories, symbols / objects, texts, officiates, sacred places, etc. that are entailed.* Atheism has none of these things.

One facetious response to this accusation is that Atheism is a religion in the same way that health is a disease or that peace is a war or that not collecting stamps is a hobby — that is, not another instance of it but the absence of it, the antithesis of it. This is amusing but also negative, not in the sense of being 'bad' or 'destructive' but in the sense of defining it in terms of what it is not instead of what it is. Atheism is not religion; it is non-religion, the absence of religion. But Atheism is more than non-religion; it is an affirmative stance, a condition of intellectual, personal, and moral freedom. In the same way, health is not just the absence of disease nor peace just the absence of war, but health and peace are positive conditions of strength, of well-being, of ability to do things and to live and enjoy your life. So too, Atheism is a psychological and existential condition of strength and well-being and ability to live and enjoy life and use your mind and trust yourself.

It has always been unclear to me what the intention of calling Atheism a religion really is. If Theists think religion is good, then that is high praise; in fact, we should then qualify for federal funds and tax exemptions too. If we are a religion in any sense, we are entitled to toleration, First Amendment protections, and all the prestige that Theists think religions deserve. I'm sure they do not mean that. Probably they mean that Atheism is dogmatic, self-assured, intolerant, authoritarian, and other bad things. But if they think that those things are descriptive of religion, how can they be proud of their own religion? Are they really saying, 'Oh, you are just dogmatic, self-assured, intolerant, and authoritarian like us'? In other words, when they call Atheism a religion, do they mean that as a compliment or an insult? Perhaps they should rethink that particular criticism.

There are also those who think that Atheism is a claim in its own right, and an extreme claim at that. I know some Atheists who maintain that they are not Atheists because they do not adamantly and unswervingly declare that there is no god. They say, 'I don't believe in god, but I am not an Atheist.' What else then could they be? Some of these people are intelligent, articulate, even scientific folks, but for some reason they are under the impression that Atheism is something it is not. I have even tried to talk to them about it, but they stay stubborn in their conviction that Atheism is some strident and therefore indefensible position. One quoted to me a dictionary definition of Atheism as the insistence or certainty that there is no god. I responded to him that dictionaries are not always right, that they are often compiled by Theists, and that I as a self-conscious Atheist ought to know what I think. He was unswayed and, like many a Theist, discontinued the conversation: "Well, that's just the way it is."

Some 'freethinkers' or 'Agnostics' or 'Humanists' prefer those terms to 'Atheist' because of the stigma attached to the latter. I more than understand the stigma of Atheism, although most of it is wrong to the point of being funny if it were not so serious. Theists and even some crypto-Atheists

(Atheists who hide or deny their Atheism) believe that we are evil, immoral, licentious, unpatriotic, satanic (which is a religious concept!), criminal, and other pejorative terms like that. The truth is that there is no evidence that we are any of these things — certainly not in greater proportion than the rest of the (theistic) population, and some of them are just plain wrong. There is nothing unpatriotic about being an Atheist; I like to think we are the epitome of the principles of individual freedom and pursuit of conscience upon which America was founded. Most Atheists are not noticeably immoral but are typical householders, co-workers, neighbors, spouses, and friends — and besides, morality is always measured against some specific moral code, so if we are 'immoral' by the Christian moral standard, so what? In fact, it does not say much for Theists who think that their religious commandments are all that keep them from running amok. The fact that most of the time no one can tell an Atheist from a Theist suggests that we are not running amok. And the fact that preachers of many faiths in many countries are presently under scandal for rampant sex abuse of minors attests to the reality that religion is no guarantee of morality.

Even if Atheists are not demonized, we are often condemned and legally discriminated against. Following the 2002 federal court decision ruling that "under God" in the Pledge of Allegiance is unconstitutional, which it is, even public officials like Senator Robert Byrd called us "pernicious atheists," and the plaintiff in the case, Dr Michael Newdow, received hateful and sometimes threatening telephone calls. We are routinely castigated and told to get out of this 'Christian god-fearing' (and supposedly loving) country. And several states in this union actually still have language in their constitutions or other laws excluding Atheists (and non-Christians) from political office or other civil rights. Can you imagine if Byrd had singled out a racial or other group for his opprobrium, say, referring to African-Americans as 'pernicious blacks' or feminists as 'pernicious women'? Would we tolerate hateful and threatening messages to gays or the disabled or Jews? Would we accept the exclusion of any of these groups from civic life just because of their group membership? Of course not. Why then Atheists?

In the chapters that follow, I will illustrate what Atheism really is and how we Atheists should represent it publicly. I will show why Atheism is not only a good idea but almost certainly the right idea. We will investigate arguments for and against god(s), the process of reasoning to sound conclusions, concepts of Atheism and Agnosticism, science and religion, cultural relativism, and political and cultural issues of church/state separation, toleration, proselytization, and living an Atheist life. My goal and my hope is to show that Atheism is an affirmative as well as a true outlook and to guide people either to recover or to cherish their natural Atheism.

A Note on Usage

In this book I will regularly use the term 'god(s)' instead of 'god' or 'God,' as I have already done in this introductory section. I do this because, counter to some common arguments, 'god' is a general term for any very powerful spiritual being, and 'God' is the proper name of the Christian god. (By the way, this realization demolishes the foolish argument that references to 'God' in American politics, say, in the Pledge or in school prayer, are 'ceremonial deism' or even 'traditional rather than religious'; 'God' refers specifically and unmistakably to the Christian god, and Christians know it damned well.) Atheism, at least as it ought to be conceived, does not pick on Christianity or the Christian god. It questions the reality of all gods, whichever religion advances them. Therefore, to be accurate, and to remind the reader constantly that the Christian god is not the only one in town, I refer to god(s). When I refer specifically to the Christian god or when I quote from others who do, I will use the form 'God.'

Likewise, in the chapter on First Amendment 'separation,' I use the term 'church(es)/state separation' for the same reason. There is not one single church that is trying to get established or that the Constitution separates itself from, but many. *There is no such thing as 'church' just as there is no such thing as 'god' or as 'religion.'* Rather, there are churches, gods, religions. The use of 'church(es)/state' reinforces for us not only the reality that there are lots of churches out there but

PART I

The Foundations

CHAPTER ONE

Twelve Steps to Atheism

'Hello, my name is David, and I am an Atheist.'

Such is the typical greeting at one of the many twelve-step type groups that clutter the country. However, the word 'Atheist' is usually substituted at these meetings with some other opprobrious term like 'alcoholic' or 'drug addict' or 'sex addict.' In every case, the word is intended to be negative, and the point of the exercise is to admit your problem as the first step to recovery from it. The declaration above is not negative in any way, however, but is a pronouncement of positivity, health, and liberation. This chapter, instead of providing twelve steps to *recover from* anything is intended to provide twelve steps to *recover something* — namely, one's natural-born Atheism. The 'steps' in this case are twelve arguments or reasons — some classic, some contemporary — why Theism fails and Atheism is the only sustainable alternative.

This chapter is not intended to give thorough treatments of all the arguments discussed. That would be beyond the scope of any single chapter and probably any single book. It is also not intended to give the most scholarly possible treatments of the arguments. For more thorough and scholarly treatments, there are many excellent books that deserve serious study, including George Smith's *Atheism: The Case Against God* (1989), Michael Martin's *Atheism: A Philosophical Justification* (1990), and J.L. Mackie's *The Miracle of Theism* (1982), among others. Readers wishing to consider the arguments below in greater depth are encouraged to consult one or more of these texts. However, the following pages present a compact encapsulation of the reasons to recover from Theism.

Step One: The Burden of Proof

This step is preliminary to all other steps, in fact preliminary to all right use of reason. That is, before one can begin to argue one must know *how* to argue — the rules and requirements of argument (see Chapters Two and Three). The most basic such rule is the *burden of proof* — that is, whose job it is to marshal and present facts and arguments to support their case and when that case has been successfully prosecuted.

It is often mistakenly asserted that Atheists must prove their case; when an Atheist states that he or she does not believe in god, a Theist will respond, 'Can you prove there is no god?' Even worse, the occasional sophisticated Theist will meet you with the argument that 'you cannot prove a negative.' However, logically and rhetorically, the Theist is wrong on both counts. A simple formulation of the burden-of-proof concept is that *the party who makes a claim has the burden to prove or justify that claim, not the party who questions the claim.* (Elsewhere we will discuss the issue of whether Atheism, even 'positive Atheism,' is making a claim at all and of what sort.) In the case of a religious argument, it is the Theist who makes the claim about god's existence or attributes, and therefore it is he or she who must back up that claim. So, when the Theist asks you to prove there is no god, you are under no obligation to do so whatsoever. Further, it is not true that it is impossible to prove a negative. *It is unnecessary to prove a negative*, but if you can, then the case against the claim becomes even stronger, perhaps conclusive. For example, if someone accuses you of a crime (that is, makes a claim of factual truth), you can prove the negative (your innocence) by providing an alibi, producing witnesses who saw the event, or otherwise proving the impossibility or self-contradiction of the accusation.

In fact, let us pursue this analogy, for the American courtroom is a model of evidence and argument procedures. Let us imagine a prosecutor who asserts a charge, like 'X did the crime' or 'There is a god.' The charge is the positive claim — a truth claim that the statement embedded in the charge is true. The defense attorney rejects the charge as untrue. In our system of justice, we maintain that one is innocent until proven guilty. So the prosecutor must present his best evidence and argument for the truth of the charge. The defender can and in most cases should refute that evidence and argument as best he or she can and even introduce counterevidence and counterargument if possible. However, it is in the final analysis unnecessary that this be done. The defender could sit with feet up on the table without uttering a word, and ideally if the prosecution does not prove its case beyond a reasonable doubt, the defendant goes free. In other words, the defense (the 'negative') has no burden on it — literally, nothing to prove. Notice too that, since guilt naturally means the truth of the initial charge and innocence means its falsity, the presumption of innocence equates to a presumption of falsity: *a claim is false until proven true.* This is what Antony Flew (1984) means by "the presumption of atheism."

This courtroom analogy illustrates precisely how the theistic argument should and must proceed. Indeed, if Theists actually believe the truth of the god-claims they are making and are not just representing claims procedurally (just as not all prosecutors do or must believe the charges they press, though they must still represent them), then theoretically the Theists must have already considered the evidence and argument and found it compelling, or else they have not thought through the matter at all or are talking out of faith rather than fact (hardly the kind of prosecutor that the state would want on the case). Therefore, the thoughtful Theist has evidence and arguments and must be called upon to produce them.

The presumption of falsity (including Atheism, which is 'the falsity of Theism') is ultimately only a restatement of the basic premise of skepticism. Radical or philosophical skepticism may posit that all human knowledge is impossible, but that is not what we mean here, and that extreme position need not concern us for now. A more moderate or practical skepticism posits simply this: *do not accept any proposition as true without sufficient reasons for supposing its truth.* As we will see in a much later section some thinkers, like Pascal and James, have held the position that in the absence of sufficient reason to judge something true or false one should judge it true, but this argument is wrong and not even practical. They naturally are referring to Theism, in fact to Christianity in particular, but theirs is merely a profession of faith, not a real or even possible general maxim. Do they think that, whenever we meet an unsettled situation where the evidence has not decided truth or falsity, we should leap to embrace the claim as true? For example, if somebody claims that his potion cures cancer but there is no research on its effectiveness, should we buy and drink the liquid?

Of course not, and that highlights the point of the burden of proof. It is simple mental hygiene to withhold our assent to and 'faith in' any claim until there is good reason to give it. There are too many claims on our credibility to welcome them all into the ranks of the true; there are too many claims to consider them all, let alone assent to them all. First, we must decide which are even worthy of consideration — which offer some chance of being true, are coherent and not self-contradictory (see below), are compatible with the body of knowledge already established, and do not contravene reality as we know it — before we submit them to consideration, which means rational/empirical testing.

As we proceed through the subsequent 'steps,' perhaps this axiom sums up the skeptical-legal approach one should take toward any truth-claim, religious or otherwise: the only necessary — maybe even the best — argument against something is a lack of argument for it.

Steps Two through Four: The Classical Logical Arguments for Gods

For a thousand years or more theologians, particularly Christian theologians, have been formulating logical arguments to prove the existence of their god. These arguments founded themselves purportedly on logical necessity or empirical evidence, and that, in addition to the fact that they have been repeatedly represented by some of the best theistic minds of the West, means that if they fail, it is to be strongly inferred that all such arguments will fail. These classic arguments are known as the cosmological, the ontological, and the teleological.

Step Two: The Cosmological Argument

The so-called 'cosmological' ('cosmos' meaning 'universe' or 'universal order') argument is the first we will undertake, since it is the first logically. It occurs in various forms, but all of its forms derive from one basic mystery — that anything exists at all. Allegedly, the universe and everything in it requires an explanation or, in other words, a *cause* or a *foundation*, which is god(s). The best-known version is the 'first cause' argument. It maintains that every thing requires a cause for it to be, and so everything (the universe as a whole) requires a cause for it to be. That cause cannot be part of the universe (since a cause must always precede its effect). Finally, there cannot be an infinite succession of causes. Therefore, there must be a first uncaused cause that is outside of or separate from the universe, which we call god(s).

Another version of the cosmological argument is the 'sustaining cause' or foundational version. This is the argument that Aquinas develops in his *Summa Theologica* but that is often mistaken for the chronological first-cause notion. The idea is that every thing depends upon something else for its existence; in other words, for each existing thing there is something 'under' it that provides the 'ground' for its existence. As above, the universe (as the totality of things) also requires a ground, and that ground cannot be any part of the universe, and there cannot be an infinite series of grounds. Therefore, a god exists as the ultimate ground or foundation or 'cause.' The third and final version is the 'contingency' version. It takes a slightly different tack, although it still rests on questions of how the universe could possibly exist. Every thing is contingent, that is, it might just as easily not exist as exist; for example, it is equally conceivable that I might not have existed as that I do exist. I am, like every other thing in existence, not necessary. The universe too as a whole is contingent and could conceivably not exist; it is not necessary. But if at any time the universe had not existed, it would not exist today, since something cannot emerge from nothing. The only possibility is that some 'non-contingent' something exists — something that has no beginning and no end — and this non-contingent something (god) makes all contingent things possible.

It should be apparent that these three versions arise from some of the same assumptions and suffer from some of the same weaknesses, although there are also some unique aspects of each. Most fundamentally, all three operate from the premise that the universe, the totality of existence, *needs* an explanation. This is stipulated, not demonstrated. It may be that the universe merely *is* and makes the explanation of any particular thing possible and interesting. But it might be a false analogy to suggest that the universe (the whole) is like any particular existent (its parts). Does the universe need a first cause or a foundation? Is the universe contingent? An affirmative answer must be justified before the cosmological argument advances.

The first-cause and sustaining-cause versions also add the assumption that an infinite succession or regression is impossible. This might seem like a commonsense view but, as Kant showed in his critique of reason, both finite and infinite universes — temporally and spatially — are equally incomprehensible to us. Is an infinite series impossible? That is unproven. There is a famous anthropological story, attributed to various cultures, about a religious belief that the world rests, for example, on a turtle's back. The curious anthropologist asks, 'What does the turtle stand on?' The informant answers, 'On the back of a larger turtle.' When the anthropologist asks what that turtle stands on, the informant responds, 'It's turtles all the way down.'

This is clearly, to us, an unsatisfactory and incomprehensible cosmology, but it is obviously not inconceivable, since our informant conceives it. But we demand an end to the progression — to an 'ultimate turtle,' if you will. And we get one — god. However, to show that this too is an unsatisfactory and incomprehensible cosmology, we need merely ask the question, 'What is the cause/ground of god?' A well-meaning Theist will tell us that he is his own cause or ground. But we have never seen and cannot rightly imagine an uncaused cause or a self-grounded ground. This is a nonanswer. It is word-magic at best and a malignant anti-answer at worst. In fact, the entire cosmological argument depends on the claim that such a thing cannot be. Further, if some being can be self-caused or self-grounded, why could not the universe be also? If we are going to imagine something violating every supposed tenet of our experience, why not cut out the middleman and attribute that quality to the universe itself?

Another concern is the lack of any discussion of the mechanism or relationship between the cause/ground/necessary being and the caused/grounded/contingent universe. It would be legitimate to demand an answer to the question, 'How does god cause/ground/guarantee the universe?' If we are to accept this extraordinary explanation, we are within our rights to request more detail. Finally and perhaps most significantly, even if any one of these three versions is true, it tells us nothing in particular about this alleged god-being. There is certainly nothing about Christian theology in the argument; this god could exist but yet be the Muslim god or one of the Hindu gods or a Greek or Norse or Native American or any other god, or it could be an impersonal energy or the devil. In fact, if we consider the first-cause argument again, it does not even insist that this god exists *now* but that it existed at the beginning (a similar case might be made for the contingency argument, although Theists might counter that he is still necessary today just in case the universe were to disappear). One advantage of the sustaining-cause version is that it seems to require a presently existing god for the universe to exist today, although even that might not be completely true. In other words, the sustaining-cause argument depicts a vertical series of causes with god(s) at the bottom today, while the first-cause argument represents a horizontal series of causes (a timeline) with god(s) at the beginning in the past. Thus, if the first-cause argument succeeds, it does not prove there is a god today, and none of these arguments can prove there is a god like the Theists, let alone the Christians, envision.

To make matters even worse, recent advances in our scientific understanding of the world have thrown the very notion of cause into question. Particularly the discovery of the quantum nature of subatomic reality has substituted a statistical or probabilistic view of events for the old familiar deterministic or 'causal' one. In other words, where it has been traditionally argued that some prior condition A is necessary and sufficient for (the 'cause' of) event B, quantum physics shows us, with great predictive accuracy, that no particular prior condition is either necessary or sufficient for some physical events such as radioactive decay, the behavior of electrons and photons, and potentially for the appearance of the physical universe itself out of a background of quantum fluctuations. As physicist Victor Stenger has stated, "In the quantum world ... things can simply happen ... I have shown that directional causality, or causal precedence, is in fact a classical, macroscopic concept that does not apply at the fundamental level of elementary particle interactions, where fundamental interactions make no distinction between cause and effect" (1995, 228). In such a view of reality, a 'cause' is neither always adequate to explain an event — even the *big event* — nor required to explain an event. Reality, at some level (perhaps at the level that really counts) is nondeterministic and noncausal. Another physicist, Taner Edis, extends this new understanding of nature by considering it not deterministic and not random but *historical* — that is, from any set of prior conditions, various events are possible, but only one event actually happens. The actual historical event, whether the appearance of a subatomic particle, a human war, or the emergence of the universe, "seems stubbornly contingent: the course of events could have been otherwise, and the only way we can see why our history took place is to recount the individual events" (2002, 137). The ultimate result is a physical reality that is related to but not predetermined by 'causal connections,' one that exhibits some freedom, some unpredictability, some uncertainty.

It seems, then, that the cosmological argument is not much comfort to the Theist. It reads more like a misuse of terms like 'infinite,' 'contingent,' and even 'cause.' In all its versions it does not answer the question of how the universe is possible but merely aborts the questioning: 'It's god(s), end of discussion.' To put it succinctly, it offers as the comprehensibility of the universe an incomprehensibility.

Step Three: The Ontological Argument

Our third step, and the second classical argument for a god, is the 'ontological' argument, in which 'onto' means 'being.' That is, this argument affirms the existence of a god on the basis of the relationship of the god's nature to Being itself. The original formulation of the argument comes from Anselm of Canterbury (1033–1109), who wrote in his *Proslogium* that God must necessarily exist, that it is in fact self-contradictory to state that he does not. Since self-contradiction is one of the fatal flaws in any proposition, we must take this challenge seriously.

Anselm starts with a definition of god as "a being than which nothing greater can be conceived." In order to have a debate at all, both the Theist and the Atheist, he says, must have this conception. But where does the conception come from? There are only two possibilities: either from the mind or understanding itself (*i.e.*, subjectivity) or from external reality (*i.e.*, objectivity). Now, something that exists only subjectively, that is in the mind, is less great than something that exists objectively in reality, because it lacks one quality — existence. Therefore, in order to be the greatest conceivable being, a god would also have to have the quality of existence. To put this another way, God's essence includes existence. If this is true, then God's nonexistence is by definition inconceivable and self-contradictory; Atheism is then not only wrong but absurd and literally unthinkable. The Atheist who still maintains the nonexistence of Anselm's god is accordingly "dull and a fool."

This may sound like a compelling case, but like most compelling but unsuccessful cases, problems can be attributed to the definitions and the premises. In fact, such powerful theologians and philosophers as Aquinas and Kant have rejected the ontological argument for various reasons. The first reason we might raise goes back to the very definition of god that Anselm employs. This definition begs its conclusion, for if we define god otherwise than as 'that than which nothing greater can exist,' the implication of existence vanishes. For example, if we define god as an all-good, all-loving being, then it is quite conceivable to presume that such a being does not exist. In other words, if you build existence into the definition of something, then obviously existence would appear to be one of its qualities: if we define invisible pizza as the food than which no greater food can be conceived, then by Anselm's reasoning it would have to exist — yet it does not.

This raises a second and more sophisticated objection. Anselm's logic assumes that a conception must have some correspondence to reality (or else it would be easy to presuppose that the Atheist could have an idea of a god without there actually being a god). But philosophy has criticized the correspondence theory of reality, and on a more mundane level we all know that it is simple and common to have ideas with no 'real' correspondent at all. For example, I can have a concept of a chicken-man without there actually being a chicken-man. Easily dismissed, Anselm might say, because this idea is inferior to real objects by lacking the quality of existence. But what if I have an idea of the greatest conceivable chicken-man, than which no greater chicken-man can be conceived? Like the invisible pizza above, by definition it would *have to* exist. This is not a silly objection, as one of the first criticisms of the ontological argument came in Anselm's own time, when Gaunilo countered with the case of the greatest conceivable island. More to the point, if Anselm's logic is sound, then an ancient Greek could define Zeus or Chronos as the being than which none greater could be conceived, and Zeus or Chronos would thereby by definition have to exist. But in actuality humans have many ideas that do not represent reality in any way; humans have the preternatural ability to combine or extrapolate ideas into concepts that never existed and never will.

To make it even worse for Anselm, the conceptual power of humans is not only much greater than he allows but also much poorer. In other words, when one claims to have an idea of something, is it really true that one has a clear and coherent idea? The answer seems to be no. Humans stumble through life much of the time with only fuzzy or even contradictory notions in their heads, notions that could not possibly correspond to any reality, let alone give rise to that reality. In particular, many people have no clear idea of what they mean by the concept of god, and it goes without saying that different people have very different understandings of the concept. Such an idea cannot possibly be used to support any argument from subjectivity to objectivity, from conception to existence, in regard to god, since we cannot even claim perfectly to know or to agree on what that word means. Finally, if Anselm is correct that humans cannot conceive of a being greater than god, perhaps that is just a limitation of human understanding or imagination. Maybe a being greater than man could conceive of an even greater being — or else the whole 'nothing greater than' idea is just word-play. To use the human mind as the measure of all ontological possibility is a scary thought.

At the most sophisticated level, Kant for one claims to refute the ontological argument on the ground that existence is not a property at all, and so the whole line of reasoning is corrupted. Rather, he says, existence is that which makes properties possible; if something does not exist, then it has no properties. But to call 'existence' a characteristic of some thing, on a par with 'redness' or 'squareness' or 'bigness,' is to misrepresent the term. The conclusion to draw from this thinking is that there is no contradiction in conceiving the nonexistence of a thing's properties if we conceive the nonexistence of the thing; the only contradiction would be to conceive the nonexistence of the properties along with the existence of the thing. To give an example, we could define 'leprechaun' as a green-wearing, pipe-smoking, gold-hoarding little man, and so, if leprechauns exist, those are their properties. However, if leprechauns do not exist (which is completely conceivable), then those properties do not exist, and there is no contradiction. Existence is a *condition of* the properties, not *one of* the properties. So, if we say that god is defined as an omnipotent, omniscient, omnibenevolent being, and he exists, then that is his character. But if he does not exist, obviously those characteristics do not exist either. And 'existence' itself is not a characteristic at all but a conditional. Therefore, it is not at all inconceivable (and certainly not dull or foolish to conceive) that this or that being — even a being with the allegedly greatest characteristics — does not exist.

Ultimately, as we encountered in the cosmological argument, even if the ontologists were completely correct — that god is the being than which no greater being can be conceived — this would still not justify the Christian religion or any other particular religion. So, the ontological argument, like the cosmological argument, cannot be used as a support for Christianity specifically in any case.

Step Four: The Teleological Argument

The final classical argument for the existence of a god is the *teleological* argument — *teleo* meaning 'end' or 'purpose' in Greek. This argument takes a different form than the previous two and is one of the most popular theistic arguments today in its modern guise. In short, it is not so much a logical argument for god(s) as a supposed evidence of god(s). In addition, it is an 'argument from analogy' between things that we are familiar with and understand and things that we are not and do not.

The basics of the teleological argument are fairly simple: the universe and the myriad things in it evince 'purpose' or 'design.' Purpose is not accidental but 'purposive' or intentional; design implies a designer. If we, for example, look at the way an eye is specialized for sight, or at the elaborate and precise relations between parasites and hosts, or at the very disposition of the earth in space, we see that these things are no accident but are exactly the way they need to be, exactly the way we would choose them and design them if we could. If there is 'Intelligent Design' in the universe, then there must be an intelligent designer, and this is god.

That this is an analogical argument is clear, and Theists are quite direct about the analogy. Human artifacts are designed — they show a specialization of parts (a 'complexity' or 'fitness' that is not random) and a relationship of means to ends (a deliberate 'functionality'). The classic statement of the teleological argument comes from William Paley (1743–1805), who mused in his *Natural Theology* about a walker coming upon a watch on the ground in a heath:

> When we come to inspect the watch, we perceive ... that its several parts are framed and put together for a purpose, *e.g.* that they are so formed and adjusted as to produce motion, and that motion so regulated as to point out the hour of the day; that, if the different parts had been differently shaped from what they are, of a different size from what they are, or placed after any other manner, or in any other order, than that in which they are placed, either no motion at all would have been carried on in the machine, none which would have answered the use that is now served by it .... [T]he inference, we think, is inevitable, that the watch must have had a maker; that

there must have existed, at some time, and at some place or other, an artificer or artificers, who formed it for the purpose which we find it actually to answer; who comprehended its construction, and designed its use.

Now, analogies are notoriously troubled types of arguments, in fact, in the final analysis, analogies are not arguments at all but instructional devices: they are intended to impart understanding of the unfamiliar by likening it to the familiar. However, an analogy is not a *proof* of anything — I could say that a lion is like a linen closet, but that does not make it true — and any analogy is only intended to go so far — a lion may be like a linen closet in some ways but not others. If we make the mistake of equating the two terms in the analogy, we have sabotaged our own reason.

So, the first question we must ask is, 'Is the analogy between human artifacts and the natural world a good analogy, and is it being used within the confines of analogical thinking?' Does an eye or a symbiotic/parasitic relationship or a solar system resemble human creations? Well, in some ways yes, in some ways no. There is demonstrably a formation and adjustment of elements such that alteration, replacement, or removal of elements might render the whole nonfunctional. In other ways, of course, these other 'creations' are not like human products at all. Nature does not manifest the same process of conceptualization and implementation that human creations do: humans proceed out from an infrastructure with a 'blueprint' in mind, and humans usually create substantial works in teams (perhaps explaining the 'polytheism' of most traditional societies — different gods for different jobs!). In human-designed works, it is possible to see half-finished works and works-in-progress, while nature does not show such things; to turn a theistic saw against itself, a half-finished eye or a platypus-in-progress would not be worth much.

Another incisive question would be whether there really is order or design in nature. It is possible, even likely, that the amount of order or design is much overstated. Clearly, nature is not 'perfect' in the way that a well-designed engine, for instance, is. Nature is, in fact, rather sloppy, profligate, and ad hoc, more in the way that something accidentally derived would be than something intentionally (let alone supernaturally) designed would be. Richard Dawkins (1996) gives the convincing example of the human eye, that bugbear of creationism, which has the light-sensitive cells lying under a layer of other cells, rather than exposed directly to the light, which would seem more sensible; it is as if visual cells developed through a process of opportunistic trial and error rather than divine plan and work 'well enough' if not perfectly. If one looks out at the visible universe as a whole, there is certainly structure and grandeur, but not much perfection — and it is even difficult to discern what 'perfection' would mean in this context. There are certainly a lot of flaws, a lot of ugliness, a lot of pain and suffering in the universe that belie an intelligent, or at least a benevolent, creator.

We should ask, as science has, whether order or 'perfection' would even be evidence of design — whether order is only possible as an outcome of design. Of course, Darwin's evolutionary theory arose to answer that question and answered it very well: natural objects can acquire the appearance of design by purely natural processes. Cats are well-designed as hunters not because some spiritual being made them thus (in fact, in biblical theology, the creator did not design them as hunters, since death was not yet in the world and hunting entails death, although why he gave them sharp claws and teeth is unclear!), but because millennia of existence in an environment favoring certain traits have 'perfected' those traits by selective force. To give a more trivial but enlightening example: what could be more 'random' and unintentional than shaking up an object? But take some iron filings, place them on paper with a magnet underneath, and shake, and the random agitation will result in orderly patterns flowing from nothing more than the natural magnetic field's action on the ron — unless one wants to insist that some god(s) stepped in o arrange the iron in orderly patterns. In other words, what ttle order we do observe in the world can be quite adequately :plained by natural processes.

Finally, Theists who appeal to design arguments must e the inevitable question: if everything requires a designer t is greater than itself, then who or what designed their ? Predictably, they will answer that their god was not designed but was always in existence, not requiring a designer. But if that is so, then their first premise — that all things need a designer — is false, and if some things do not need a designer, then maybe the universe did not need a designer either. And, what is worst of all, if humans, life, or the universe were truly designed in any familiar sense, they would not only evidence complexity or perfection but *purpose*. Even if we acknowledge that god(s) designed the wonderful machine of galaxies, humans, or puppies, we would still be left with the question: why? What is this design designed for?

A word is called for about the recent notion of 'Intelligent Design.' Having failed utterly to get religion accepted into mainstream education and science in the form of 'creation science,' Theists have switched course — although still trying to manipulate the prestige of science on behalf of old-fashioned religion — in promoting Intelligent Design or 'ID.' ID masquerades as serious science, investigating problems of cellular or molecular processes, for example, and arrives at the determination that these processes are once again too complex or perfect to have evolved randomly. How one sets the standard of complexity at 'too complex for nature' is beyond me, but nevertheless, they conclude that only an intelligent designer could account for the results. In a way, this is a teleological argument without the god, although some ID writers do posit god as the solution; others just leave it at some unspecified designer. It should go without saying that this is not science — since science attempts to identify a process, not just a lack of one — and that as an argument it is subject to all the criticisms that we just formulated against teleology in general. In other words, it's not true (since it does not really say anything), and it would be irrelevant if it were true. We will return to this discussion in Chapter Seven.

Steps Five through Nine: The Empirical and Social Arguments for Gods

If the logical arguments for the existence of god(s) fail, or at least if they are insufficient, there are other arguments to which the Theist can turn. These arguments stand (or fall) on other grounds, in particular on actual or putative observations and facts, whether made by oneself or by observers and authorities in another place and time, or on real or alleged social effects and consequences. These arguments include appeals to scripture and other religious authority, miracles, personal experience, morality, and benefit.

Step Five: The Argument from Scripture or Authority

Step Five leaves behind the classical and mostly logical world of arguments for god's existence and enters a realm of more empirical or even social reasons to believe in a god. One such argument trotted out perpetually is the argument from scripture or religious authority. This argument is extremely simple and extremely persuasive to certain people; it states merely that a trustworthy source — even a god-given source — gives us our religious information, so naturally it is true and we should accept it. This is an incredibly flawed and truly dangerous stance to take, as we shall see, but first let us note that there are two issues at hand — the issue of scripture as authority and the issue of authority in general. Let us examine these more closely in turn, starting with authority in general.

It is common practice for us humans to accept that, because an authority states so-and-so, it must be true. We can define 'authority' here as 'one possessing a legitimate claim to knowledge or power in a certain realm on the basis of training, experience, office, or other personal or professional characteristics.' For instance, if a doctor tells us we have a disease, he ought to know, because he is a doctor. Or if a police officer pulls us over for speeding, he has a right to ticket us, because he is a policeman. We would not let our friends or some guy off the street diagnose our illnesses or punish our legal infractions;

we would not even let a doctor ticket us or a policeman operate on us.

However, let us state in no uncertain terms here and now: *an argument from authority is not an argument at all*. In other words, it is logically fallacious to accept something as true *just because* an authority asserts that it is the case. It is easy to illustrate why. First, the authority could be wrong. Many, many authorities have been wrong, about everything from the safety and effectiveness of this or that drug or diet to the very shape of the earth. Second, authorities disagree. It is purely anecdotal evidence to quote Dr. Smith that you should only eat carbohydrates, since Dr. Jones says that you should never eat carbohydrates. In other words, it is usually if not always possible to challenge an authority or list of authorities with a counter-authority or counter-list of authorities. Theists have addressed me personally with a list of 'intelligent men and scientists' who believed in god, and I can produce my list of intelligent and scientific Atheists. Neither proves anything.

As with our doctor and police officer, an individual may be an authority in one area but not another; authority, in other words, is not a universal or generalized trait and does not transfer between realms of knowledge or skill. So if a Theist produces a Nobel Prize–winning physicist who is a Christian, a legitimate response is to ask, 'Okay, he is an authority on physics, but what makes him an authority on religion?' Finally, all authority is in the end secondhand information ('testimony,' Hume would say, as we will discuss below). There is no way on the face of it to assess the accuracy of the authority's pronouncements. Instead, when the authority speaks, the process of reason *commences* rather than consummates.

There are those who happily suggest that science is little or nothing more than authority-worship and therefore itself is like a religion (a curiously self-denigrating suggestion!). And it is true that in science we often listen to authorities — but not so as to automatically or blindly embrace their pontifications, for the reasons we just explored. *In principle*, if not in actual practice every time, we accept their authority because it is possible to verify or falsify their sources and their conclusions or because we assume that others have already attempted such verification or falsification. This is a big 'in principle,' for most of us do not and never will have the skill, technology, or opportunity to conduct our own tests, and we must rely on the scientific community to fully and fairly perform the tests for us. We sometimes mistakenly presume that results or conclusions have been tested before they are announced, or even that the scientists are competent and objective, but such is not always the case. Hence the potential danger exists of, at best, hasty unfounded science, and at worst bilious pseudoscience.

These concerns transfer to the specific situation of scripture as authority, with additional and fatal concerns of its own. For one, scripture is always secondhand testimony — something that (allegedly) happened at some other, usually remote, time and place; even worse, it is biased testimony, something like the reports of a scientist who is working for a tobacco or pharmaceutical company. People who write scriptures are predisposed to believe a religion's claims (they are creating those very claims!), and editors and compilers of scriptures (those who set the 'canon') naturally only select the texts that conform to and advance the belief. All of these issues make scripture suspect from the outset. Finally, there is no verification, attempt at verification, or possibility of verification of the claims in the texts; you must take them at face value or not at all.

Another concern in scriptural authority is the appeal to prophecy as supposed confirmation of the truth of the text. This appeal is fallacious as a logical matter and mostly if not universally false as an empirical one. If one scientist prophesied that someday we would discover elementary particles called bleens, and later another scientist announced that he had discovered bleens, that would not prove that bleens are real, and it would certainly not mean that the first scientist was a prophet. At any rate, most 'biblical prophecies' are so vague as to have no real cognitive or predictive value; if a verse reads that a power will rise in the west, that could mean anything or nothing (e.g., west of what?). Other prophecies pick and choose from the verses to construct an apparently convincing façade, and many see fulfillment of prophecy only in retrospect.

There is no need here to belabor the point that scriptures are full of internal contradictions and errors. Those who would live by the absolute truth of their texts would die by the falsi-fication of any part of them. But to move beyond that well-known and well-established point (the reader can find exten-sive lists of Bible errors and contradictions elsewhere, for example McKinsey 1995; Green 1982; Smith 1995), it is false when most people assume that we are talking exclusively about the Christian Bible. Why privilege the Christian Bible? Other scriptures exist in the world and are held dear by large num-bers of the faithful. Almost as many people in the world believe the Qur'an as the Bible, and the Qur'an asserts that God never had any sons. Why not base your argument and your faith on the Bhagavad Gita, the Buddhist sutras, the Book of Mormon, or the myths of any traditional religion? In other words, the ultimate flaw of any appeal to authority, including scriptural, is that you have already determined in advance what your authority will be and have already placed your trust in it; you have preselected an authority that hap-pens to support everything you do and want to believe.

In the end, the problem of the Bible or any other sacred text as authority is that, if you are not already a believer in its truths, it has no authority. To non-Christians (including Atheists), the Bible is no authority at all, just as to Christians the Qur'an or the Hindu Vedas are no authority. Nonbelievers don't care what somebody else's text says. This is why I per-sonally do not get into biblical disputes with Christians and why I would urge other Atheists to do the same. I don't care what the Bible says — it is not my authority — and so its claims are not worthy of my serious consideration, any more than any other texts or myths in the world. We Atheists have no burden of proof to refute the Bible.

Step Six: The Argument from Miracles

Miracles constitute a different kind of approach to the theistic question: not just an argument for god but a supposed *evidence of* god. Before getting into this discussion, here is one problem to keep in mind — if a single idea or concept claims to explain everything, then it really explains nothing. In other words, if when all is going well according to natural laws, then that is a sign of god, and if when something happens that is unusual or exceptional, then that is a sign of god too, then everything serves as evidence for you. There is no way to separate the real evidence from the false or imagined.

What precisely is a miracle? Is it an unusual event? But lots of unusual events occur within the range of reasonable expectation; it might snow in the summer, or the Red Sox might win a World Series someday. Would these be miracles in the sense of a god's intervention, or just highly unlikely scenarios that are nevertheless statistically possible? Perhaps a miracle is a supernatural event. But that definition begs the question, for if we have predefined what is natural and what is not, then anything that falls under our definition of not-natural would count as a miracle for us. And what exactly would not-natural or supernatural mean other than a violation of the laws of nature? But this presupposes that there are such things as laws of nature, that we know what those laws are, and that we recognize a violation when we see one. Besides, perfectly natural events, like finding money in the street or having a baby, are often described as miracles.

Theists who use this definition to lay a foundation for arguments from miracles do not realize how much territory they have ceded to science and reason and yet how shaky their ground is. It is science that is concerned with and informed about laws of nature, not religion. What exactly is a natural law? It is not like a political law — it is not a prescription for behavior but a description of behavior. Natural laws are inductive statements about how nature appears to function (we will speak more of this below in our discussion of design arguments). But in acknowledging natural laws, Theists get themselves in a bind, for they often criticize rational knowledge of nature as fallible, which it no doubt is, while they depend on it to adjudicate miracles apart from 'natural' occurrences. As a ridiculous but typical example, Theists often attack inductive scientific or even prescientific knowledge like 'the sun will come up tomorrow' as uncertain and fallible, yet if the sun did not come up tomorrow they would call that a miracle. But you cannot have it both ways: if human knowledge is so fallible, maybe we were wrong about the sun coming up every day, so tomorrow's non-sunrise was actually a perfectly natural phenomenon — one that we were erroneous to predict in the first place. So the Theist's ascription of a miracle depends in an odd way on reason's and science's understanding of what nature is and does.

Furthermore, miracle-talk generally evinces a basic ignorance of statistical reasoning. In any set of results, exceptional things will happen a certain percentage of the time. That is why the bell curve is bell-shaped. 'Typical' results occur most of the time (that is why the bell curve is highest in the middle range), but 'atypical' or rare events occur with lesser but some frequency and compose the 'tails' of the curve. This is why statisticians apply tests of significance to their results; the question is, how likely is it that this result would occur by chance? By chance, it is possible that it could snow in summer or that a terminal disease could spontaneously remit — and they do — but these should be 'low-percentage' events, perhaps one in a hundred or one in a thousand. If they occur with greater frequency, then we have something to think about (but then of course diseases that clear up a large portion of the time are not designated as 'terminal diseases' in the first place). But what miracle-seekers often do is to pick out the extreme results — predictable in any normal distribution — and claim those as miracles or violations of normal circumstances when they are in fact part of normal circumstances!

Finally, miracle-seekers tend to choose only the confirming examples from the range of experience rather than, of course, the disconfirming one. This is purely anecdotal and therefore utterly useless as evidence. For instance, if one person is cured after a visit to Lourdes, they tend to attribute special significance to that result, ignoring all the people who are not cured, let alone the numerous people who are actually harmed or killed there. Such evidence-stacking makes the whole business irrelevant.

Miracles, if they are anything, must be unlikely or unexplainable things, for if they had any other explanation, they would not be interventions of god(s) and therefore not evidence of god(s). David Hume, one of the first great skeptics of modern history, wrote in his classic essay 'On Miracles' that we must judge miracles by the strong rules of evidence. Most people hear of miracles secondhand, so again miracle-talk usually exists as testimony, not personal experience. So, Hume asks, why and on what conditions should I believe the miracle claims? It is always possible that the testimony is mistaken or is even a lie. He answers that extraordinary claims require extraordinary evidence, and in the absence of that evidence the miracle claim should be rejected. Thomas Paine, author of *Age of Reason* and *Common Sense*, is even more direct: "We have never seen, in our time, nature go out of her course; but we have good reason to believe that millions of lies have been told in the same time; it is, therefore, at least millions to one, that the reporter of a miracle tells a lie." (*Age of Reason*, Part I, 63–64).

Step Seven: The Argument from Personal Experience

Our commentary on arguments from miracles and the nature of testimony raised the issue of personal experience, which is itself often appealed to in claims of god-belief. In fact, personal experience is commonly the ultimate and unassailable ground for belief, since it again seems to be direct evidence of a god rather than a mere intellectual rationalization or exercise, and since it seems unimpeachable — if I experienced it, I experienced it, no matter what objections the doubter might have. It is somewhat outside of the scope of the present work, but this very type of argument is an interesting and potentially dangerous aspect of contemporary culture, especially American culture, in which subjectivity is accepted as reality: if I feel it, it must be true. It is almost un-American these days to discount someone's personal opinions and feelings, even if those opinions and feelings go against fact and reason, and even if those opinions and feelings are being offered as grounds for objective and public truth claims.

Be that as it may, let us note first that to call any experience a 'religious experience' is to beg the question yet again. If I hear a voice in my head or have a mystical feeling or see a beautiful sunset and call that a religious experience, I have imposed a meaning on it and prejudiced the evaluation of it as an experience. Now, Richard Swinburne (1998), a leading contemporary theistic philosopher, has distinguished four types of 'religious' experiences:

1. Experiencing an ordinary object as a religious object (*e.g.*, taking thunder as a sign from god)

2. Experiencing a religious object publicly (*e.g.*, seeing an angel or hearing god where everyone can see or hear it)
3. Experiencing a religious object privately (*e.g.*, seeing an angel or hearing god where only you can see or hear it)
4. Experiencing an ineffable sensation of some sort that cannot be described in words (*e.g.*, a feeling of oneness with the universe *etc.*).

The trouble with these sources of experience should be painfully apparent. Type One experiences could easily be and no doubt are mistakes, projections, wishful thinking, or over-interpretations; is every thunderclap a sign from god, or just some, and if just some, which ones and how do we distinguish, and why can't god be more direct with his signs anyhow? Type Two experiences essentially never happen, except perhaps in the sense of reflections in windows that look like the Virgin Mary or stains that look like the profile of Elvis; but these again are overinterpretations or projections, and any actual public appearance of god or his emissaries would be a lot more compelling. Type Three and Four experiences happen or are claimed fairly often, but the point is that there is no way to verify that they happen, let alone to verify their 'religious' significance. There could be and are many other ways to explain them, if and when they occur.

Hence, we can actually dismiss personal experience as a basis for theistic belief with no more difficulty than the other 'empirical' claims. First, to everyone except the subject of the experience, the experience is nothing but testimony and hearsay; the person 'says' that he 'heard' god speak, but I do not know that for a fact and cannot check it. Second, even for the subject, the experience is mere raw data; if I hear a voice, how do I know that it is the voice of God? It could be the voice of Allah, Vishnu, Buddha, Satan, or my cat; each is equally (un)likely. Third, religious experiences are so different for different people that it serves as a red flag for us; the occurrence and interpretation of such experiences seems closely related to personality and culture, so much so that we can explain and dismiss them as culture-bound. In other words, if Christians have personal experiences of God, Jesus, and Mary, and Muslims have personal experiences of Allah, and Hindus have personal experiences of Brahma or Shiva or

Vishnu, then either an awful lot of gods exist (to take the experiences seriously), or people just experience what they want or expect to. Ultimately, if we argue from personal experience, then we must either take all personal experiences seriously — which is almost impossible to do, since they are often mutually contradictory — or explain why we only take certain ones seriously — which will expose our prejudices, preconceptions, and commitments.

Finally and most decisively, even if such experiences are occurring, there are other and more likely explanations for them. They can be dreams, daydreams, hallucinations, inserted memories, misinterpretations, or overinterpretations. That is, they can have perfectly natural causes, if they are even anything remarkable at all. Several recent books, in fact, have made the case for brain states associated with religious experiences, although some have made the fallacious claim that the experiences are more than the brain states (*i.e.*, that the experiences and states refer to some 'objective reality' outside the brain). In the laboratory, researchers can recreate almost all of the 'religious experiences' reported by subjects, without any corresponding external realities (*i.e.*, no gods, just electrodes and drugs).

In conclusion, personal experience is no more sound a basis for religious belief than any other evidential claim we have considered. Philosopher Michael Martin put it well when he mentioned the confusion between a source of belief and a justification for belief — if a person has an 'experience,' that person may base his/her belief on that experience, but the experience is not actually a good justification for any belief, let alone the specific one that he/she no doubt holds. Such experiences, like all other evidence, must be subjected to the rules of evidence and the burden of proof, not blindly and unproblematically accepted and wildly and idiosyncratically interpreted.

Step Eight: The Argument from Morality

In the theistic world, when all else fails, it is possible and likely to turn to the argument from morality or benefit; in other words, if you cannot prove that religion is true, perhaps at least you can prove it is necessary or advantageous. However, not even these weak and desperate maneuvers really stand against criticism and analysis, and even if they did, they would be poor excuses to practice something that one did not firmly believe, if believe at all.

Many Theists agree that morality is impossible without god(s). Their argument takes two forms — first, that there are moral laws and man is a moral species, therefore god(s) must exist as the lawgiver or creator of our human nature, and second, that without god(s) there would be no grounds for morality and humans would be evil immoral libertines ... like Atheists are. Therefore, they conclude, people should believe in god(s) even if those beliefs cannot be proven true; truth here is subordinate to effect. Basically, both of these approaches are empirical arguments, so we can treat and refute them as such.

It is true that humans live under moral laws or guidelines. However, every society has its morality, but each is different. What is deemed good in one society is often deemed bad in another; for instance, killing is immoral in most societies (under most but not all circumstances), but head-hunting is or was a valuable and appropriate behavior in some societies. In other words, morality is not absolute or universal, despite what Christian Theists in particular think, but relative. Rather, as Nietzsche stated, "there are altogether no moral facts." So if there is a god, he/she/it has either given humanity lots of conflicting moral guidelines or none at all. More likely, humans give themselves moral codes wherever they live because humans are a moral — that is, a social — species. We see the rudiments of morality and orderly society in our primate cousins and even in 'lower' animals, so there is no need to search beyond our physical and social nature for the explanation of rule-governed behavior.

If in fact theistic belief were conducive to moral action, we would expect and demand that religious individuals or societies be more moral than nonreligious ones. In addition to the problem that morality is relative (indisputably the Taliban in Afghanistan considered their actions moral), there is no evidence whatsoever that the predicted effect is present. One need only look at the current scandal in the Catholic church (but hardly only in the Catholic church) for proof positive of this result; priests may be no more, but they are apparently no less, likely to commit child abuse than anyone else. America as a society may be a religion-soaked place, but we suffer from much more crime and vice than most less religious societies like Canada, France, Britain, Australia, or Japan. Crime and carnage are actually committed every day in the name of god and religion in many theistic societies.

Furthermore, it is false and foolish to say that Atheists are amoral libertines. In fact, Atheists commit less crime, are less fanatical, and are generally mild and reasonable people. The few bad Atheists in history, like Stalin, prove nothing — there are bad Atheists and bad Theists; if Theism does not make a measurable difference in this regard, then the argument fails. And surely this very argument does not say much for the personality of Theists; are they saying that without god and religion they would run amok? I had a friend years ago who said, after graduating high school, that he wanted to sleep, party, play rock music, and chase girls all the time. However, reality set in rapidly, and those dreams of wanton hedonism soon gave way to work and marriage and family. Such is the condition of Atheists — we do not live lives of wild and reckless abandon. We are mostly busy being citizens, workers, partners, and parents, like everyone else in the world.

It might even be argued that the whole claim of morality based on religion is flawed, since rewards and punishments do not make behavior moral but only coerced. In the psychologist Lawrence Kohlberg's stages of moral development, reward-and-punishment thinking is the lowest stage, far below reflective or principled behavior. If a god puts a spiritual gun to your head and says 'Follow these rules or else,' the resultant behavior is neither free nor moral. Coerced behavior may be very orderly, but, as the communist regimes showed us, orderly society is not necessarily moral society.

Even worse for the Theist, over two thousand years ago it had already been shown by Plato that the moral argument for god(s) was flawed. In his dialog *Euthyphro* he found that the relationship between god(s) and morality was not a simple one. The participants, Socrates and Euthyphro, argue around in a circle about what makes a behavior desirable to the god(s): is an action good and just and honorable because the god(s) ordain or prefer it, or is it ordained or preferred by the god(s) because it is good and just and honorable? If the former, then morality is arbitrary, since whatever the god(s) would ordain or prefer would be accepted as moral by humans, even if that included killing (as it often did in the Old Testament and often does today in practice). If the latter, then certain actions are 'naturally' or 'objectively' good and just and honorable, and therefore (1) deity itself is bound by this 'natural morality' and subject to it, not the author of it, and (2) humans by their own efforts and reason could arrive at this objective morality without the aid of god(s).

In the end, it is clear that morality is man-made — and that humans have made it many times in many different forms. In addition, morality can be based on many things. Religion is surely one source of morality, but it is also possible to base morality on reason or human nature or social obligation or lots of bases. Atheists do not have a single shared moral code, but virtually all Atheists arrive at roughly the same morality as most Theists, but by a different course; about half of the Ten Commandments are a pretty good idea. I don't need a god to tell me that killing is socially and psychologically undesirable in most cases. Reason can and does get humans to a viable moral place that is just as well-grounded as any religious code. Religion adds nothing to the mix.

Step Nine: The Argument from Benefit

Some apologist Theists, after yielding all this ground, still maintain that we should believe nonetheless. They admit that all the Theist arguments fail and that there is no 'reason' to believe. In fact, sometimes the very unverifiability, even irrationality, of Theism is taken as an argument for belief. Tertullian in the second century CE wrote: "And the Son of God died; it is by all means to be believed, because it is absurd. And He was buried and rose again; the fact is certain because it is impossible." This is dizzying illogic, but more than that, it is a precarious basis for belief: if absurdity and impossibility are our criteria for belief, then how do we decide which absurdities and impossibilities to believe in?

The two most famous 'challenges to believe' come from Blaise Pascal and William James; they have been discussed and dismissed repeatedly since their formulation, but they continue to rear their ugly and ridiculous heads in theistic disputes. Pascal offered his well-known 'wager,' in which he insisted that, since reason cannot settle the issue of god's existence, we should approach the question like a bet — if we bet there is a god we could win big but have nothing to lose, but if we bet there is not a god, we could lose big but have nothing to win. The flaws in this position are obvious. First, even if the idea of a wager is right, it does not indicate *which* god we should believe in. If we bet there is a Christian god but there is really a Hindu god, then we lose even though we put our money on Theism. In other words, Pascal has set up one of the clearest examples of a false dichotomy. Second, it is not true that Theists have nothing to lose; even if the only two choices are Christianity and Atheism (which they are not), still if Christians bet wrongly, they lose time, money, freedom of thought, and peace of mind (always worrying about some imaginary god and devil). They also get shame and guilt, false knowledge, and false hope. On the other hand, it is not true either that Atheists stand to win nothing: if we bet on Atheism and win, we receive freedom of thought and action, freedom from shame and guilt, true knowledge, and the right to build and inhabit our own human world.

William James described the other main system for believing in light of the inadequacy of reason. Reason cannot, he posits, help us choose, yet choose we must. In such cases, "Our passional nature not only lawfully may, but must, decide an option between propositions, whenever it is a genuine option that cannot by its nature be decided on intellectual grounds." In other words, when evidence and logic cannot adjudicate, we can appropriately turn to feelings, hopes, and such to make our choice. But this is a dangerous if not incoherent position, for a variety of reasons. We know all too well that 'the heart' is not a very discriminating organ, and we can be led down treacherously false and unhealthy paths by following emotions over reasons. Also, our passions are not unbiased judges for our choices, since they are informed by what we already believe or at the very least by what is available in our cultures to believe (in other words, few Americans would choose Zeus or Odin!). James thinks he has answered this question by distinguishing between 'live' options and others that are not live, but he never does and never could explain why some options are not live for some people in some places and times. Finally, letting the passions make our decisions about theistic questions does not prove anything about truth, only about the emotional appeal of the choices.

This pretty clearly illustrates the problem with arguments from benefit: they do not *prove* anything. Even if the argument is valid — and I think we have shown that it is not, on empirical grounds — it does not mean that there is a god, only that the psychological effect of thinking there is one is advantageous. And it cannot distinguish between one god-belief and another; if believing in the Christian god or the Muslim god or the Hindu gods each produces benefit, how do you choose between them? If they all work equally well, then it is probably not them but us! Finally, the futility of this argument is highlighted by the fact that, if there really is a god of any kind, it is hard to imagine that he/she/it would be impressed by this approach to belief. The Christian god, for instance, demands faith, commitment, and devotion, not idle belief of the sort characterized by 'Oops, I better believe, just in case.' Such a believer is not a believer at all; he is just taking out spiritual insurance, and the god will know it.

Steps Ten through Twelve: The Arguments Against the Existence of Gods

Our first nine steps have been a liberation from the tyranny of classic and contemporary arguments for god(s) and/or belief. Having established that there is no compelling or even convincing reason to accept any of the god-talk we hear from any religion, we may stand fairly comfortably on our Atheism. But can we go further and advance our own arguments to strengthen our conviction that Theism is a futile and bankrupt claim? I think that we can, and I have selected three final arguments to make the case.

Step Ten: The Incoherence or Contradiction of Religious Language

Theists will often ask, as if it were an argument for their side, whether we can prove the nonexistence of god(s). Usually, our response is that we do not have to, as we cited above in Step One, the burden of proof. Their argument amounts to the principle that, if you cannot disprove something, you should believe it, which is patently silly. Another form this complaint takes is that you 'cannot prove a negative,' so if you claim that there is no god, you are making an unsupportable or illogical claim. On the same principle as we just mentioned, you do not have to prove a negative; you only have to prove a positive. But is it really true that you cannot prove a negative?

In the well-established realm of logic, there are in fact two ways to 'prove a negative,' or better yet to prove that a claim has no merit. These methods involve the nature of the language in which the claims are made and measure the coherence and consistency of that language. Claims that are incoherent or self-contradictory in their language are necessarily invalid and false.

Incoherence as the quality of some language, for example religious language, entails that the claim or the terms of the claim have ambiguous meaning or no meaning at all and are not worthy of consideration (some philosophers of language separate incoherence and ambiguity, but we will treat them together for our purposes). Many if not most people, when they say something like 'I believe in god' or 'I believe that there is a god,' assume that others — and even they themselves — have a clear conception of the word or phenomenon 'god' when neither has such a conception at all. If you ask Theists to define god, they will either balk and say that god is unknowable and ineffable or they will offer inconsistent and conflicting definitions. But of course, without a settled definition of terms, argument or even discussion cannot proceed, so we should always require Theists to define god.

If Theists cannot agree on what god is, then Atheists really have nothing more to do. The very word and idea is confused and ultimately meaningless, and therefore any further talk about god must be incoherent and invalid. I think it is good to remember that there is no such thing as Theism but only Theism*s*, and that accordingly Theists have as much or more to settle with each other as with us Atheists, as we will see in Step Twelve. But what if god is mysterious and unknowable? This, alas, is another refuge of the confused, for how can one coherently talk about, let alone believe in, the unknowable? How could one possibly 'know' that one's claims and beliefs are legitimate and founded? For example, if god 'works in mysterious ways,' how can we know for sure that he/she/it is working at all? If I said that my car worked in mysterious ways, in that sometimes it starts and sometimes it doesn't, that would be the definition of *not working*! If god sometimes answers prayer and sometimes doesn't, sometimes intervenes in human affairs and sometimes doesn't, how can we know which is which? We cannot. Therefore, since the very words and concepts Theists use appear to be incoherent, we may be able to dismiss their claims out of court before the argument even starts.

Contradiction is a clear and straightforward notion. A term or concept cannot contain definitions or characteristics that contradict or cancel each other. We can, for example, 'prove the negative' with absolute confidence that there is no such thing as a 'married bachelor,' since a bachelor is by definition unmarried. What then is the definition of god? If Theists could even agree, they might settle on such traits as infinite, perfect, eternal, all-knowing, all-powerful, all-good, and incorporeal. Before we get started, it is more than possible that these characteristics are themselves incoherent: what does it mean to be 'infinite' or 'all-powerful' or 'incorporeal'? Are these even real things or merely negations or exaggerations of familiar experiential concepts like 'finite' or 'powerful' or 'corporeal'? Can any human really grasp the meaning of the superlatives attributed to god?

But let's assume for present purposes that the god-traits have actual meaning and that the god supposedly has all these traits. Is it not contradictory to be an 'incorporeal being'? Is it not contradictory to be all-powerful and all-good in view of the nature of life and reality, which contains so much suffering and evil (this is the problem of theodicy, to which we will turn in Step Eleven)? Is it not contradictory that god could be all-powerful but that there could be other powerful things too, including Satan and even humans, with our puny but real powers? Is it not contradictory that god could be perfect and eternal, for perfect things by necessity want or need nothing, yet the Christian God seems to have bothered to create the world and seems to have a personality that loves and angers and gets jealous (all signs of an imperfect nature) and even worse has changed his mind about sacrifice, retribution, and other issues? And is it not contradictory to imagine a god that is all-knowing but that supposedly allows 'free will' — or that could create such an imperfect world with imperfect human beings who need to pray to get his attention, and then punish them for the natures that he himself gave them?

In conclusion, any talk that is incoherent or self-contradictory is, by logical necessity, to be set aside and rejected without further dispute. If religious language — god-talk — is incoherent and/or self-contradictory, it is invalid and false by logical necessity, and our analysis indicates that it is very likely if not certainly both. Therefore, we can say that we have 'proved the negative' by proving that the terms of the positive are empty and confused and that only by negating them does sense ensue. As a final demonstration of this principle, imagine trying to argue that there is such a thing as a blurg. If the blurg-believer cannot produce a coherent and noncontradictory definition and description of the thing, regardless of what other arguments or evidence he may marshal, we are reasonable to maintain that there is no such thing as a blurg to begin with.

Step Eleven: The Problem of Evil

One of the most unshakable problems for Theism over the centuries has been the problem of evil, or what is known as 'theodicy.' The problem goes back to our discussion of self-contradiction, in particular in relation to the empirical reality of the created world: if god exists, and if god is all-good and all-powerful, then why does evil exist? The Hellenistic philosopher Epicurus said it best, three centuries before Christ but already after the logic of gods and evils had become troublesome:

God either wishes to take away evil, and is unable, or He is able, and unwilling; or He is neither willing nor able, or He is both willing and able.

If He is willing and is unable, He is feeble, which is not in accordance with the character of God.

If He is able and unwilling, He is envious, which is equally at variance with God.

If He is neither willing nor able, He is both envious and feeble, and therefore not God.

If He is both willing and able, which alone is suitable to God, from what source then are evils? Or why does He not remove them?

Theists have naturally struggled with this question and have come up with some clever answers for it. But do they really convince?

Christian apologists in particular have attempted to distinguish two kinds of evil — natural and moral. Natural evil might more accurately be referred to as 'bad,' since supposedly there is no ill will involved (unless the devil did it or God himself did it); these consist of natural disasters, pain and disease and the like. Moral evil pertains more to the 'evils that men do,' so let us consider them first. Why is there moral, that is intentional, evil in the world? Theists actually have a ready solution — free will. That is, evil is either the result of ungodly behavior that humans in their freedom but ignorance choose to do to each other or the consequences that God unleashes on humans for that behavior. This is a pretty comprehensive theological explanation, but other questions persist. Why, for instance, did God, who should have known better, make such a flawed creature as man, who would likely if not certainly use his free will to his own detriment? There are even philosophers of religion who argue that God could have made an improved human who still possessed free will — one who was more likely to choose freely the course of good. By analogy, when we as parents raise good children, children who are more prone to act morally and positively, we have not thereby taken away their free will.

Also, while it seems potentially justifiable that free will would bring down evils on individual evildoers, it seems much less justifiable when the evils befall innocent victims. Why would a god allow me to use my free will to do evil to you? If this god is powerful and good, and if you are righteous in his eyes, surely he can and is inclined to protect you? Among humans, a parent who can protect one child from the evils of another but does not do so is a bad parent; how less so a god? Let us also grant that god, as creator and lawgiver, has the right to punish; are not the punishments assigned — eternal damnation and torment — totally out of proportion to the crime, which is after all the crime of being the creatures that he made us to be? And finally, as we observed in Step Ten, if a god really is all-knowing and all-powerful, is there such a thing as free will at all, or is that just an illusion and excuse?

The problem of natural evil is more elusive. Theists often start with free will again: the very fact that there is pain, sickness, and death in the world at all is due to the original act of human free will, the 'original sin,' and not only humans but plants, animals, and the earth itself pay the price. Truly this punishment is in another dimension from the crime, like beating a child nearly to death at her first mistake, then leaving all subsequent errors and crimes undisciplined! But God does as he wishes, no matter how irrational or disproportionate. Theists will also argue that the evils are part of a bigger plan that we cannot see. But, if we cannot see it, we cannot know this is true. Besides, it is difficult to see why suffering is necessary to any such plan or why an all-powerful and all-good being could not achieve the same results without the evils — couldn't figure out a better plan.

The suggested answer to this dilemma is that either the good outweighs the evil or that the evil is somehow necessary, for instance to produce higher-level good. It has been proposed that if there were no disasters or suffering, there would be no opportunity for compassion or courage or heroism, and that these are greater goods than the evils are evil. First, this too is pure speculation, and we cannot know if it is true; it sounds like rationalization, quite honestly. But granting for the moment its truth, why must sometimes hundreds or thousands suffer and die to teach a lesson — and the same lesson over and over? Is the lesson really worth it, and if it is, is there not another way to convey it? Second, this might justify human suffering, but why nonhuman suffering? Why should puppies and pine trees suffer and die? Surely animals and plants do not learn compassion and heroism, and their suffering too often happens away from human eyes for it to have any salutary purpose for us. And, in the end, why does a god who created the whole universe with a thought need to use such blunt and heavy-handed methods to achieve such slight and usually failing ends? Why teach puny humans a pointless lesson by clumsy means like earthquakes, floods, hurricanes, and horrific diseases? The tools do not fit the job, and the ends do not justify the means.

Ultimately, the problem of evil remains. Explain or justify it as you wish; even insist that anything god does is good by definition. Still, the effects down here on earth are the same — pain, misery, and strife imposed on innocent and guilty alike, under the apparent indifference, neglect, or even intentional cruelty of this powerful good god. If such a god really does exist, it's hard to accept how he/she/it deserves our praise.

Step Twelve: The Sociological or Statistical Argument

A number of the steps climbed so far have alluded to the differences and disagreements between various religions — varying and conflicting scriptures/authorities, personal experiences, moralities, *etc.* This fact highlights a grave error in much of American debate about religion: the tendency to conceive of the issue as Christianity versus Atheism. I would like to advance a more uncommon but more decisive claim — that the best argument against Theism is not Atheism but *other Theisms!*

In modern, tolerant society, individuals, even religions, tend or at least pretend to accept the coexistence of others with dissimilar and even mutually exclusive beliefs. Not all, of course, hold this position; some condemn at least certain others, if not all others, and what little tolerance there is in the modern world has been hard-won at a high price, as we will discuss in a later chapter. Still, we like to pride ourselves on our tolerant attitudes. However, at the heart of every religion is an exclusivistic claim — that it has the truth, the only truth, the only good, the only solution to life's (and after-life's) problems. If this were not the case, why would followers not leave and choose another belief? But if all beliefs are 'okay,' why privilege yours over all the others? Although today's believers do not like to admit it — in fact, they might actively deny it — each religion's exclusive truth claim is a refutation of all the others. If Christianity is right, then Islam is wrong (Islam, by example, teaches that God never had any sons, so if that is true, Christianity is wrong to its core), or if Hinduism is right, then both Christianity and Islam are wrong, and so on *ad infinitum*.

The 'statistical' argument thus goes like this. Say that there are 100 religions in the world, which is an extremely conservative estimate. Each of these religions makes an exclusive truth claim, such that if it is true, the others must be false. Grant too that each claim is equally likely (how could we know otherwise?). In this case, each religion has a 1% chance of being right; then it also has a 99% chance of being wrong (if any of the other 99 religions is correct, it is wrong). Therefore, whatever you choose to believe, there is a 99% likelihood you are wrong. If the number of religions in the world is 1,000, then your likelihood of being wrong rises to 99.9%. But, if we accept that there is only a 50/50 chance at best that there is a god at all (*i.e.* Atheism), then the likelihood of being wrong rises to 99.95%. A recent survey of religions counted over 33,000 sects just of Christianity, giving each a 99.993% chance of being wrong. In other words, the chance of any particular religion being correct, all things being equal, is the reciprocal of the number of religions in the world — an infinitesimally small number. In the end, it is almost certain that, whatever religion you choose, you are wrong.

The point of this final argument is that there is in reality no such thing as 'Theism' but only 'Theisms.' Theists often try to obfuscate the issue by claiming that the vast majority of humans believe in god, but they fail — passively or actively — to appreciate that these many Theists do not believe the same things but quite disparate and incompatible things. Rather than allowing them to claim each other in support of their beliefs, we should annex them all as arguments against each other. Granted, this is not an argument against the existence of god(s) *per se*, but it is an argument against each particular claim of the existence of god(s), and since each religion is a new specific claim, the argument from 'other Theisms' is all we need to defeat each claim when it appears. So, whenever we are in debate with Theists, we should remind them that not only do Atheists disagree with them but that the majority of Theists do too!

As a final comment, the 'sociological' argument from 'other Theisms' is the main reason why Atheists should stop squabbling about Christianity and the Christian Bible. Rather than engage in Bible debate, I tell Christian debaters that I do not care what the Bible says, any more than they care what the Qur'an or the Bhagavad Gita says; those sources are only authorities to the people who already believe in them, and those people have to demonstrate why their texts are authoritative in the first place. This cannot be done without advancing other criteria that are just as relative as the texts themselves. So, we should force Theists to face their own diversity — and their own contradictory, self-canceling diversity — instead of taking them on one by one. In the end, they have not only the burden of proof but a double burden of proof: not only to prove that *a* god exists but to prove that *their particular* god exists. This, if six thousand years of recorded history is any indication, they cannot do. And perhaps it will even plant a seed of doubt or skepticism in their own heads.

Conclusion: Claiming Your Natural Atheism

These twelve steps have shown that there is no good reason to take any god-claim seriously and that there is good reason to maintain the 'presumption of Atheism' against all such claims. If one follows all twelve steps and takes them to heart, thinks about them, and practices them, then one can be assured of being on the road to recovery. But what is there for Atheists and Theists alike to recover?

For Atheists, you can recover your certainty, your confidence that your conclusions are sound and your positions justified. You can also recover your sense that you are a good person, that religion does not monopolize the moral ground. You can recover your right to use your reason and to trust it to guide you through treacherous territories where falsehood and fanaticism lurk. Most importantly, you can recover your natural right and capacity to define your own morality and to construct your own world of meaning.

For Theists, you can recover your reason which your religion has asked or compelled you to abandon. You can recover trust in your own mind and senses, in the natural world, and in human nature and society. And you can, with your recovered faculties, take that first tentative — even painful — step into the world without gods, which is the only world there is.

CHAPTER TWO

Thinking About Thinking — A Short Course on Reason

In the ongoing exchanges between Atheists and Theists, 'thinking' and 'knowing' and all their forms and vagaries are perennial subjects at issue. Various thought-related terms like critical thinking, reason, freethought, and logic are regularly floated by or aimed at each other. Atheists of course are notorious for — and usually proud of — being 'rational' and 'logical,' and these terms are often intended by anti-Atheists as epithets more than compliments, suggesting a kind of disregard of if not disdain for the more 'emotional' or 'intuitive' side of human nature. This is clearly untrue, as we will explore subsequently, but the charge is an effective one, particularly among Christians, who often distrust or dismiss human mental abilities as irrelevant, inadequate, or even counterproductive to the spiritual quest. They may be right, although emotion, 'feeling,' intuition, and faith are no steady guides on the road to truth — including 'spiritual' truth — as we will posit and prove below.

Our task in this chapter is to explore the domain of and dispel some myths about thought and reason; we also want to consider how to use reason well. Let us begin by examining the constellation of related terms surrounding thought. Critical thinking, for instance, is something we all value, I presume, and it is something that we attempt to teach in school. I talk about critical thinking in my own teaching. Without being too technical, to think critically is to ask yourself and others, 'Why do I/you think that?' I tell my students that to think critically about the course material, all they have to do is ask why I say the things I say or why they should accept them. In other words, critical thinking is scrutiny of the information and opinions (of others and of yourself) and the process of arriving at such information and opinions; simply put, what is the basis for holding that position or coming to that conclusion?

Freethought can be defined as thinking, usually pertaining to religious matters, that is 'free' to question facts and assumptions, that does not accept authority, tradition, popular opinion, or personal desire or interest as sufficient grounds for a position or opinion. Freethought insists that thinking must be liberated to ask any question and follow wherever the answers lead; thought that presumes or demands its own destination in advance cannot be free, since that destination may be wrong. As Thomas Jefferson said, "Question with boldness."

Logic is a particular tool for thought, which we will discuss at length below — a method for arriving at good conclusions based on the best available evidence. That brings us to reason, which is a concept much lionized and maligned in the whole Theist/Atheist enterprise. Curiously, on both sides reason is often misunderstood as some separate, mysterious, exclusive form of thought. Atheists and other 'rationalists' may themselves mystify it, passively or actively, as some unique power of the mind — a kind of thinking apart from other kinds of thinking. Theists, predictably, often have a jaundiced view of it, seeing it as a particularly inhumane or destructive application of mental activity. Both views misrepresent reason and present it as more foreign and distinctive than it really is.

Reasoning is one of many things that the human mind can do (and is probably not the most common!). Among the various 'uses' or powers of mind are the pursuit of beauty, of pleasure, of fun, of problem-solving, and of persuasion. Problem-solving is something that all living things, at least all animals, of necessity do, and it entails judging or acting effectively on available information. Persuasion is a specifically human vocation, attempting to convince others that one's own judgments or actions are correct. Beauty, pleasure, fun, and other such interests will not be discussed here, although even the most hard-headed Atheist (like myself) would be foolish to denigrate their reality and appeal, and few if any do.

There are many ways to approach or accomplish problem-solving and persuasion. Humans can and do make decisions and actions on the basis of emotions like love or fear, of desires, of beliefs, and of preconceptions and prejudices, among others. Then there is reason. Reason is the process of arriving at conclusions and courses of action on the basis of facts and arguments. It takes what is known or can be demonstrated and attempts to move with certainty from the known to the unknown. Reason operates from knowledge to produce new, confident knowledge. While this sounds important and unique, I want to hold that reason is not one kind of thinking or knowing separate from other kinds but that *reason is thinking*. Reason and critical thinking and freethought are one and the same; any kind of 'thinking' that is not reason or does not follow the dictates of reason is not thought at all but something else mistaken for or masquerading as thinking. If the goal of thinking is true and justifiable judgments and actions, then only reason offers a credible guarantee of reaching that goal. Of course, people can engage in other processes that resemble or pretend to be thinking, such as expressing a taste, holding out a wish, or advancing a belief, but these and related activities are not thinking because they do not proceed through a 'thought process' nor arrive at new knowledge that was not included in or entailed by the sources from which the 'thinking' emanated. In fact, they do not arrive at 'knowledge' at all.

Reason is first and foremost a method. One can reason about anything, including feelings and beliefs; if one has any doubt about this claim, consider the work of Thomas Aquinas, who reasoned extensively (although not always well) about Christian beliefs in his work. And, as just stated, reason can be performed well or poorly. But regardless of the quality of one's reasoning, reason is a dimension apart from things that are not thinking at all — like asserting, pleading, threatening, cajoling, testifying, and the many disguised forms of non-thought that buzz around us every day. Here I concur with, though paraphrase, George Smith, author of *Atheism: The Case Against God*, by suggesting that 'rational thought' and its supporting procedure of 'rational demonstration' are not special types of thought and demonstration but are themselves *thought* and *demonstration*.

Reason is the faculty by which man acquires knowledge; rational demonstration is the process by which man verifies his knowledge claims. A belief based on reason is a belief that has been examined for evidence, internal coherence, and consistency with previously established knowledge. There can be no propositions beyond the "limits of reason." To advocate that a belief be accepted without reason is to advocate that a belief be accepted without thought and without verification. (110)

The one place I would vehemently part company with Smith is in applying the word 'belief' in any of these contexts, as we will see in a later chapter.

The Process of Reasoning

Reason is the process of moving from facts to conclusions by means of argument. An argument is a series of statements or 'propositions' designed to establish the truth of a claim or a conclusion; the argument uses such statements as 'reasons' for arriving at other, newer statements. An argument need not be a 'debate' but can be merely one side 'presenting its case'; the classic example of this is the U.S. Declaration of Independence, which presents its argument for the justification of American independence from England, without asking for a response from King George.

Propositions are clearly central to reason. A proposition is a sentence that can be shown to be either true or false; we could refer to it as a 'truth claim.' Propositions are thus distinct from other kinds of utterances such as questions, commands, exclamations, and so on which are not propositional, that is, which do not make a claim; such utterances may be persuasive — even highly so — but they are not 'rational.' But propositions are only one of two essential components of any good argument. They are the 'content,' if you will, or the grounds of the argument, the things that are advanced as true and upon which the argument will stand. The other component is the 'form' or the relationships between the various grounds and the final conclusions of the argument, or what is typically called the 'logic' of the argument.

Therefore, a 'sound' argument is one in which all of the grounds are true and all of the logic is valid. Obviously, then, there are two completely distinct issues in any argument — truth of grounds and validity of logic. Let us refer to the grounds of the argument as its 'premises,' or statements that directly support the conclusion. The truth of the premises depends on how well the premises correspond to reality (the 'correspondence theory' of truth or knowledge is simplistic and controversial, but it will suffice for now). In other words, if one premise of my argument is that cats are black, then it is important for the success of my argument that cats really are black. The validity of the logic entails that the conclusions of my argument follow for certain from the premises, that I have not made any bad or unwarranted connections between premises and conclusions. If the logic is good, then true premises should lead inexorably to true conclusions. For instance, if I premise my argument on the statement that cats are black, and I then posit that Fluffy is a cat, it should follow by necessity that Fluffy is black.

Thus, a sound argument passes two tests — the test of content or truth and the test of form or logic; if an argument is sound, then the falsity of its conclusion should be theoretically impossible. It should be apparent, accordingly, that the first rule of argumentation is never to challenge the conclusion but to attack either or both the premises or the logic. A successful refutation of either will bring an argument down, regardless of how good the other is. This raises a crucial point: truth is not validity, and validity is not truth. An argument may have accurate facts and be faulty, or it may have impeccable logic and be wrong. There are, in reality, two entirely independent ways in which arguments fail.

Good premises may lead to bad conclusions via bad logic. For instance, if I say, 'crows are black, and my cat is black, therefore my cat is a crow,' this is clearly wrong, although both of my premises are true; in combination, and as a justification for the conclusion, however, they are flawed. Similarly, good logic may lead to bad conclusions via bad premises, in the sense that the premises are false or unproven or themselves subject to argument. As an example, the argument 'God punishes sinners, you are a sinner, therefore God will punish you' is an unsound if not false argument since it is undemonstrated — merely asserted — that God punishes sinners or even that there is such a thing as sin or God. If the premises are true, then the conclusion is sound (since the logic is valid), but there is no proof that the premises are true; they call for yet another argument to establish their truth before they are appropriate as grounds for the present argument.

In the end, based on the quality of its premises and its logic, an argument or conclusion is either sound or unsound. A sound argument is necessarily true. An unsound argument, however, is not *necessarily false*; it is simply *not necessarily true*. It may, ultimately, be true or false. But that is precisely the point: since there is so much uncertainty at the end of the argument, it is essentially useless as an argument. Since it may be (accidentally or coincidentally) true but we cannot be sure, it is no secure position to take or to build further arguments on.

Premises and Truth

As stated, premises are the statements or propositions used to support a claim or conclusion — the 'reasons' for justifying the argument, the 'content' or the 'truth' part of the argument. Premises can consist of such elements as evidence, assumptions, supporting arguments, authority, and explanation. No matter what type of premise is employed, it is invariably stated in words, so the definition of the words or terms of the argument is essential, as we discussed in the previous chapter. A definition is a description or account that accurately and fully distinguishes a word or concept from everything else — the 'necessary' and 'sufficient' conditions of the thing (*i.e.*, it must have these characteristics and it requires no others). For example, if we were to proffer a definition of 'human,' it might include or be based on physical characteristics (erect bipedalism), behavior (tool-making or language), or other distinctive traits (a soul). However, if other beings were found to share these characteristics (say, apes can make tools or use language) or if the characteristics themselves were found to be false or unsubstantiated (say, there is no such thing as a soul, or at least no proof of it), the definition would be inadequate. Definitions can be synonyms for the word or concept, examples of it, or stipulations (like 'parallel means that two lines never intersect').

As we mentioned in Step Ten in our Twelve Steps to Atheism, an argument can fail before it even gets out of the dock if there is a problem with the terminology. If the terms of the argument suffer from incoherence or self-contradiction, then the argument is necessarily unsound and cannot lead to a firm determination of truth. Incoherence includes vagueness, ambiguity, and meaninglessness. Vagueness occurs when the meaning of a word or proposition is unclear; for instance, if we were to take the statement 'Thy rod and thy staff, they comfort me,' I would maintain that no one knows quite what that is supposed to mean. What does comfort mean in this context, and how do a rod and a staff bring it about? Ambiguity is similar but different in that the word or proposition has two or more possible meanings; a good example of ambiguity is a statement like 'biting dogs can be dangerous,' which could refer to dogs that bite or people who bite dogs. Meaninglessness is the extreme case where words or statements are advanced that have no meaning at all; if someone said, 'glorgs are good,' I would have to reject the statement as unprovable, since I don't know what a glorg is. The same case might be made for the statement 'god is good,' since I might have no idea what god is. Other religious language — in fact, all religious language — may ultimately fail as meaningless, including terms like 'heaven,' 'hell,' 'sin,' 'eternity,' 'soul,' and so on.

A self-contradictory term or proposition, as we know, is one that has two or more characteristics that could not possibly coexist. For example, if someone said, 'god is a married bachelor,' we could reject that claim out of court, since it is contradictory. Similarly, the claim that god is omnipotent and omnibenevolent may be self-contradictory, especially when held up against the facts of the natural and social world. If so, then no such being could possibly exist, since the characteristics are mutually exclusive.

So, simply stated, if the premises of an argument show incoherence or self-contradiction, the argument must be unsound and probably false, maybe even nonsensical. But let's grant the premises are not, at least at face value, either incoherent or self-contradictory. Next we must evaluate the merits of the premises in terms of their truth. The first kind of premise that we listed above was evidence, which may be a fact or observation or other kind of information. Evidence consists of examples, events (uncontrolled information), experimental data (controlled information), hypothetical cases, analogies, testimony, and statistics. The difference between events and experimental data is an important one. An experiment (another of those words that gets overused and overmaligned) is a special case of fact-gathering in which deliberately contrived situations are designed to yield particular observations. The point is to 'control' or exclude as many variables as possible in the situation in order to determine the relationship between a manipulated ('independent') variable and the resultant ('dependent') variable. Experimentation is the hallmark of science, but not all science is experimental, and not all experiments are scientific. Events, being uncontrolled, are somewhat less reliable as evidence, since we cannot rule out the effects of uncontrolled or even unknown variables; many facts are only available to us as events (such as historical occurrences or the big bang), and they may be wonderfully important to our knowledge, but they are also more slippery to process.

Analogies and testimony are useful but much more suspect as evidence. An analogy is a comparison between two unlike things based on one or more traits that they share. When someone says that the universe is like a watch in that they were both designed, they are not stating a fact or making an observation but proposing an analogy. Analogies are neither true nor false but rather strong or weak. The strength or weakness depends on the accuracy of the depiction of the relationship between the two things and the aptness of the relationship to the present case in the argument. So, if someone says, 'watches have lots of parts, and the parts work in conjunction, and the watch was designed' and 'the universe has lots of parts, and the parts work in conjunction, therefore the universe was designed,' they are making a weak analogy. Not all things with lots of parts are designed, and there is no evidence that the 'parts' of the universe 'work' in any familiar sense of the term; also, it is easy to understand what 'designed' means in the case of watches (we see humans make watches), but it is not so easy to understand what the concept means in the case of the universe (we've never seen anyone make a universe). Testimony, as we have noted, is an account offered by a 'witness' to an event which, while important and useful, is questionable and ultimately defeasible on the basis of the credibility of the witness, the likelihood of the report, and the corroboration of the report by supporting evidence. Testimony, like analogy, can never be sufficient evidence on its own — as many wrongly convicted defendants would readily agree.

Statistics are also a special case, one that uses a subset of instances to generalize about a larger set or even all of reality. For example, if we discern that 50% of test cases demonstrate trait X, then the implication is that 50% of all possible cases would do so. There are some clear issues in this type of evidential reasoning, however. The first is sampling: have we in fact collected a representative cross-section of the larger set we are trying to learn about so that we can extrapolate the findings of the sample to the whole set? If our sample is 'biased' in some way, then our generalization will be flawed and subsequently useless. It should go without saying that a small sample is always more suspect than a large one. It is always possible that a small sample has drawn a nonrandom selection of subjects into the test. And in the worst case, a 'sample of one' is often used to assert some truth when we cannot even begin to know how representative it is of 'typical' circumstances. So if I claim that I prayed about my illness and got better, that sample of one provides nothing more than anecdotal evidence. This is why it is difficult to generalize and draw conclusions about, say, the creation or design of the universe; we only know of one universe, and maybe it is not typical of all universes!

Second, the method of testing or evaluating the sample is critical: have we used the right measures, asked the right questions, probed the sample accurately and fully? Obviously, one of the problems with and criticisms of statistics is that the tools you use to collect statistics determine the outcome; as we have discovered to our chagrin, if on a survey a researcher asks 'Are you an Atheist?' versus 'Do you believe in god?' versus 'Do you believe in a personal god who sits on a throne in the sky?' the results will vary widely, making the statistical results difficult to read and apply. Finally, interpretation and representation of statistics are problematic. With hard numbers in hand, it is still possible to misunderstand or to mislead by, for example, emphasizing minority results (say, reporting that 'prayer has medical effects' when the effect was 10% or 20%, well within the realm of chance), conflating results (say, reporting that '95% of people believe in god,' when they believe wildly different things about wildly different gods), or using charts and graphs to visualize statistics to downplay or exaggerate trends or relationships (say, focusing in on a small region of values to make the differences seem more profound, or on a large region of values to make the differences seem more trivial).

James Lett (2001) has done a nice job of summarizing the "six rules of evidential reasoning" by which we can judge the quality of the evidence (or purported evidence) that is presented to us in arguments. The first rule is falsifiability: "It must be possible to conceive of evidence that would prove the claim false" (1). This is a familiar and basic aspect of knowledge, especially scientific knowledge, and has been common parlance at least since Karl Popper's work on the philosophy of science. If it is impossible in principle (whether or not it is something we can do or are likely to do) to prove a claim false, then there is no way we can ever reliably establish its truth or falseness. Anybody could advance any wacky evidence and compel us to accept it, since it is immune to testing. Lett mentions two ways that the rule of falsifiability is violated: either by making an "undeclared claim" which, being "so broad or vague that it lacks any propositional content," suffers from incoherence, or by using the "multiple out" which entails "an inexhaustible series of excuses intended to explain away the evidence that seem to falsify the claim." He offers young-earth creationism, UFOs, and psychic powers as relevant examples.

His second rule of evidence involves logic, so we will leave that until later. The third rule concerns comprehensiveness, in that the evidence "offered in support of a claim must be exhaustive — that is, all of the available evidence must be considered" (3). The most common violation of this rule is the use of selective evidence — only accepting or presenting the facts that strengthen your case — and discarding disconfirming evidence. For example, 'researchers' may only report the cases where prayer seemed to make a positive difference in health, leaving out the cases where it made no difference or perhaps even a negative difference. This leads to the fourth rule, that of honesty, which simply asserts that the evidence "must be evaluated without self-deception." This rule is in part an extension of the rule of falsifiability in that one should not make excuses for the failure of one's data; the new and significant aspect of the rule is how one evaluates one's own data and follows it unflinchingly to its conclusion. Being honest with the evidence "means that you must accept the obligation to come to a rational conclusion once you have examined all the evidence"; if the "weight of the evidence contradicts the claim, then you are required to abandon the belief in that claim" (4). This rule speaks to those who set out with a conclusion in mind and intend to prove that conclusion no matter what the facts say.

Rule Five refers to replicability: "If the evidence for any claim is based upon an experimental result, or if the evidence offered in support of any claim could logically be explained as coincidental, then it is necessary for the evidence to be repeated in subsequent experiments or trials" (5). In other words, a single experimental result is never adequate to establish a fact or prove a case. There is always the possibility of statistical variation, random outcomes, experimenter error, or other confounding phenomena. The danger of violating this rule has been apparent lately, as scientists — some reputable, some not — have occasionally and publicly rushed to announce results that were refuted shortly thereafter by retesting. If a result is valid and reliable, it should and will occur with regularity every time the same test is conducted; otherwise, something is amiss, and quite possibly some other explanation exists for the results.

The final rule is sufficiency, which states that the evidence "must be adequate to establish the truth of that claim, with these stipulations: 1. the burden of proof for any claim rests on the claimant, 2. extraordinary claims demand extraordinary evidence, and 3. evidence based upon authority and/or testimony is always inadequate ..." (5). We have previously discussed all of these issues, so they should be clear and certain. In particular, rejection of or skepticism toward a claim or piece of evidence is not a claim or piece of evidence in itself, and therefore it bears no burden of proof. The rule of honesty would demand that someone who makes a claim but cannot or will not accept and meet the burden of proof for it does not have evidence at the same level as the claim, cannot muster other than authoritative or testimonial evidence, and should withdraw the claim from our consideration — and probably apologize to us for wasting our time.

As we admitted above that authority and testimony might serve as premises for any argument, along with evidence, we have noted now (and in the previous chapter) the weakness of these particular phenomena. In fact, in an important way, authority is testimony: it is the testimony of one who claims to know for himself or herself based on special skill or experience. Authority and other forms of testimony are worthwhile as *inputs* to the process of reasoning, but they are not sufficient grounds themselves to build any reasoned argument on. Presented with authoritative or testimonial 'evidence,' the reasoning process begins as we weigh the truth, trustworthiness, and usefulness of that evidence. We often, in real life and in argumentation, defer to authorities and eyewitnesses, mainly to save time or because we trust them, but their reports are always challengeable and defeasible in principle and usually in practice.

Assumptions and supporting arguments deserve a word before we move on. Supporting arguments are obviously subarguments that are designed to support the major argument, and as such they are subject to all the considerations outlined above. Assumptions are the implicit premises of an argument, usually unproven and often unprovable. In order to judge the soundness of the argument, assumptions need to be made explicit and tested like any other truth claims. For example, in the theistic 'design argument,' one assumption is that all orderly things are designed and all designed things require a designer; in the cosmological argument, the assumption is that all things that exist require a cause and that a chain of causes cannot be infinite. While these assumptions seem intuitively appealing, that is their danger — that we take unsubstantiated assumptions as established facts and not challenge them to find that they are in actuality prejudices, preconceptions, or old wives' tales.

Logic and Validity

The second element of a sound argument, and the one that most people are probably more familiar with, is its logic or, as we described it, the valid relationships between the premises and the conclusions of the argument. If the logic of the argument is good, then the conclusion 'follows' necessarily from the premises. Like reason itself, people commonly mystify logic as some strange and scary kind of thinking or misconstrue logic as the whole of reason. In fact logic is simply a set of tried-and-true rules for how to combine propositions into trustworthy units. The 'rules of logic' may not be equally familiar to everyone, but everyone practices an implicit or naïve kind of logic all the time. And logic is not identical to reason; it is part of the reasoning process — the middle part — and is about getting from 'here to there,' from facts to conclusions, legitimately and dependably.

The most basic form of logic is joining two premises to produce a conclusion, and this structure is known as a syllogism. The classic syllogism in logic is 'All men are mortal, Socrates is a man, therefore Socrates is mortal.' In this formulation, 'All men are mortal' is the major premise (making a general statement about a class or set of phenomena, in this case men), 'Socrates is a man' is the minor premise (making a specific statement about a member of a class or set), and 'Socrates is mortal' is the conclusion. The logic of this argument is valid, because if all members of set X have trait Y, and Z is a member of set X, then Z should and must have trait Y. The argument will be sound if the premises are true — if it is true that all Xs are Y and that Z is an X. In this particular case, that seems fairly certain.

Syllogisms of this sort represent what is known as deductive logic or simply deduction, or an argument in which the major premise is based on a rule, law, definition, principle, or generalization. An alternative structure of logic is inductive logic or induction, in which the major premise is based on observation or experience. However, it can be demonstrated (as we will explore below) that all deductions can be expressed inductively, and all inductions can be expressed deductively. In fact, if you think about it, the major premise of our classic deductive syllogism — that all men are mortal — is inductive at least to a degree: we might define or stipulate that all men are mortal, that mortality is part of the definition of 'man,' but more likely we are making an observational statement that all men that we have known or heard about so far have been mortal. Hence comes the difficulty with induction and therefore with deductions that rest on inductive premises.

But let us discuss deduction first. Deductive logic starts from some premise, however arrived at, and attempts to extract from it consequences that are implicit in or required by it. In other words, we say that the conclusion necessarily follows or arises from the premises; the conclusion is self-evidently true based on the premises. Whether the premise is strictly a definition ('All bachelors are unmarried') or a mixture of definition and observation ('All men are mortal') or a mere stipulation ('It is evil to harm people'), if the minor premise establishes a specific membership in the class or set referred to in the major premise, then we can with absolute certainty ascribe the trait of the latter to the former. It might be noticed that there are two ways to express a deductive argument, either as a syllogism (all Xs are Y, Z is an X, therefore Z is Y) or as a conditional statement (if all Xs are Y, and if Z is an X, then Z is Y). The variation in structure has no impact on the logic or soundness of the argument. One important limitation of deduction is that, generally if not universally, it does not produce 'new knowledge' but merely draws out the consequences from things we already know. We may be surprised, perhaps, by the implications of the knowledge we already have — we may not have thought its consequences all the way through — but in the end deduction gives us certainty but not a lot of productivity.

Induction is different not only in form but in function. Inductive logic starts from a premise based on or derived from observation or inference and extends or generalizes these to reach its conclusion. An observation is something we know from experience or hopefully from a (consistent) set of experiences; for example, we have seen humans die before. An inference is an application of what we know to something that we do not know; all humans that we have observed *so far* have been mortal, so we infer that all possible humans that we *could ever know* would be mortal. Some types of inferential thinking include applying statistical results to a wider or universal population, as should be apparent upon reflecting on our analysis of statistical evidence above, and assigning causality (which was the great problem for the philosopher Hume, who noted that we see events like one billiard ball hitting another and then that second billiard ball moving but that we do not 'see' cause — it is a mere inference from the consistent conjunction of two events or observations). Induction thus depends essentially on generalization or extrapolation.

Basically, induction stands on the comparison between two sets of events or phenomena. The strength of an inductive argument depends, therefore, on (1) accurate and comprehensive observation of the events or phenomena, (2) a strong causal link between the variables, and (3) the similarity of the specific and the general or extrapolated cases that are being compared. In other words, an inductive premise based on only one observation, while it might be completely correct, would have a lesser likelihood of being correct than one based on multiple observations; the single observation might be a fluke or an error or a misinterpretation; presumably, over repeated trials and observations, chance would rule out some outcomes and a dependable pattern of events would emerge. This is one problem with, say, praying for money and then finding money in the street; based on one case, it would be tempting to induce that prayer always works, but if the praying behavior were repeated without consistent results, we would have to modify or reject our original induction. Also, induction raises the issue of cause and correlation, or what is sometimes called the '*post hoc ergo propter hoc* problem': just because something occurs with or after something else does not mean that there is a causal — or any — relation between them. If I do a rain dance and then later — minutes later, hours later, days later — it rains, that does not establish a causal relationship between the two things, even though it might be seductive to think so. Finally, induction depends on the observed or known cases and the inferred or unknown cases being as similar as possible. One way of saying this is that if some observed sample of Xs are Y, 'all else being equal' or 'there being no significant differences,' then all Xs are Y. However, if all else is not equal or if there are significant differences, the induction will be flawed if not hopelessly false.

Interestingly, as we mentioned above and hopefully already illustrated, an induction can be and often is used as a premise in a deduction. One way to treat the syllogistic premise that all men are mortal is to simply stipulate it to be so: part of the definition of 'man' is 'mortal.' In another more accurate way, though, the premise is an inference from experience: all the men we have known or heard about have been mortal, so we infer or extrapolate that all men are mortal. This is a highly likely inference, we would admit, but it is not impossible that we might find one or more cases of immortal men; then our syllogism would change from 'all men are mortal' to 'some men are mortal,' with dramatic logical consequences; we could not be sure now whether Socrates is mortal or not simply based on his manhood. And this raises the fundamental concern about inductive logic: while it does generate 'new knowledge' — things that we did not know until we made our observations — it does not grant us 100% certainty of our conclusions. The conclusions will only be as reliable as the observations and the inferences, and if the observations are incomplete, biased, or skewed; or if they are not causally connected but merely coincidentally or accidentally associated; or if they are not entirely relevant to the general case we are trying to make, then our conclusions will be less than certain. One other possibility, of course, is that conditions may change between the occasion of our observation and the occasion of our conclusion. One common criticism of 'scientific' knowledge, which is usually inductive (based on experimental observation), is that it is not absolutely certain, and this is true: to take a trivial example, we know that the sun rises every morning, but in fact we do not 'know' this, we induce or infer or extrapolate this from our previous experience. 'All else being equal,' we can reasonably expect the sun to rise tomorrow morning, but if things are not equal — if the sun explodes or something stops the earth's rotation, *etc.* — then it will not rise. But this would not prove that our previous inductive conclusion was 'wrong,' merely that circumstances had changed so that our induction no longer applied.

Fallacies

In the reality of practical argumentation, complex arguments can be a combination of deduction and induction, even a hierarchy of nested syllogisms with multiple premises, hidden assumptions, and convoluted and tricky logic. Each argument requires a new effort at analysis and deconstruction, to see what evidential and logical mistakes it may commit. However, there are some familiar and well-established logical mistakes that any reasonable person should be able to recognize instantly, unless they are couched so confusingly or deceptively that the logic is not readily observable. These familiar, and to many people fun, mistakes of reason and critical thinking are the 'fallacies,' that is, failures or errors in the relationships between premises and conclusions that render the conclusions questionable or invalid or even patently false. These are some of the flaws that make arguments unsound, even if the premises are true.

Both form and content, evidence and logic, have their fallacies. Propositional fallacies are errors in meaning, clarity, or sense of premises or truth claims; we have seen some of these possible fallacies already, such as unfalsifiability, lack of comprehensiveness, dishonesty, non-replicability, and insufficiency, including the specific case of shifting the burden of proof. Logical fallacies are naturally errors in the linkage between premises and conclusions, in how the argument moves from or processes premises to reach conclusions. They are essentially *non sequitur* errors: their conclusions do not follow from their premises but are made to appear as if they do. The following list and discussion will be by no means exhaustive, but it will illustrate and warn against some of the favorite and most common fallacies.

Evidential Fallacies

Common evidential fallacies or fallacious abuses of evidence or truth claims come in at least seven varieties.

1. Anecdotal evidence is a supposed fact or bunch of facts, including stories or personal reports, often without context, which is/are at least not comprehensive or sufficient and often also dishonest, non-falsifiable, and non-replicable; an anecdote offered as evidence might be 'My aunt Tilly prayed for chocolate pudding, and the home served chocolate pudding that evening.'

2. Amphiboly is the use of vague or ungrammatical language, making the very premise incoherent or ambiguous. For instance, the common claims that 'belief in god makes life better' or 'all prayers are answered' and their variants are impossible to test or verify because their terms are so nonspecific.

3. Ad hominem attacks attempt to discredit the evidence by discrediting the person who presents the evidence. This is a particularly common and venal strategy against Atheists; one familiar poke is "Nietzsche was an atheist and he went insane, so atheism must be bad or wrong." One special type of *ad hominem* fallacy is the *tu quoque* or 'you too' nonargument, which goes something like "I can't prove that special creation happened, but you can't prove that evolution happened either."

4. Appeals of various kinds constitute efforts to establish the truth of the premise by invoking its source or some other characteristic of the premise rather than any actual evidence for it. These include the following approaches:

    a. appeal to authority, as in "Einstein believed in god, so there must be a god";

    b. appeal to tradition, as in "We have always used leeches to cure illnesses, so they must cure illness";

    c. appeal to majority opinion, as in "Most people believe in god, so there must be a god";

    d. appeal to antiquity or the great age or continuity of a phenomenon, as in "The Roman Catholic Church has existed for thousands of years, so its doctrines must be true";

    e. appeal to novelty or the new and improved status of a phenomenon (the exact opposite of the appeal to antiquity), as in "Modern science has found a neurological basis for god, so there must be a god";

    f. appeal to success, as in "Bill Gates is rich and he believes/does it, so it must be true" or "Christianity has spread around the world, so it must be true."

5. Sweeping or hasty generalization involves taking one or a few instances and making a general inference on their basis. For example, 'All atheists are bad people' or 'All Atheists are communists' are fallacies, as are what we already referred to as *post hoc ergo propter hoc* ('after this, therefore because of this' or misplaced causality) statements, like 'Communists are Atheists and communist regimes were evil, so Atheists are evil.'

6. 'No true Scotsman' fallacy seeks to dismiss the evidence by maintaining that the facts disqualify the case from even being evidence: 'Child abuse by priests is not proof of any failing in religion, because no true Christian would ever abuse children.'

7. 'Straw man' fallacy attempts to set up a definition or condition so odious that it is difficult to defend or easy to refute; in particular, defining Atheism as the 'denial of god' or the 'certainty that god does not exist' creates a false characterization of Atheists that we should not argue with but reject.

Logical Fallacies

Another complete and well-known set of fallacies deals not with the truth claims as such but with the relationships between the truth claims and the conclusions, that is, the 'form' or logic of the argument. Important logical fallacies come in at least eight varieties.

1. Affirmation of the consequent is an error in which the possession of a characteristic is used to justify including something into a category of things that possess that characteristic. A good deductive syllogism, as we said, takes the form 'All Xs are Y, Z is X, therefore Z is Y.' A fallacious affirmation of the consequent would take the form of 'All Xs are Y, Z is Y, therefore Z is X.' An example will make the fallacy clear: all crows are black, Fluffy is black, therefore Fluffy is a crow. The problem with this argument is that perhaps Fluffy is a black cat; blackness alone does not entail or require crow-ness. There are other black things beside crows. A theistic example of this fallacy would be the following: all designed things are complex, the universe is complex, therefore it must be designed. The problem with this argument — the heart of the 'argument from design' in all its forms, including the contemporary 'Intelligent Design' form — is that it does not state and cannot prove that all complex things are designed. It merely claims (a problematic claim) that all designed things are complex. There may, therefore, be some complex things, like coastlines or river courses, that are not designed. Thus, the entire argument from design is based on a fallacy.

2. Denial of the antecedent makes the mistake of denying a trait to a subject because the subject does not belong to a category that has been recognized to possess the trait. It takes the form 'All Xs are Y, Z is not an X, therefore Z is not Y.' To take our crows again, this would be to say that 'All crows are black, Fluffy is not a crow, therefore Fluffy is not black.' But this conclusion is false, since Fluffy is a black cat. The fallacy here is conflating 'all Xs are Y' with 'only Xs are Y': clearly, crows are black, but they are not the only black things around. If it were true that only crows are black or all black things are crows, then the argument would be sound and Fluffy could not possibly be a black cat. A theistic application of this fallacy might be 'If you have a personal experience of Allah, then he exists; I have never had a personal experience of Allah, therefore Allah does not exist.' This in fact highlights the major failing of arguments from personal experience: I may have had the experience but not you, or you may have had the experience but not me, but none of it proves anything.

3. Fallacy of composition mistakenly presumes that if one part of an argument is true, then the entire argument is true. A good example would be '[some] science supports the Bible's claim that the universe is only six thousand years old, therefore everything in the Bible is true.' The problem with this argument, besides the fact that it uses scientific evidence selectively if at all, is that it could be used to justify a completely contradictory claim, such as '[some] science supports Hinduism's claim that the universe is billions of years old, therefore everything in Hinduism is true.'

4. Fallacy of division, the opposite of the fallacy of composition, maintains that whatever is true of the whole must be true of its parts, for example, 'Christianity has a strong moral component, therefore Christians must be moral people.' This is no more necessarily true than to say that a car can drive you to the store, so a spark plug can drive you to the store.

5. False dichotomy or the excluded middle sets up a simple either/or situation (which usually does not exist in reality), so that if it can be shown that one position is wrong, the other must be correct. Theists love to do this with evolution or big-bang physics: "If evolution is false, then special creation must be true," or even worse, "If Darwinian evolution is false, then special creation must be true." What this argument fails to consider, though, is that there may be and generally are other possibilities, including not only other scientific or naturalistic explanations but also other religious explanations; the defeat of evolution would not guarantee Christian correctness, since maybe Hindu or Buddhist or Shinto or Australian Aboriginal cosmogony is correct.

6. Appeal to ignorance disguises incredulity or lack of imagination as argument; it is especially noticeable these days in the 'Intelligent Design' camp. ID proponents largely say nothing more than 'we cannot see how such complex things could have developed by natural processes, so there must be an intelligent designer.' This argument is ignorant on two counts: first, just because they cannot understand or accept it does not mean it is false, and second, they are ignorant (or sometimes deliberately evasive) about what this designer is or where he/she/it came from. Just asserting that 'there is a designer' is not information or explanation is any useful way.

7. Fallacy of interrogation or of presupposition is a form of begging the question and is one that Theists have personally tried on me. The idea here is to phrase a question in such a way that the terms or concepts that you want to establish are built into it. For example, when a Theist asks, "Well, if you do not believe in god, then who made you?" he or she is committing this fallacy by insinuating that someone must have made you. This type of question should not be answered but dismissed.

8. Circular reasoning is one of the most pervasive and obstructive fallacies in argumentation; it uses a claim to prove or justify itself, which is perhaps the most fallacious thing of all, since the claim is what is in need of proof or justification. This often takes the form of using one part of the argument to prove another part. The archetypal formulation of such an argument would be 'The Bible claims that Jesus died and rose again, and the Bible says that it is the truth, so Jesus must have died and risen again.' Of course, the truth of the Bible is exactly what is in dispute, so no Theist can use the Bible to prove the truth of the Bible as a whole or any single claim in it. Any argument can only be settled by evidence and logic outside the disputed claims of the argument; even more, any self-referential claim can appear true if you commit circular reasoning. Why not 'The Qur'an claims that God never had any son, and the Qur'an says that it is the truth, so God never had any son'?

Conclusion

Thinking is never an easy thing to do, and it is certainly not the only thing that humans do. No doubt, we evolved over millions of years not so much to think and to reason as to solve problems, persuade others to accept our solutions, and to act. Thinking and reasoning are one way to solve problems, persuade others, and determine actions, but they are not the only way by any means. In fact, habits, feelings, beliefs, and 'culture' (as discussed in Chapter Four) serve as all-too-handy, prefabricated problem-solving and action-determining mechanisms. In fact, much of human life is designed explicitly for minimizing individual decision-making — for making solutions and courses of action routine, automatic, 'thought-free.'

These mechanisms function well enough when circumstances are familiar and predictable, but (1) circumstances are not always familiar and predictable and (2) 'well enough' does not mean 'well' and it absolutely does not mean 'true.' If we are less concerned with truth than with getting through our day or through a sticky situation, instincts, habits, feelings, beliefs, and cultural patterns may be enough. But none of these things can get us to truth with any acceptable degree of certainty. Among these flawed decision-making processes is faith.

There is only one way to arrive at true judgments about any subject at all with any degree of certainty, and that is by reason. This is why reason is the only type of thought that deserves to be called thought: reason demands facts, weighs those facts for truth and correspondence to reality, and then processes those facts to obtain trustworthy knowledge. Other forms of 'thought' may trip over truth accidentally, but they cannot with any degree of assurance establish or demonstrate that they possess the truth. For example, it may be correct in the end that god is a man who sits in the sky and sent his son to die and will reward or punish eternally for our failings in this life. However, given the evidence from physical reality, and the at-best inconsistent evidence of divine existence, and the laws of logic, and the alternative views of deity and religious interpretation in the world, there is no trustworthy way to prove, to 'know' this truth; those who 'have' it would literally have stumbled across it, and it is equally likely that some other view of deity (the Muslim, Hindu, Buddhist, or animistic) is true — yet they could not 'know' with certainty that they were right either!

Reason certainly has limitations; things that do not admit of being 'true' or 'false' cannot be treated with reason. Feelings, tastes, and desires are neither true nor false; they are thereby not rational. We will explore the consequences of this fact in the next chapter. And reason can certainly go wrong, and we have discussed how in great detail — either by building its case on false or flimsy premises or by linking those premises with flawed or fallacious logic. Hopefully now we are better equipped to avoid these mistakes. But, when conducted well, there is no better way of knowing — there is no *other* way of knowing — than reason.

CHAPTER THREE

Proofs and Principles —
Unreason, Religion, and Relativism

Consider these situations: a person argues that a god exists because he has had a personal experience of the god, or a person claims that a god exists on the grounds that belief in god gives her life meaning and empowers her, or a person maintains that he does not have to prove the existence of his god at all because the vast majority of people already accept the existence of god and that instead the nonbeliever has to prove the non-existence of god. Having previously surveyed both the arguments for and against the existence of god and the rules of reason, the problems with these assertions should be obvious. The purpose of this chapter will be to explicate how to dissect specific arguments of these sorts — how to distinguish reasons from 'good reasons,' reason from unreason, the true or false from the neither true nor false, and the absolute from the relative.

The Other Burden

We introduced the concept of burden of proof in Chapter One, describing it as the challenge that claimants have to justify their claims. This challenge is not unique to religion but applies to any kind of factual or 'truth' claim. We said, and I rigorously defend, that only the maker of positive (i.e., 'there is an X') claims bears a burden of proof. 'Skeptics,' that is, people who merely question or reject a claim, have no burden of proof in any way, since they are not offering an assertion (i.e., 'there is no X') but simply a doubt (i.e., 'I do not see any basis for the claim that there is an X' or 'what are your reasons for claiming that there is an X?'). As such, on the legal model, as we saw, the 'defense' has no work to do; rather, the 'prosecution' (the claimant) must either justify or withdraw the charge.

There are many people, though, who still attempt to share if not shift the burden of proof in the area of religion and the existence of god(s). Some Theists, more or less maliciously, demand that the Atheist — who is merely practicing good skepticism — give his 'reasons' for not believing. Later in this chapter I will explain the flawed principle behind this demand, which should end the debate once and for all. However, others, like the one imagined in the first paragraph of this chapter, stand on other ground: they insist that the Atheist has a burden of proof because so many people already hold the god-belief and therefore it is the Atheist who is asking the majority to release their often long and deeply held convictions. Now, there is a flawed principle in this argument as well, but there is also a point to it.

I have even seen rationalists and skeptics accept a share of the burden of proof on this basis — not that Atheists are advancing positive claims (which is never true) but that they are asking people to jettison a widely held positive claim. This is in fact an issue for Atheists, as it is for any 'minority' or 'innovating' party that is challenging the *status quo*. Galileo suffered from this burden in relation to the Ptolemaic and Catholic view of the universe, and Einstein suffered from it in relation to the Newtonian view. Of course, we know that it is a fallacy to assume that the *status quo* is true just because it is popular or ancient or authoritatively given. That is why this 'other burden of proof' is really not about *proof* at all but about *persuasion*, which is a significantly different beast.

To the best of our knowledge today, the Galilean/ Copernican system is true and the Ptolemaic is false, and the Einsteinian theory is universally true while the Newtonian is 'true within its range of application.' But these and many other new and unfamiliar ideas were often met with initial resistance. Even after they had satisfied their 'burden of proof' in the sense discussed above and in Chapter One, they often continued to be resisted. This is because there is a real and substantial difference between being *true* and being *convincing*. 'True' is a rational status, referring to accurate facts and valid logic; something can be true whether I know or accept it or not. 'Convincing,' however, is a psychological status, referring to how compelling and decisive the idea seems to a particular audience.

It can and does arise that *the truth may not be convincing.* For example, the foundations for the new truth may be incomprehensible to the audience. When Galileo first proposed that the earth moves while the sun stands still (which is itself not quite right), many people simply could not imagine this being true. The earth feels stable, while we see the sun 'rise' and 'set.' Even more impressively, when Einstein theorized that the very space in which heavenly bodies move is curved by the masses of those bodies, many people could not (and still cannot) picture such a thing. Quantum mechanics is another good example of a notion so counterintuitive in ways that it is beyond the grasp of most lay folks and even many scientists. The new truth may also conflict with other preexistent truths or beliefs. Einsteinian physics at least in ways contradicted Newtonian physics, which was extremely successful and well acknowledged. Darwinian theory at least in ways contradicted the generally believed theistic understanding of creation. The controversy over evolution also illustrates another phenomenon that prevents an idea from being persuasive, which is the emotional or psychological content or implications of the idea. A large percentage of Americans find evolution unconvincing not because the evidence is not there, but because the whole notion is insulting or demeaning in their eyes to human dignity.

Do these and other similar objections make the new concepts or theories any less true? Absolutely not. But they do make them less persuasive, and in this sense the innovator, the doubter, the questioner does bear a certain burden, even though it is not quite a burden of 'proof.' We may have all the proof we need. Anyone who knows the hominid fossil record is aware that the proof of human evolution is overwhelming; the whole argument about a 'missing link' is a chimera, as we have found innumerable links in good succession in a virtually unbroken chain going back millions of years. Still, some people resist accepting the 'truth.' And this is where the 'burden of persuasion' comes in: to present and disseminate the facts so that resisters can and must know them, to explain the situation sufficiently clearly so they can comprehend it adequately, and to soothe the emotional and psychological objections — or, if nothing else, render those feelings sufficiently tolerable or irrelevant — so they can embrace or at least live with the implications. Perhaps, for instance, human dignity is not all that it is cracked up to be, or perhaps we can find a new dignity in our kinship with the rest of the physical world. Certainly, almost all humans have made peace with the fact that the earth is round and revolves around the sun, without giving up our sanity or sense of human purpose.

The upshot of the contrast between 'being correct' and 'being convincing' — between proof and persuasion — is that humans tend to be conservative in their thinking. This is probably not an unexpected or even completely undesirable thing. As the Declaration of Independence puts it in reference to politics, matters "long established should not be changed for light and transient causes," and humans are more disposed to persist in their old beliefs and truths "than to right themselves by abolishing the forms to which they are accustomed." This is probably even a good thing ultimately, or else we would be constantly chasing after the latest fad and 'fact' offered by scientist and charlatan alike. Humans also get not only cognitively but emotionally attached to their ideas and understandings, whether they are fundamentalists or physicists. People invest their hope, their love, their money, and their reputations and careers on specific issues and do not let them go easily. This sometimes makes science seem as 'dogmatic' as religion (an odd criticism when raised by a Theist!), but the real root of the thing is the natural human propensity to conserve cognitive content and to need a strong dose of persuading to dislodge them from their convictions. The fact that scientists eventually do get on board with new theories, while Theists cling to ancient received 'knowledge,' only highlights the difference between them.

So when Theists demand of Atheists to 'prove that there is no god,' what they are often actually asking for is persuasion — persuasion to change their minds about something that was settled for them a long time ago, that was maybe never even a question for them. Unfortunately for new and threatening truths, the burden of persuasion is much higher than the burden of proof. Think of it this way: if a human could arrive at intellectual maturity without having adopted or perhaps even having been exposed to any religious beliefs, that human would be in a position to make an objective, neutral evaluation of the 'proof' put forth by Theists and Atheists. In that case, the proof would be persuasive, and the burdens would be equal. But people — the majority, as it turns out — who are already committed to the 'truth' of their religions are going to be (appropriately, in a sense) much harder to persuade of their wrongness and of the convincing quality of the case against god(s). Similarly, Atheists and other freethinkers are going to be much harder to persuade of the truth of this or that particular religion, having already seen and struggled with the issues dealt with in Chapter One.

A final distinction is worth considering. Our imaginary Theists at the opening of the present chapter gave a couple of their reasons for believing in god(s). We were unconvinced. That is because there is a critical disparity between *reasons* and *good reasons*. In a way, this is nothing more than a restatement of some basic foundations of logic. When someone offers an explanation, one form of that explanation may be giving reasons (other forms may include making analogies, constructing definitions, *etc.*). The reasons, as we know, may consist of facts/observations, arguments, or interpretations. But not all reasons are equally good, as we also know. If someone says, 'I am eating M&M's for my illness because they look like pills' or 'because they taste good,' that indeed may be their reason, but it is not a good reason. Similarly, if someone says, 'I believe in god(s) because the universe looks designed to me' or 'because it makes me feel good,' that too may be their reason, but it is not a good reason. *A good reason is a sound argument*, with all that it implies: careful observation, valid logic, disqualification of alternative explanations, importation of no unnecessary assumptions or corollaries, freedom from personal preference or prejudice, and so on. In an ideal world, good reasons would be convincing, since there would be little or no option but to accept their conclusion, but mere reasons would not and should not be. Furthermore, if it needs saying, stating someone's reasons for their beliefs or actions is not equivalent to justifying or endorsing their beliefs or actions: I can say, 'His reasons for doing X are Y and Z' without suggesting that those are good reasons for so doing. For instance, I can say that Massachusetts Puritans burned citizens because the former believed they were witches and the Bible says not to suffer a witch to live, but that does not mean that I accept any or all of their 'reasoning.' I perceive their reasons, but I do not accept them as 'good reasons.'

True, False, and Neither

Another area of some controversy and confusion is the very notion of true and false. We have said, and analyzed extensively in the previous chapter, the rational process of sifting truth from falseness. Propositions, we stated, of the form 'there is an X' or 'X is Y' are either true or false; in fact, the entire discipline of logic and perhaps of philosophy is designed to deal with and evaluate propositions of this sort. Every proposition, then, if it claims that some entity exists or that some entity possesses this or that quality, should be provable as either true or false.

As we argued in the last chapter, and as we will argue in a later chapter, reason — and its special applied form, science — deals with the factual, the observable, the demonstrable, the propositional, the true or false. In fact, I said and I repeat that only reason deals trustworthily and dependably with the true or false. Other human faculties — like emotion or taste or faith — may arrive at true statements too, but they do so arbitrarily, accidentally or incidentally, and they can never demonstrate their truthfulness; even when arrived at by other means, they can only be evaluated, tested, and justified by reason. However, it is a fact — and not an undesirable fact — that not all of human existence is propositional. As mentioned at the outset of the previous chapter, humans do a lot of things other than make truth-claims. They also ask questions, give orders, state preferences, express emotions, and such. What is the relation of reason to these phenomena?

Theists, poets, and other romantics often assert that the heart (or other part of the anatomy) has a reason that reason cannot grasp — a 'mind' of its own. This line of thinking is often taken to imply or prove that the heart, by which is meant emotion or taste or faith, can have its own knowledge, its own truth. Reason, intellect, the 'mind' that really is mind, cannot understand and certainly cannot refute this 'other' truth.

However, the heart does not have reason, and it certainly does not have mind. It does, nevertheless, have its own processes. All propositions are sentences with a subject and a predicate, like the classic 'The cat is on the mat.' They are either true or false. But not all sentences with a subject and a predicate are propositions. For example, 'Is the cat on the mat?' is not a proposition, it is a question. 'Put the cat on the mat' is not a proposition, it is an imperative. And 'I like the cat' or 'That is a pretty cat' is propositional in one manner but nonpropositional in another. So what is the truth status of such utterances?

What possible sense would it make to research the truth status of a question? How could I ever determine whether the question 'Is the cat on the mat?' is true or false? What would the determination possibly mean? The answer to the question — either 'Yes, the cat is on the mat' or 'No, the cat is not on the mat' — is propositional and therefore true or false, and with the proper observation we can know which. But the question as a question is neither true nor false. Since it is not a truth claim, the issue of truth or falsity is utterly irrelevant. Similarly with an imperative like 'Put the cat on the mat,' the statement is neither true nor false. Statements on the order of 'I like the cat' and 'That is a pretty cat' are in a gray area somewhere between, or straddling, propositional and nonpropositional. In other words, if I really do like the cat, then saying that I do is making a true statement; if I do not like the cat, then my words are a lie. And we could, in principle, assess the truth status of the claim, perhaps by observing how I treat the cat; if I am nice to it and feed it and take care of it, then it might be reasonable to conclude that I really do like it. As a self-report, it is either true or false. But why do I like it? Why do I think it is pretty? I might say that I like it because it purrs or because it makes me happy or because it is pretty (which is a circular argument). Yet, someone else might say he hates the same cat because it is ugly or because it makes him unhappy or, most troublingly of all, because it purrs.

So, in terms of validating whether I am truly representing my feelings about the cat, the sentence is a proposition. However, in terms of the basis of my feelings themselves — in terms of the sentence as an expression of my likes or dislikes

— it is not a proposition. If that seems confusing, then consider it this way: a sound argument should lead consistently and necessarily from true facts through valid logic to sound conclusion. Now consider how I arrive at liking the cat: the cat purrs, purring is a good reason to like a cat, therefore I like the cat. The premise of the argument (the cat purrs) is true and indisputable. But the logic (purring is sufficient for liking) is flawed, since someone else — a cat-hater — may despise purring and dislike cats accordingly. So this cannot constitute a sound argument for liking the cat. In other words, an argument should and must lead everyone inexorably to the same conclusion, or else it is not a sound argument. But no list of the traits of my beloved cat, or my beloved wife, or anything else that I love, is sufficient to lead to the conclusion of love. The same holds for every kind of preference, taste, desire, or other personal reaction. It is 'illogical' to say that my wife is nice and smart and beautiful and *therefore* I love her. Perhaps the best proof of this is that there are lots of nice and smart and beautiful people in the world and I do not love them, and not everyone loves my nice and smart and beautiful wife. Love, preference, taste, desire, *etc.* are thus *not rational.*

We alluded to this notion in our analysis of reason. Not everything that humans do and think and feel is rational. That is okay; it is even good. Rational things are not the only worthwhile things in the world. They are, however, the only *certainly true* things in the world. If I say that I love my wife but am mean to her and hit her and so forth, it could well be that my claim is false; if I say that I love her and am good to her and give her gifts, it probably means that my claim is true. But I did not arrive at my love for her by reason. The heart does in fact have its own ways, but they are not reason. We all know very well that some people love others whom they clearly should not. We all know that love can persist even when circumstances are unloving. I still like the cat even when it throws up on the mat. Such emotions, as well as preferences and tastes, are not rational.

Various analysts use the terms 'rational' and 'irrational,' sometimes along with 'nonrational,' in various ways. Some of these semantic systems are useful, some are not. I would like to suggest that we limit the term 'rational' to arguments or conclusions that have been demonstrated true or false on the basis of facts and logic. That is, I think, a standard connotation based on everything we have said about reason, thinking, and true or false propositions. The statements and sentiments that we have just been describing are not rational in this proper sense, then, but they are not false or bad either. In fact, they are not true or false; they are neither true nor false. Truth and falsity do not apply here. I will call such sentences or the mental/emotional states to which they refer 'nonrational' because they have nothing to do with reason. They are not arrived at by reason, and they cannot be tested by reason. That does not mean, emphatically, that they are bad or worthless or inferior to reason. Some of them are really quite wonderful. It is just that we can never refer to them or validate them as 'true.'

However, lest you wonder what any of this has to do with religion, we have not exhausted the typology of human thoughts and feelings. There are also those sentences and claims that look like propositions in that they take the form 'there is an X' or 'X exists' or 'X is Y' but are not rational propositions. Some examples would be 'there is a god' or 'god exists' or 'god is good.' These statements are in fact propositions, in the sense that they are either true or false ('god is good' is a little trickier, since 'good' is a value judgment and depends on a subjective evaluation). However, the person who maintains these claims, the Theist, does not have adequate fact or valid logic on his side to reach or defend them. The only possible way to reach such conclusions is by flawed or fallacious thinking — which again does not always prove that they are false but does always prove that they are unsound. For instance, Theists may say, "The Bible says there is a god, so there is a god," but this is fallacious. They may say, "The priest/minister/church says there is a god, so there is a god," but this too is fallacious. They may say, "I have had a personal experience of a god, so there is a god" but this, like the others, is fallacious. And they may say, "The idea of a god makes me happy and makes me feel empowered, so there is a god," but this is worse than fallacious; it is utterly irrelevant.

For claims such as these, which are propositional but which have not been and cannot be arrived at by reason, I reserve the term 'irrational.' As propositions, they are either true or false, which makes them completely unlike nonrational statements, which are neither true nor false. It is perfectly fine to indulge in and enjoy the nonrational; some of life's sweetest treasures are nonrational. But the irrational is to be avoided. Irrational statements masquerade as truth (or at least truth claims), but they have no rational foundation whatsoever. Insofar as we can test the thought process that leads to such statements, they test out as either demonstrably false or undemonstrable at all.

In summary, we can say that,

- rational statements are either true or false, and we can in principle know which;
- nonrational statements are neither true nor false, and that's okay;
- irrational statements purport to be propositions, but they fail the test of rationality. They are flawed and likely false, and if they happen to be true, it is by accident.

Rational things, like facts and theories about objective and empirical subjects, can be known; *only* they can be known, and *only they constitute knowledge.* Nonrational things, like love, hope, taste, preference, desire, *etc.* are not 'knowledge' but are no less valuable and wonderful for it. Irrational things, like statements about unsubstantiated beings, forces, or dimensions are not knowledge, have a high probability of being false, and give us no method for separating the true from the false. They subsist on nothing but faith.

Look for the Principle

Reason is, for many people, a highly abstract and mystical thing, when in actuality it is extremely practical and familiar. Everyone uses reason every day in multiple forms to solve ordinary problems and sort out ordinary claims on our credulity. In most areas of daily life, we would never think of violating the normal constraints of reason; for example, we would not, hopefully, buy a cleaning product, food item, or medical procedure without examining its ingredients, effectiveness, side effects, or very existence. As an extreme illustration, if a man in a white coat (presumably a doctor) told us he had an invisible pill that would cure our ills if we just believe in it, I fervently trust that we would laugh and walk away. Accordingly, if we were truly objective about religious claims, then if a man in a black suit or gown told us that an undetectable being would make us happy and save our lives if we just believe in it, we would laugh and walk away. The claim is too preposterous to even consider.

Nevertheless, many people do consider it and accept it anyway, or perhaps they do not consider it yet accept it anyway. So our inclination simply to walk away and declare the whole discussion ridiculous is insufficient as an arguing technique and a social choice. Theists will either think that they have won or that we are just being obtuse and stubborn, and they will certainly not be convinced, which is the whole point of argument in the first place. In the previous two chapters we have presented most if not all of the key arguments for (finding them deficient) and against (finding them sufficient) god(s), and I would like briefly now to demonstrate why those arguments succeed or fail and how to use them in practice.

As we said in regard to reason and argument, the number one rule should always be not to argue with the conclusion but with the premises or logic. If we can find the fault in one of those, the conclusion must collapse, although Theists will generally not allow that to happen. But even more so, many of the arguments that Theists employ in defending Theism are defeasible in one easy step. It is a step that all atheistic polemicists should remember and exploit. It is merely this: look for the principle at the root of the argument.

A few examples will suffice to show what I mean. Let us consider first the fundamental rule of all argumentation, the burden of proof. We have discussed a couple of times already why Atheists bear no burden of proof logically (while they may bear a burden of persuasion, which may be massive). If we simply assert that we share no burden of proof, Theists will often dismiss us as evasive or sidetrack the original argument with a secondary argument about the burden itself. This matter can be settled definitively by looking to the principle behind the burden of proof concept. It is this: the burden of proof contends that one should not accept a claim as true until there is adequate reason (evidence and logic) to accept that it is true. Therefore, the burden is on the proponent of the claim to produce that reason. If one were to insist that the burden lies on the party refuting the claim, then the principle behind that position would be that one can or should accept a claim as true until there is adequate reason to reject it. This is of course exactly what the Theist is maintaining — that if you cannot disprove god(s), you should believe in god(s). The obvious and self-defeating implication of this principle, though, is that you (and the Theist too) could and should accept not just that god-claim but all god-claims as true until they are proven false. And since, by their own admission god-claims cannot be proven false, then not only we but they are compelled to believe in every god that was ever professed by humans in history!

This is patent nonsense, and the Theist will quickly deny it, but it is the inevitable consequence of the shift of burden of proof. In fact, it is worse than that, since the issue is not restricted to religious questions. If the burden really does lie, even partially, with the 'skeptic,' then we would all be required to accept every claim about every topic from medicine to UFOs to magic crystals just because someone advanced the claim. We would either embrace every absurd statement that was made to us or spend all of our time fending off these absurdities. If someone said, "God is an undetectable hamster," we would have to agree or search for the (unavailable) evidence to refute the suggestion. In other words, the principle that the negative side bears the burden of proof — that you can or must believe until counterevidence is produced, that is, that it is true until proven false — is impossible to support, dangerous to advance, and an utter failure. A few test claims addressed back to the Theist, such as leprechauns, aliens in your head, and undetectable hamsters should make the point uncomfortably clear.

Other examples work in a similar fashion. Why is the appeal to personal experience as an argument for god(s) a fallacy? The answer again is the principle behind the argument: if someone has an experience of something, that experience is sufficient proof of the existence of that thing. Unfortunately, people have experiences of all sorts of things. If we were to take the principle seriously, which we do not, then every religion's experiences would be proof of the truth of that religion. Buddhists have personal experiences of nirvana and buddha-nature. Hindus have personal experiences of Brahma and Shiva and Vishnu and Hanuman and Ganesh and many other gods. Muslims have personal experiences of Allah. Wiccans have personal experiences of witchcraft and other spiritual beings and forces. Native Americans had regular personal experiences of spirits in their 'vision quests.' If the principle is to be normative, then all of these experiences must be 'true,' and all of the gods, spirits, or forces to which they refer must also be real. Few if any Theists want this outcome.

Of course, as in the case of the burden of proof, the issue is not limited to religion; personal experiences of all kinds of bizarre nonreligious phenomena are frequently claimed, and often in our society subjectivity is accepted as sufficient grounds for truth (as we will discuss in a later chapter). Some people hold that they have had personal experiences with aliens, or talking dogs, or Bigfoot, or Elvis, or ascended masters, or an endless number of wacky things. But if the principle of personal experience is good, then we must take all of these experiences as evidence of empirical phenomena too. We obviously do not, and we apply reason to evaluate which experiences are transparent fakes, hallucinations, or mistakes and which have at least a slight chance of being real. Then we test those for veracity. To do otherwise would be, quite literally, insanity.

Most of the additional faulty principles behind arguments reduce to similar *ad absurdum* results. The appeal to authority or to scripture ('you should accept the opinions of authorities or scriptures as true') leads to the same consequences — you should accept not only priests but ministers, rabbis, imams, boddhisattvas, yogis, witches and warlocks, and every other 'specialist' who makes an assertion (including scientists!), or you should accept not only the Bible but the Qur'an and the Bhagavad Gita and the Buddhist sutras and the Book of Mormon and every other scripture as the word of truth. That is impossible, because they are mutually contradictory, and no Theist believes or wants it to be true. Popular opinion, anecdotes, tradition, antiquity, success and other grounds for belief fall away in the same manner, since the principle behind them would force us to accept things that we do not want to accept and that we know better than to accept.

One additional argument that deserves a comment is the claim that god(s), or the supernatural in general, are 'unknowable,' therefore nothing can be proved either way. Of course, this is not an argument at all but a charm against arguments ('You can't disprove my belief — and I can't and don't have to prove it — so leave me alone to believe as I want'), but it is patently self-refuting. Notwithstanding the fact that the claim of unknowability is itself a religious claim — who says the divine or supernatural is unknowable? — ascribing unknowability to it is to make a positive knowledge claim about it. Unknowability is a quality of god(s) that a believer claims to know, even while he or she persists in making other claims, like god(s)' goodness or power or very existence. But more to the point, the principle under this pseudo-argument is: if something is unknowable, that is sufficient grounds to reject any attacks on it. The consequences of this 'argument' are, again, absurd. I could call vampires or dragons unknowable, and that would preclude any disagreement on the subject. I could call my own psychic powers or those of my invisible dog unknowable and thus privilege them from debate. Any claim of any kind could be shielded from inspection and refutation simply by assigning it the *trait* of unknowability. The fact that it is impossible on principle ever to distinguish the unknowable from the nonexistent actually serves the Theist or supernaturalist and is the whole point of the argument.

Most of these are fallacies of evidence, as described in the previous chapter, but the process works for fallacies of logic too, such as excluded middle, appeal to ignorance, and circular reasoning. The fallacy of the excluded middle propounds that it is wrong to conclude that X is true simply because Y is false or just unproved. The principle that must be affirmed by those who commit the fallacy (as when they say, 'well, evolution is wrong/cannot be proved, so Christian creationism must be true') works perfectly well in reverse ('Christian creationism is wrong/cannot be proved, so evolution must be true') and also opens the debate up to other Xs (such as 'evolution is wrong/cannot be proved, so Hindu creationism/Mayan creationism/extraterrestrial life-seeding must be true'). The appeal to ignorance rests on the principle that anything I cannot imagine or explain must be false and that *any* alternative I posit is superior, but this is naturally wrong and dangerous. And circular reasoning, which takes many forms, boils down to 'X is true because X says it is true,' which spirals into a world of trouble and contradiction, since anything could in theory be used as support for itself.

So, in all of these cases, the principle at the heart of the error manifests two essential problems: first, that the principle does not take us dependably and exclusively where we want to go but threatens to run off in all directions simultaneously, and second, that to make it go where we want to go we must add secondary and arbitrary qualifications. For instance, if a Theist makes an appeal to scripture, arguing that the Bible is a good guide to truth, then the only way to prevent the principle of the argument from running wild is to attach capricious standards for judging the Bible superior to other scriptures.

The common Christian tools in this case are Bible prophecy, the 'uniqueness' of the person of Jesus, or the antiquity and number of authors of the document. But why choose those particular standards? Bible prophecy is, of course, a matter of contestation itself, since many of the 'prophecies' are not prophecies at all but misapplications of one verse to a later verse, and an important contingent of prophecies has failed to come true. Besides, other religions make or claim successful prophesying. The 'uniqueness' of Jesus is equally up for grabs, since it has not been and probably cannot be established that such a person even existed. But supposing that he did, the fact that he is allegedly a man-god means a lot to Christians but little to Muslims; in fact, Muslims generally hold Jesus in lower esteem than Muhammad because the latter was purely human and yet was a perfect prophet of god.

Antiquity and multiple authorship are problematic criteria. There are many books as old or older than the Christian Bible, including Egyptian, Mesopotamian, Indian, and Greek texts; are they all true — and the older the truer? And who is to say that multiple authorship is superior to single authorship? The Qur'an is purportedly a work of a single author (Allah, through his messenger Muhammad), which would seem to introduce fewer 'points of failure' into the document. And the fact that dozens of authors would agree with each other (which, by the way, they do not nearly as well as Bible-believers think they do) proves nothing. Don't you think that the later authors of the Bible had read the earlier ones and that some group or committee looked over all the possible candidates for inclusion in the canon and chose the ones that agreed with each other? We know for a 'gospel' fact that there are other books — heterodox or nonconformist books — that were rejected from the canon, like the apocryphal and Gnostic gospels. So other texts were written contemporaneously but rejected because they did not agree. Agreement was a matter of picking and choosing.

Thus, the only way to rescue the flawed principles of these fallacious arguments is to introduce arbitrary standards designed to rule out all of the implications one wants to prevent. But since those standards are completely *ad hoc* and unsupported, there is no reason to take them seriously either. The only sane course is to avoid arguments with contradictory and out-of-control principles like the ones above and, when we encounter the arguments coming from Theists, to point out quickly the morass that their argument leads them into. By so doing, we withdraw a plank on which they are accustomed to stand and expose the vulnerability, absurdity, and even insanity of some of their most precious arguments.

On Cultural Relativism

There are altogether no moral facts. — Nietzsche

Several times already in this book I have addressed the issue of knowledge and truth *vis-à-vis* belief, and we will encounter it again in later chapters on knowledge and belief, science and religion, and toleration and truth. In the final section of this chapter, I would like to return briefly to the topic of 'true, false, and neither' from earlier in the present chapter to discuss the implications of this insight for cultural relativism. This will also prepare us for the next chapter, which is devoted to the question of freethought and anthropology as partners in a new and problematic view of culture, of which religion is a part.

Cultural relativism is one of the most misunderstood and maligned notions in all of scholarship, yet it is so useful and so demonstrably real from the anthropological perspective that it is sometimes difficult for me to see what all the fuss is about. It is a concept especially despised and condemned by conservatives and those who think they have 'the truth.' This is not surprising. Cultural relativism, sometimes bundled with ethical relativism and other relativisms, deprives them of the absolutism and certainty that they so cherish.

Cultural relativism is often taken, particularly by Christians and conservative politicians, to mean 'anything goes,' everything is equally true (or untrue), and there is no absolute truth. As such, it is a stab at the heart and a slap in the face of Christianity (and almost every religion), which claims to possess the 'one absolute truth,' as well as of popular conceptions of the identity and philosophy of America, where certain practices and values are good and real and true. Christianity, for example, variously maintains that killing is always wrong, monogamy is always good, and homosexuality is always bad. American culture, being hugely influenced by Christian values, tends to appropriate most of these, adding values of tolerance and diversity and fairness and individualism, *etc.* These morals and values, Christians and most Americans believe, are good for us and good for everyone — true for us and true for everyone.

Cultural relativism, as seen in the next chapter, is a hard-won and not-always-comfortable realization that not everyone in the world thinks and believes and values and acts like we do. It tended to await contact with societies that are radically different from our own, such as during European exploration and colonization, to learn and imbibe. But it was also apparent even in more parochial circumstances, such as when orthodox Christians in medieval Europe were confronted with heterodox Christians (and non-Christians) in their midst who would simply not recant their heresy no matter how much persuasion and force was applied to them. The result, however, was anything but open-eyed and open-armed toleration but rather persecution and intensified absolutism.

It is, nevertheless, a *fact* that people in different places and different times have different morals, values, beliefs, and 'truths.' This is akin to the fact that species evolve, whatever process you attribute the fact to or however emotionally you feel about it. Natural selection is one mechanism for the fact of physical evolution, and cultural relativism is one philosophy or reaction to the fact of cultural diversity. It is by no means the only possible reaction: conversion and genocide are other, vicious, and common results.

Cultural relativism, then, starts from the realization that cultures — beliefs, behaviors, values, *etc.* — are different in different eras and locations. It does not, contrary to the alarmist whining of frightened absolutists, mean that 'everything is true' or that 'there is no truth.' What it means is this, and nothing more: every judgment, every understanding, every value is relative to some point of view. It does not mean that all points of view are equally valid or good; that would be a value judgment too, in fact an impossible and meaningless one to make. Good for what? Good at what? That question too is relative.

As a particularly stark example, in some traditional cultures, head-hunting was a normal practice. Killing people and taking their heads as trophies or ritual objects was expected. A great warrior or shaman would have heads in his possession. Now, if an American, from our non-head-hunting culture, walked into the site of the heads, he would evaluate the situation in terms of his American values: nice people do not have severed heads in their homes, so this must be the home of a bad person, a criminal, maybe even a psycho-killer. He would be wrong. Imagine if a headhunter were to walk into the home of George Washington or the pope and notice the absence of severed heads. He would probably conclude that this was the residence of a man of little or no military or spiritual prowess, maybe even a coward or an insignificant man. Where are the heads? He would be wrong too.

The problem is not that either or both cultural positions are right or wrong but that they are not applicable to each other. Headhunter values and norms cannot be used to understand the behavior of Americans, and American values and norms cannot be used to understand head-hunters.

This is not to say that head-hunting is better or worse than not head-hunting; the cultural relativist does not make such determinations, although the members of a society do. But the results of that determination are inconclusive and not surprising: head-hunters think head-hunting is better, Americans think non-headhunting is better. All they have done is to reaffirm their particular cultural values.

'But isn't head-hunting *really* bad or immoral?' the typical American or Christian complains. What does 'really' mean? It is immoral to us, not immoral to them. Other examples abound; in fact, in actuality this is the stuff that culture is made of. To most Americans, child marriage and polygamy are socially dysfunctional or immoral; to many other cultures, they were or are the norm. To most Americans, infanticide is bad and monotheism is good, but to many other cultures infanticide is acceptable (if not exactly good) and monotheism is wrong or inconceivable.

So what do we do? Who is right? Or do we just have to throw our hands up in the air and surrender that all value judgments are impossible? The answer is that no one is right or wrong but that we do not have to abjure all judging and evaluating and valuing. Cultural relativism does not say that judgment is impossible; *it says that judgment is always done from some moral or normative perspective.* We can judge from an American or Christian perspective, but we must be aware that we are being judged by others from other perspectives. The way that our actions and values appear to us may not be the way that they appear to other people on the planet. And this is a profoundly important fact, not just for the Theist/Atheist debate but for all of our international diplomacy and military policy.

What does all of this have to do with reason and religion? The answer will become clearer as this book progresses, but it can be anticipated and explained here. Cultural relativism makes sense and is crucial to grasp because some things — such as values, norms, morals, beliefs, and so on — are neither true nor false. They are, like the statements we analyzed above, non-rational. In fact, a very great deal of culture, including much of religion, is non-rational and thus not resolvable in some objective and absolute court of truth. They are irresolvable. Even more, there is nothing to resolve, because there is no 'true' or 'correct' moral or value position, only alternatives. The only possible meaning for the idea of 'judging' values or morals is 'holding them up to a value or moral standard,' but that process would be relative too: which standard shall we hold them up to? Christian? Muslim? Headhunter? While we might not like ('value') all of the options equally, they are all possible options to apply.

So the question, 'Is killing really wrong?' is as nonrational as other questions like, 'Is polygamy really wrong?' or 'Is infanticide really wrong?' or 'Is homosexuality really wrong?' All questions are nonrational by definition, but questions of normality or morality or value are nonrational *and relative* — only answerable from a particular moral perspective of good or bad, not from an absolute logical perspective of true or false. In fact, notice that the question cannot be asked in the form of 'Is polygamy true?' That question could only mean, 'Is there such a thing as polygamy?' in which case the answer has to be yes. 'Polygamy exists' is a rational proposition and a true one. 'Polygamy is wrong/immoral' is a nonrational statement; more than that, on closer inspection, it is not a proposition at all but an imperative: 'you/we should not commit polygamy.' Like 'thou shalt not commit adultery' or 'honor thy father and thy mother,' these are orders or commands, not propositions, so they are nonrational and neither true nor false. Morals cannot be true or false. Morals are not facts, as Nietzsche stated, but rather instructions or orders. Morality can never be said to be 'true.' Morality must, thus, be relative; the only way it could be absolute (the same for everyone everywhere in every time) would be through the successful imposition of one particular set of morals or values on everyone else, most likely by force. Tomorrow, Christian morality may be absolute, if it destroys every other morality and establishes itself in their place, but today it is not. And on second thought, since no moral system can change the systems of the past, no system has a ghost of a chance of claiming or establishing absoluteness.

Cultures, however, talk about other things besides morals. They also talk about empirical matters such as the shape of the earth, the age of the universe, the existence of various kinds of beings, and much else. The opponents of cultural relativism sometimes appear to think that it claims that all cultural notions are equally true or valid. Especially under the influence of the deconstructionists and postmodernists, it became standard procedure to make truth relative. But our discussion of relativism so far has had nothing to do with 'truth,' very explicitly. Things that are neither true nor false are relative to the nonrational systems from which they arise. Truth — fact — is a whole other universe. Christian literalism teaches that the world was created a few thousand years ago; Hindu literalism teaches that the world was created hundreds of billions of years ago. The Bible mentions unicorns, and Chinese culture has a prominent place for dragons. Extreme (and confused) relativists, if any actually exist, maintain that believing is being: if Christians believe that the world is six thousand years old, then it is six thousand years old 'for them.' If Hindus believe the world is billions of years old, it is billions of years old 'for them.' Unicorns exist for Bible-readers, dragons for Chinese, griffins for Englishmen, leprechauns for Irish, and so on *ad absurdum*. There is no truth, there is no reality, only what people think.

This is utter nonsense, and it is based on a misunderstanding that this chapter has been written to clarify. Nonpropositional statements are neither true nor false, and all morals/values talk is non-propositional. Therefore, whether a practice or idea is 'good' or 'bad' is relative. But propositions are either true or false — not both and not neither. A statement like 'the world is six thousand years old' or 'unicorns exist' or 'Jesus was born of a virgin' is a proposition and is therefore either true or false. It may be exceedingly difficult, maybe even impossible in practice, to determine which, but it is either true or false. And if, for example, it is true that the world is six thousand years old, then it is false that it is any other age. In other words, if Christianity is right about this, then Hinduism is wrong, and if science if right about it, then both Christianity and Hinduism are wrong. But — and this is the critical factor — *propositions are not relative; propositions are either true or false. Fact is not relative; values and morals and beliefs are relative.*

And so we see that religion, like all of culture, is composed of two kinds of statements — moral/value statements (like 'thou shalt not kill' and 'god is good') and factual statements (like 'the world was created in six days' and 'Jesus was born of a virgin'). The first type of statements, from a rational point of view, need not concern us; they cannot be proven or disproved, they can only be believed or not. The second type of statements concerns us greatly, since they are either true or false. Religion, naturally, generally takes them as true. Of course, there is one other possibility that we will consider at more length in a later chapter — that the propositions are actually allegorical, not 'true' at all but 'poetic' or 'mythic' or 'symbolic.' If that is the case, then they do not detain us either: if Christians want to believe that the creation story is an allegory about nature, including perhaps evolution, then it is of no interest to us rationalists, although it adds nothing to the understanding of the universe. A natural understanding would serve the purpose just fine. But when they do — and certainly they do — take religious stories as fact, then they have entered the territory of reason (formally, of science, as we investigate at length in Chapter Seven), where they must defend their claims and see those claims either supported or defeated. They cannot argue that their beliefs are 'true' and that they are simultaneously impervious to reason. That is a self-destructive contradiction.

Conclusion

This chapter has ranged over a variety of topics, with a common unifying theme — what is a matter of truth and reason and what is not? We have seen that truth does not depend on being convincing, even though if truth wants to prevail it must succeed at breaking through preconceptions, prejudices, and prior commitments (rationally achieved or not). In the world of logic and reason, it is enough to be proven; in the human world it is also necessary to be persuasive. Unfortunately, facts and arguments are not always the most persuasive means for moving human minds and, consequentially, hearts. As we will discuss in the last chapters of this book, humans are much swayed and influenced by nonrational factors like emotions, tastes, and yes, beliefs.

We also made the crucial distinction between rational, irrational, and nonrational. These are old words assigned to new meanings, and not all scholars use them exactly as I do. However, the three types of phenomena — true or false and held with reason, true or false and not held with reason, and neither true nor false and unrelated to reason — are philosophical or epistemological essences that must be recognized and segregated before clear thinking can proceed. In particular, matters of fact as determined by science and objective observation are rational, matters of belief as determined by religion or ideology are irrational, and matters of feeling, subjectivity, preference, taste, and desire are nonrational. It can never be said that the nonrational is true or false, only that it is good or bad — and then only from a certain point of view. It can be said that the irrational is true or false, but even when it is true, since no rational process can be identified to arrive at the position, we cannot call it knowledge and we can only consider the correctness of it to be accidental.

We also discovered that behind many fallacious arguments lurks a principle that cannot possibly be applied and complied with. These principles, when seen as such, clash in absurd and contradictory mandates, such as that you must believe every authority or every scripture or every personal experience. When presented with one of these arguments by a Theist (or anyone else), instead of trying to respond to the argument, it is preferable to expose the principle before their eyes: 'So, you are saying that personal experience/authority/scripture is a valid proof of religious truth? Well then, what about this experience/authority/scripture? Are they true too?' Their feeble attempts to set standards for proving one belief (theirs) over all the others can be exposed as such as well.

Finally, we took a better look at the subject of relativism, learning what it does and does not assert on the basis of categories of rational, irrational, and nonrational. Cultural relativism applies only to the nonrational parts of culture — the value/norm/morality parts — which cannot be said to be 'true' but only good or bad from a particular cultural perspective. Cultural relativism does not say that judgment is impossible, merely perspectival. However, every culture, of which religion is one domain, also contains propositional content that is either true or false and is therefore *not* relative. Careful observation and accurate interpretation — that is, reason and, in its formal instance, science — can make the assessment of the truth or falsity of such propositions, and we are not compelled to embrace an 'anything you believe is true' implication.

Religion, then, is by definition a combination of the rational, the irrational, and the nonrational. Its moral or value elements (which some thinkers like Stephen Jay Gould and Huston Smith take, erroneously, to be its real and whole nature), being non-rational, are not subject to rational analysis; you accept them or you don't. But contra Gould, Smith, and the like, religion also includes truth-claims about the existence of beings or forces, about the nature or character of those beings or forces, and about the origins and history of physical things. These elements, propositional and therefore either true or false, cannot provide the conditions for the determination of their own truth or falsity. Only reason can do that. When reason supports one aspect or another, that's fine, since no one says that every religion is wrong about every single point of fact. But when reason refutes one aspect or another, religion must yield on that point or persist in its identified falsehood. To persist in holding demonstrably false or unsound conclusions is the very essence of irrationality.

CHAPTER FOUR

Anthropology and Freethought —
The Loss of Certainty

I am an anthropologist by training and also by temperament, an observer of the human condition almost more than a participant. Anthropology is a distinct and important field of investigation, although one not particularly familiar to the public. Many people have seen some native tribes in a *National Geographic* episode or a scientist digging on PBS for bones, but few of them know what anthropology is or what it has to say about being human. This is unfortunate, for in a way anthropology, of all the human sciences, asks the most profound questions and offers the most profound answers about humanity.

In particular, the public — and especially Atheists and freethinkers among the public — do not tend to grasp the importance of anthropology for understanding the history and very possibility of freethought and Atheism. I wish that I could go so far as to claim freethought as a result of anthropological investigation and analysis, and partly, as we shall see, anthropology is a cause of much of contemporary cultural criticism. However, more to the point, anthropology as a discipline and as a perspective is not so much a cause as a parallel or simultaneous outgrowth of the identical spirit and attitude that made freethought possible and vital. For what is freethought but the will to question received truths and follow evidence wherever it may lead, regardless of authority, tradition, popular opinion, or personal preference? And what science goes further than anthropology in describing alternatives to — and therefore criticisms of — one's own all too often taken-for-granted cultural norms and truths? In a crucial way, anthropology is freethought in practice and in full flight.

What is Anthropology?

Anthropology is a fairly young science, having been formalized only in the last century, although its roots go back another fifty to a hundred years. It has tended to focus on small-scale traditional cultures like the ones that Europeans 'discovered' in the Americas, Africa, Asia, and the Pacific Islands. As such, one might think that it has little to do with modern folks like ourselves or with our particular social issues. However, nothing could be further from the truth, since all of these societies — no matter how remote or how exotic — are composed of humans just like us, and what they do could be what we do.

Anthropology, as its name suggests, is the study of humanity (*anthropo* = 'man' or 'humanity,' *logy* = 'study' or 'words'). More precisely, it is the study of humanity in all of its diversity — diversity in body and diversity in behavior. Many sciences study humans, from the social sciences of psychology, sociology, economics, history, *etc.* to the natural sciences of biology and chemistry. However, these other sciences tend to focus on 'us,' that is, modern Westernized urban humans; of course, they may include non-modern, non-Western people in their discipline, but usually as a subfield like 'cross-cultural' psychology or 'world' history. The attention is on ourselves.

Anthropology looks beyond ourselves, and at the same time expands the definition of 'ourselves' to include the 'Other' — the remote, the foreign, the exotic, the 'non-us.' In doing so, it asks a profound question that other sciences do not and that perhaps even it did not intend to ask: what is necessary and what is possible for humans? That is, it considers the full range of human potentialities, looking for any generalities or universals about human lifeways while keeping attention on all the specific differences in how humans think, feel, and act. When we encounter peoples with different — even shockingly different — ways, we are compelled to ask why and sometimes how they do those things.

Again, anthropology shares its subject matter, humanity, with many other fields. But anthropology is unique among them in its 'perspective' or approach to that subject matter. This anthropological perspective is made up of three key elements. First among them is its comparativism or cross-cultural investigation; it seeks to know humanity in all its manifest forms and to make what comparisons or generalizations it can. Second is its holism, taking each part of a group's way of living as connected to every other part and always looking for the relation of those parts to each other and to the natural environment in which the group lives. Third — and most importantly and controversially — is its relativism. Relativism has been criticized, and mischaracterized, but as we recently saw in essence it is a simple and unimpeachable idea: values, morals, and beliefs are relative to a particular social context, to a particular society, such that what is moral in one society may be immoral in another. This is not a theoretical nor even a debatable assertion; it is a fact. Head-hunting is (or was) normal and acceptable, even laudable in some societies but a hideous act in others. Polygamy is the rule in some societies, while it is punishable by law in others.

Relativism is rejected usually for one or both of two reasons — that it advocates an 'anything goes, all things are equal' attitude or that it abandons 'absolute' morality or truth. The first charge is wrong, but the second is right. Relativism does not maintain that 'anything goes' but merely reports that this goes here and that goes there. It does not say everything is acceptable or everything is good; in fact, 'everything is good' is a value judgment too. Rather, it instructs us that every judgment of value and normality is made from some point of view. If someone asks, 'Is polygamy good?' the only possible sensible response is 'According to whom?' Of course, relativism has been abused lately by those who claim that even *facts* are relative — that is, if one group or individual thinks the world is flat, then the world is flat *for them*. This is not what cultural relativism means at all, and this is a specious application of the concept of relativism, as we discussed in the last chapter.

Nonetheless, if morality, value, and 'social truth' are judgments from some particular social perspective, then it does follow that we must abandon the notion of absolute morality. This is naturally a huge problem for absolute moralists, like Christians, who like to believe that their moral rules and sanctions apply to all humanity. As of today they do not, and the only way to make them apply would be to enforce them on all humanity, which is what the missionary project is all about. But until the day comes when one group's morals and values displace those of every other group, morality and value will continue to be relative. Even on that far-off day, the history of cultural diversity will still be testament to the relativity of morals and values.

The organizing principle of the anthropological endeavor is the concept of 'culture.' Culture, in its broadest sense, simply means 'raising' or 'growing,' as in rearing children or growing crops; in its narrowest sense, it has tended to mean 'high culture,' like opera and ballet — that is, 'raising' people from 'lower' tastes to 'higher' ones. But anthropology uses the term in an intermediate sense, as the particular ways that social groups 'grow' people to be members of that group. E.B. Tylor (*Primitive Culture*) in 1871, at the very dawn of modern anthropology, coined a definition of culture that still works today; culture, he wrote, "is that complex whole which includes knowledge, belief, art, morals, law, custom, and any other capabilities and habits acquired by man as a member of society." This definition, which makes explicit the holism of the anthropological perspective and at least implies the comparative and relativistic elements, adds two other key characteristics of culture: it is learned and it is shared. Culture is what a group of people, a 'society,' shares as its ways of thinking, feeling, believing, behaving, and creating, and it is therefore what new members (children) are exposed to and learn by being born into that society.

More recent anthropologists have continued to refine and debate the definition of culture, some emphasizing its subjective/psychological aspects and others its objective/public aspects. One influential definition, appealing to our contemporary interest in mind and symbols, asserts that culture 'is best seen not as complexes of concrete behavior patterns — customs, usages, traditions, habit clusters — as has, by and large, been the case up to now, but as a set of control mechanisms — plans, recipes, rules, instructions (what computer engineers call 'programs') — for the governing of behavior' (Geertz 1973, 44). In his apt analogy, Geertz likens culture to a computer program: like a program, a culture is a set of ways to 'process' and respond to the world, and like a computer a human is capable of 'inputting' and executing a stunning range of 'programs,' but only those which have been 'installed.' In other words, we might think of 'American culture' or 'Japanese culture' or 'Australian Aboriginal culture' as discrete programs, all executable by the human 'computer' but only if that human has the opportunity to install or learn that cultural program. To extend the analogy, a human without a culture, like a computer without a program, would be futile and unworkable, but more on this below.

Another analogy I like is that of a pair of glasses. Culture is like a pair of glasses in that it shapes how we see the world and therefore how we interact with it, even what we think or expect is actually present in it. As with glasses, people do not ordinarily see their cultures but rather they see *through* or *via* or *by means* of them, seeing the world as the culture so distorts it. Anthropology, on this analogy, then becomes the means not only to see the cultural glasses of other people and societies but to attempt to try those glasses on and 'see' or think or understand as those others do. And ultimately, it forces us to realize that we too wear cultural glasses that can — with great effort and potentially great cost — be removed and replaced by other glasses. However, this discovery, and the loss of familiar glasses and the acquisition of unfamiliar ones, can be dizzying and vertiginous. This is, I think, what Nietzsche at least on occasion meant by "looking into the abyss" and what he and other existentialists experienced as "nausea."

The Encounter with the Other

Anthropology, then, is the formal discipline of discovering other people's glasses, attempting to wear their glasses (at least for a little while), and thereby losing the comfort and certainty of one's own view of the world. Anthropologists accomplish this end through the systematic practice of fieldwork, living among and as much as possible living *like* the people of another society. I myself lived for two years among Australian Aboriginals, trying to speak their language, eat their food, practice their culture, and enter their universe of meaning and action. Anthropology and related fields have referred to this phenomenon as the 'encounter with the Other' — the other here being some divergent form of humanity.

Of course, anthropology did not discover the Other as such; humans have always known that there were 'others' out there, in the next village or the next valley or the next continent, and they generally understood that those others had different ways of life than they themselves practiced. Probably no human society has ever been so isolated that it knew of only one form of humanity. However, awareness of the other is not the same as interest in or reflection on the other, and throughout history most societies have either not taken the Other seriously (as worthy of study and contemplation, as potentially informing them about themselves) or not taken the Other to be completely acceptable or completely human at all. In fact, the wonder is not so much that almost all societies in all times and places have excluded the Other from their universe of meaning and morality as that any society ever thought to do differently. That is where the possibility of anthropology, and of freethought, comes in.

Very early on, there were some rumblings of an appreciation of the message of Otherness, although they were few and far between. The first relativistic-sounding comment in the history of world literature appears in a quote from the Greek philosopher Xenophanes, who observed: "Ethiopians have gods with snub noses and black hair, Thracians have gods with gray eyes and red hair .... If oxen or lions had hands which enabled them to draw and paint pictures as men do, they would portray their gods as having bodies like their own; horses would portray them as horses, and oxen as oxen" (Wheelright 1966, 33). This is a remarkable insight, that not only do different human groups have gods in their own image, but that different species would too. However, Xenophanes fails to practice relativism in his evaluation of this situation; he says that all of these visions of gods are misguided and wrong, since god is really only 'one' and does not have any of these characteristics. (No doubt the Ethiopians and the Thracians would have disagreed with him adamantly.) Ultimately, the ancient Greeks never developed a science like anthropology, rather seeing people unlike them as 'barbarian' and 'uncivilized.'

This situation is much more common than the potential but failed relativism of Xenophanes. In the Hebrew Old Testament of the same general era, non-Hebrews were idolaters, sinners, and evildoers; no serious possibility of acceptability without being Hebrew was entertained. Early (and late) Christianity and Islam, as well as all other religious and cultural traditions, did not do much better. In fact, the main obstacle to anthropology — and to all possible relativism and freethought — is and always has been *certainty* in one's own truth and goodness, the kind of 'one-possibility thinking' that is characteristic of all traditional and most modern societies. Cultural certainty is the death of freethought and thus of relativism, since only one kind of thought is permitted or at least valued highly; all others are by definition false or inferior or unacceptable. And naturally our own pervasive tradition, the Judeo-Christian tradition, is characterized through and through with one-possibility thinking.

The stultifying effect of this kind of thinking was to foreclose any questioning about the Others whom you encountered — they were either to be avoided or killed or converted — and to evaluate and interpret all experience, including experience of the Other, through preexisting cultural glasses or programs. Again, Christians were not so blind that they could not see differences, behavioral and bodily, between themselves and surrounding peoples. However, their inclination was instinctively to assimilate those experiences to the schemas, largely provided by the Bible, that they already possessed. For instance, when they contemplated pagans in their midst or at great distances, the existence of these Others was reconciled with biblical accounts of creation or differentiation; the other people were fallen descendants of Adam, or perhaps results of a non-Adamic creation (the controversy of monogenesis versus polygenesis), or their cultures and especially languages were a product of the Babel event.

That this closed type of thinking would lead to some fanciful conclusions is hardly surprising. From ancient times, Europeans had suffered not only from a lack of interest in foreign peoples, or even a lack of information, but a positive burden of bad information. They believed in, and reported to each other, the existence of fanciful monstrous races with no heads or one huge foot or similarly unlikely compositions (*e.g.*, Friedman 2000). Surely monsters, while titillating to the public, were not the stuff to stimulate a science of foreigners, let alone to suggest a kinship between them and us. Anyhow, even the most hardheaded Christians could not ignore the fact that non-Christian, non-European people inhabited the world nor even the anomalous archaeological features in their own backyards. Saxo Grammaticus, writing in the twelfth century of the enormous stone edifices of Denmark, opined that "the country of Denmark was once cultivated and worked by giants .... Should any man question that this is accomplished by superhuman force, let him look up at the tops of certain mountains and say, if he knows how, what man hath carried such immense boulders up to their crests" (Slotkin 1965, 6). Even into the sixteenth century men of good Christian conscience still struggled with the signs of Otherness in their countries; of the Stone-Age artifacts scattered around Europe, "Ulisse Aldrovandi...said that they were natural accretions developed by geological processes; Conrad Gesner ...that they were thunderbolts. Stone projectiles were usually called 'elf arrows' or 'thunderbolts' by laymen ..."(Slotkin, 44). In yet other cases, unexplainable but obviously non-Christian phenomena were either ignored or dismissed as demonic.

The Renaissance in Europe, however, presented another moment of enhanced awareness and appreciation of the Other, by the same means as anthropology accomplishes that awareness — practical and sustained contact. If there is a flip side to certainty, a condition that makes certainty sustainable and defensible, it is uniformity. As long as uniformity could be believed in, or enforced, certainty could be preserved. But the encounter with nonuniformity, with difference — and the closer the nonuniformity, the bigger the threat — made certainty harder to defend. Through contact with Islam and China, with ancient Greek and Roman sources, and with so-called 'primitive people,' Otherness was forced on Europeans in ways that could not be easily dismissed. The contact with Muslims and East Asians, which began as trade relations, all the same exposed people to other civilizations not only different from but in some ways superior to their own. Arabs, Turks, Indians, and Chinese were no doubt pagans and infidels, yet they were urban, cultured, happy, and advanced in their economy and technology, often beyond Europe. Whether or not they knew of the Oriental disdain for Europeans can only be speculated, but if they did, no doubt that reverse perspective caused them some discomfort. Of course, the notion of true toleration and cohabitation with these Others, especially the Muslims, was not seriously considered, but at least the fortress of certainty was breached.

Equally if not more troubling was the rediscovery of the culture of their own ancients, the Greeks and Romans. Preserved only in memories and then in scraps and fragments, it was widely assumed that the ancients, especially Plato and Aristotle, while not Christians, were 'pre-Christian' in some way, speaking to the same otherworldly truths as Christianity. However, encountering via the Muslims, who had preserved much of the original work of the ancients, the actual words, histories, and beliefs of their progenitors, this impression became impossible to sustain. The Greeks and Romans had inhabited a very foreign religious, social, and psychological world than the Renaissance Christians, forcing the latter to face the Otherness of their own family tree. Our own ancestors were Others.

Perhaps even more shattering of European cultural certainty was the experience of the Protestant Reformation that was begun in the early decades of the sixteenth century. As we will describe in detail in a later chapter, this religious schism posed a mortal threat to European Christianity and self-identity. European Christianity had struggled with diversity (labeled as 'heresy' or 'blasphemy') literally from its first days, but a general — if armed — consensus had arisen, and the full force of the medieval church was employed to patrol the uniformity. Heretical movements, though common, were typically successfully contained or eliminated. However, Martin Luther's Protestantism was a threat that would not go away. It divided Christendom once and for all — and not just once, but again and again, as new sects multiplied at amazing rates. The familiar response was naturally attempted first: force and persecution. But when the dust had settled and the blood had soaked the ground, both 'religions' were still standing and defiant, and an uneasy peace was struck. The first painful and tentative step toward 'tolerance' was taken, though not eagerly, but the more important point is this: there was now an Other right next door who would not disappear and not stay quiet. Europeans had become, in a profound way, an Other to themselves.

Also, the period of world exploration inaugurated just at the turn of the fifteenth century, intending only to find new paths to the old world, encountered a new world, or many new worlds. The indigenous peoples of America, Africa, Asia, and the Pacific — often referred to at the time and since as 'primitives' or 'savages' — were a severe intellectual challenge to Christian certainty. How could people so different from Europeans physically and culturally even exist in the world? Of course, the first reaction was to assimilate them once again, cognitively and politically; they were condemned for their nakedness and ignorance, their savagery and barbarism, while they were converted, exploited, enslaved, or terminated. An early debate within the Catholic church in regard to the native peoples is instructive. Within decades of Columbus' first voyage, the church was divided as to the disposition of the 'Indians.' Some judged them to be less than human, little better than animals, or at best fallen humans, while the more 'liberal' Bartolome de las Casas argued for their humanity and therefore humane treatment. However, if they were indeed human, then the proper response of colonial authorities was to 'civilize' them and to convert them to Christianity. Neither side considered the relativistic option — to learn from and about them, to tolerate their difference, and to leave them alone. There was no such thing as anthropology yet.

Almost accidentally, Europe gradually came to know more about these new peoples as explorers, traders, and most notably missionaries sojourned among them. Traders spent large amounts of time with natives, sometimes even marrying and raising children in their societies, but did not tend to have an academic or scholarly attitude toward them; the traders' knowledge was often deep but amateur and private. Missionaries, on the other hand, occasionally made it their business to know the cultures in a more academic way, so as to translate the Bible into their languages and to further the conversion process. At any rate, these figures, as well as an increasing number of settlers, became better acquainted with indigenous peoples and funneled that knowledge back to Europe.

Partly as a result of these experiences, Europeans became engaged in questioning their own received cultures and traditions. Starting with the Reformation and continuing with the Enlightenment, Europeans came to see their own institutions and norms as problematic, undesirable, even foreign and oppressive. European political and social realities, like the divine right of kings, the class structure, and even the doctrines of Christianity themselves came under accelerating criticism during the 1600s and 1700s. There were no doubt various sources of these criticisms — some from classical notions of democracy and human rights, some from pre-Christian European tribal culture, and even some from Christian notions of justice and the virtue of the poor — but there is little doubt that much of the criticism was energized by the observation of alternatives to European culture and politics evidenced by 'primitive' people.

Europe of the Middle Ages and early modern age was indisputably a place of inequality, injustice, class distinction, violence, hunger, and other vices. 'Primitive' people were seen in two different lights — one, as the most wretched, impoverished, lowly manifestations of humanity (Hobbes' "nasty, brutish, and short" life image), and the other, as free, natural, egalitarian, happy paragons of what humanity once was and could be again. Much of this so-called 'noble savage' image was based on romantic, wishful, or just plain silly accounts of native life, but the impact was profound all the same. Rousseau is most associated with this angle of criticism of contemporary European society. He compared savages favorably with his own countrymen and institutions, finding in the former the very archetype of free and natural humanity. Humans in a "state of nature" to him were independent and equal, enjoying "the peacefulness of their passions, and their ignorance of vice." He contrasted "natural existence," distinguished by instinct, amorality, appetite, natural liberty, and individual strength, to "civil society," with its formal justice, morality, reason, civil liberty, and general will (the "social contract").

Of course, Rousseau's stereotype of primitive society is foolishly simplistic and idealized; there is no such thing as 'natural man,' since all humans are cultured and none live in a state of raw nature, and there is no single 'savage society' but a plethora of traditional cultures — from the happy to the miserable, from the peaceful to the warlike. Also, he was by no means recommending a return to the primitive state but merely pointing out the two possible states of humanity and the costs of evolving from one to the other. In *The Social Contract*, in the section "The Civil State," he wrote:

> Although, in this state [civil society], he deprives himself of some advantages which he got from nature, he gains in return others so great, his faculties are so stimulated and developed, his ideas so extended, his feelings so ennobled, and his whole soul so uplifted, that, did not the abuses of this new condition often degrade him below that which he left, he would be bound to bless continually the happy moment which took him from it forever, and, instead of a stupid and unimaginative animal, made him an intelligent being and a man.

This is clearly not anthropology — we would never call our subjects "stupid and unimaginative" — but it is something different from anything we have seen before. Rousseau and others like him are taking the Other seriously, declaring them a worthy subject of study and discussion, and even offering them as a model of virtue — another kind of virtue besides the prevailing Euro-Christian virtue — and one that sheds light on our time and on us as fellow humans.

In the 1800s, particularly by midcentury, the concept of evolution, together with the discovery of ancient archaeological ruins around the globe; the re-reading and reinterpretation of classical Greek, Roman, and Hebrew literature and history; the gathering of cultural artifacts for private and museum collections; the rise of industrial capitalism and its observable social consequences (and the 'grand narratives' of culture criticism like Marx's historical materialism); and the practical requirements of colonial administration brought culture to the foreground and led to the birth of anthropology proper. Much of this activity was still ethnocentric in the sense of judging other cultures by one's own standards or assembling this knowledge for one's own ends, but there was a difference now, and the difference was *difference.* Differences between societies, and between historical periods within a society, were taken seriously, even expected, and were seen as relevant to us specifically and to humanity generally; a kind of 'biography of humanity' could be composed which included both them and us.

If there were clear lessons to be extracted from this experience they were, first, that all societies do in fact have a culture (there are no humans without culture); second, that culture affects how individual humans think and feel; and third, that these other cultures are as real and true to them as ours is to us, and that ours is as weird to them as theirs are to us. The era of relativism had arrived. And it was ushered in almost simultaneously in natural science (Darwin's theory of evolution and Einstein's theory of relativity), philosophy (Marx's historical materialism and Nietzsche's "transvaluation of all values"), art (impressionism, dadaism, and surrealism), and of course anthropology — the science of cultural relativism and of serious Otherness.

The point that I am trying to make, again, is not that anthropology has been the fount of cultural criticism and freethought; rather, as we have seen, anthropology as a formal discipline was a relative latecomer to the scene. The point is that both anthropology and the movements for freethought that preceded it sprang from the same sources, namely, the acceptance of Otherness and the awareness that differences in value, morality, and 'truth' are real and are not going away. Both freethought and anthropology are symptoms of the same underlying condition — the *relative* condition, the condition of *difference.* Societies that do not acknowledge or appreciate the possibility of difference, although they may be surrounded by it, will not develop anthropology, and they will not develop freethought. Both anthropology and freethought are products of living with one foot outside of one's own social reality.

However, as should be apparent, this relationship and its implications are not one-way. As anthropology and freethought come alive and grow from the fact of difference, so they also result within their host societies in a corrosion of cultural certainty. Anthropology and freethought are both manifestations and agents of this corrosion. Both of these forces remind us that our values or morals could be this or they could be that, that no way of thought or belief is forever, that none is absolute, that none is better or truer than another. They both confront society with the fact that even that society itself is temporal, constructed, subjective — 'just culture.' Freethought began as an appeal to conscience and to evidence (even if that evidence was initially still biblical authority), and it allowed and commanded one to think and to evaluate and thus to value for oneself. No doubt, no one in the sixteenth century expected it to go as far as it has today — to the very point of questioning religion itself. But questioning, once started, cannot be contained, and its course cannot be predicted. And anthropology began as the study of the remote and exotic but quickly upon realizing that the remote and exotic were humans like us (and that we are the remote and exotic to them) reflected back upon our social ways, stripping them of any special privilege or absoluteness in the vast human scheme. It was humbling — and disorienting.

In conclusion, the consequences of starting down the road of relativism and the awareness of cultural difference are profound and inescapable; they are somewhat like eating of the tree of knowledge, where one will never be innocent or certain again. This corrosive experience has the potential to unravel all of the social fabric; if culture is man-made, then why does any of it matter, or why can't I just make any value or do any behavior I want? In other words, nihilism and solipsism — the rejection of all authority and all truth — are the immanent dangers of this journey. But in a world that includes difference and interpretation and culture, what other choice is there than this road?

Culture as Virtual Reality

The point of the discussion so far has not been to prove the inevitability of nihilism and solipsism or even the virtues of anthropology but to demonstrate that it is a certain kind of society that embarks on either anthropology or freethought and that modern European society is such a society for a variety of reasons. The other point is to show that culture is a profoundly important concept for understanding freethought, religion, and human reality itself.

It seems that each human society is a world of meaning or significance or understanding/believing/valuing unto itself; each experiences the world through its own unique glasses or program. In this sense, there is no 'real world' or 'objective world' as far as human beliefs and values are concerned; there is of course a real world, but human values, morals, and norms shape our experience of it so thoroughly that there is little point in trying to talk about it anthropologically (leave that to the natural scientists and the philosophers). In a way, then, each human society lives in its own socially constructed reality.

I recall that in the late 1980s and early 1990s 'virtual reality' was a hot topic: any time now, people would be able to don clothing and helmets and have all sorts of virtual experiences indistinguishable from reality. That dream has not yet quite become actual, but maybe it is still coming. But from our point of view in this chapter, all human reality is social reality — experienced through the filters or visors of some culture system — and all social reality is virtual reality. When you get immersed in a book or caught up in a movie, you are living in virtual reality. All of us live in virtual reality all the time. Benedict Anderson (1983) has described modern nations (the "national identities" that we each partake in) as "imagined communities" of people we do not and will not know personally yet feel kinship with, and William B. Davis, the 'cigarette-smoking man' and freethinker from *The X-Files*, speaking at an American Atheists convention in 2001, has described acting as living truthfully in imaginary circumstances. Humankind's greatest gift — perhaps its only gift — is the ability to create worlds, believe in them, and live in them.

Cultural reality seems so real to us, of course, because it is there before any of us is individually and because everyone else is doing it. It is difficult to question — sometimes even to see — culture because we enter the cultural world at the second of our birth, or maybe even sooner, if our mother's behavior and feelings have any impact on us prenatally. When we first open our eyes, and every time after that, culture is there. Culture is just what everyone around you does. That is how it is shared and how it is learned. For most people it takes a monumental effort even to discover that it is there, let alone to escape it; few if any do, and that is probably normal and just as well. Even more powerfully, though, culture is not just what we think but what we think *with*; as Geertz said, culture is our acquired control mechanisms, our externally derived instincts, our program, and our glasses.

Humans then do not create and inhabit their worlds individually but collectively. Groups share a worldview and transmit and reproduce that worldview by living it with each other and with the next generation. The very 'givenness' or 'taken-for-grantedness' of culture makes human reality opaque and, for most, unquestionable; it's 'just what we do.' Anthropology and freethought are alike in being escapes, however slight and fleeting, from the centrifugal pull of social reality as self-evidently real.

Culture, the Human Mind, and Nature

Why or how is this virtualization of reality possible for humans? Geertz has offered some insights into this phenomenon as well. Essentially, the answer is that so little is given to humans by nature, by so-called 'human nature.' Rousseau in this sense was right about one thing: that "natural man" would be a stupid and unimaginative animal, if any such thing existed. And in the few instances where it appears that a human has grown entirely wild, as in the cases of feral children, what we do find is not some kind of idealized or romanticized natural person but a less-than-completely-human being.

There are two foundations for the minimal content of uncultured human nature. The first is the interdependence of biological and cultural evolution. We know now with fair certainty that, despite earlier predictions and prejudices, a humanlike brain evolved considerably after a humanlike body. Before there was a brain anywhere near the size and structure of the modern human brain, ancestors to our species were already walking bipedally and using and making tools. Therefore, the environment of human physical evolution included culture, and as we evolved into our present form, we lost many primitive characteristics, including large teeth and instincts. Humans are remarkably limited in our catalog of instincts, and these were replaced by tools, learning, and the total ways of life we call culture.

The second foundation of our limited natural inheritance is the requirement of birthing such large-brained beings. The human brain has long since evolved to be too large to be born mature, so infants are born with distinctly immature brains that mature in the outside — that is, social and cultural — world. So, just as our species evolved phylogenetically in the environment of culture, so each individual develops ontogenetically in the environment of culture. Growth and maturation entail 'enculturation' or socialization — the acquisition or learning of specific cultural knowledge and skills with which human nature is not provided.

The point is not only that humans have so much that they *can* learn but so much that they *must* learn. As we come into the world, humans are 'unfinished,' and we become finished and fully human only in and through culture. In the process, and as a result of millions of years of evolution, culture becomes virtually 'wired into' the individual; Geertz writes that we humans "are, in sum, incomplete or unfinished animals who complete or finish ourselves through culture — and not through culture in general but through highly particular forms of it" (49). There is even no such thing as 'culture in general' but only specific manifestations of culture — American, French, Japanese, Aboriginal, *etc.* — and each human individual is ordinarily exposed to and shaped by one of these. Because of this congenital incompleteness, "man is precisely the animal most desperately dependent upon such extragenetic, outside-the-skin control mechanisms, such cultural programs, for ordering his behavior" (44). Geertz goes on to conclude that "culture, rather than being added on, so to speak, to a finished or virtually finished animal, was ingredient, and centrally ingredient, in the production of that animal itself" (47). Therefore, there is no such thing as 'human nature' apart from culture: human nature, if it is anything, is the ability and the necessity to make and to inhabit — and to believe in — culture. Culture completes an incomplete being.

Implications for Religion and Freethought

Humans live, always and necessarily, in a world of human creation — there is no other — usually without even being aware of it. This world of values, meanings, morals, customs, and artifacts seems 'real,' given, natural. It is not.

Like a pair of glasses, humans see with culture, but they do not usually see culture. Computers do not know they are running a program; they simply follow the instructions. Seeing your glasses, recognizing your program, is a rare thing, achieved by few individuals in even fewer societies. It demands a certain amount of 'freedom,' a certain amount of distance from oneself. It is also probably not an entirely desirable or beneficial ability: taken-for-grantedness is adaptive in a strong sense. The very opaqueness and 'obviousness' (Geertz has even described 'common sense' as a cultural system — what is obviously and self-evidently true to everyone varies from society to society) of the human world spares us from having to remake the same conclusions and judgments over and over; as some anthropologists and sociologists have emphasized, culture provides us with a set of 'frames' or 'scenarios' with familiar and predictable patterns and outcomes. These frames or scenarios get the average person through the average life with little uncertainty and little remainder, but only so long as the conditions in which they were forged persist.

When new or anomalous circumstances appear, the first thing we humans, like all other life-forms, try to do is to apprehend them with our preexisting schemas. This usually works, or at least if it does not work, we don't realize it: if we came across huge stone structures and we believed in giants, we would naturally judge that the structures were built by the giants, and that judgment would suffice. If we discovered fish bones on high and dry mountain tops and we believed in a global flood, the mystery would be solved for us immediately — and in a way that appears to confirm our belief. It is only when confronted with constant challenges to our understanding that will simply not fit our 'lenses' that we will eventually — but not without resistance — discard them for other, newer lenses and schemas.

This is why cultural relativism in general and freethought in particular are predictably rare and fragile. Culture is really given by the society that precedes and survives us, and it is really taken by us individually. It is in the mind of the individual before the individual starts to think about it — before the individual starts to think at all. It is not something that most humans think about but something they think *with*. Thus, it is almost forbiddingly difficult for humans to turn their minds to consideration of their own culture; the process is something like pulling out one of your teeth by using your other teeth. Most people would never even achieve awareness of the possibility of such a thing; most of the those who do would never seriously entertain the idea; and most of those who entertain it would not suffer through the pain for what little if any gain is offered.

Religion is a part of culture. From an anthropological or freethought perspective, it is a human product pure and simple, and it is difficult to see, given the extreme diversity of religious phenomena, mutually exclusive and contradictory as they are, how this perspective could be wrong. Religion, like every other aspect of culture, wants to be taken for granted; it makes claims about the physical, metaphysical, and moral realities of the world and asks to be 'seen through,' not seen. Most people never question their religious truths any more than they question their physical or commonsense truths; that is the whole point of cultural 'truths.' They are not subjects for questions; they are terms for questions.

Some Atheists and other critics of religion like to use the analogy of a crutch for religion — that it is something that the weak use to get them through otherwise difficult situations. The implication is that if they were stronger (like us) they could dispense with the crutch and walk independent and free. Even this analogy, of course, raises serious operational objections: you cannot pull a crutch out from under a disabled person and expect him or her to walk. Rather, they will fall and then blame you for the accident. The real point is more profound but perhaps more discouraging: religion for the religious person is like culture for the cultural person — it is glasses, not crutches. And these glasses are not prophylactic — they do not help the person to see 'better.' *They make seeing at all possible.* Maybe an ultimate analogy for culture in general and religion in particular is not glasses but the very eyes themselves. You could not expect to pull someone's eyes out and have them see better, anymore than you could expect to take away someone's culture and have them understand and act better.

I am hardly apologizing for or defending religion here. I wish it would go away. But as Atheists and freethinkers, we need to appreciate that some methods will not achieve their goals. We will probably not convert Theists, individually or collectively, by arguing with them, much less condemning them. Arguing in the conventional sense in this case constitutes little more than demanding that they take out their eyes and see like we do, and condemning is more likely to make them protective of their eyes. It would be equally unlikely to succeed if we went to another society and told them that their culture was all wrong or that they were stupid and weak for practicing it. Of course, there are those who have done so — missionaries especially — but their success is more attributable to their control over resources and their brute force than to argumentation and criticism. Few if any American missionaries ever arranged debates with Indian tribal leaders; instead, they threatened them with hell, rewarded or punished them with material goods, and coerced them with military power.

Yet cultural relativism and freethought are possible, for they exist, however tenuously. They are possible for a variety of reasons that we have hopefully explicated by now. One reason is 'mutation,' that is, random and unpredictable changes in thought that occur, for instance, when individuals do not learn and internalize their 'given' cultures perfectly. The process of enculturation or socialization is not a certain or perfect one, and ultimately culture, although it is 'given' in the sense of already-existing, must be 'taken' by each individual — perceived, interpreted, reconstructed, and integrated into his or her personality. This is by no means an automatic or guaranteed process, as anthropologists and psychologists have discovered. Much depends on the creative genius of each individual, who must, in a way, re-create culture mentally for himself or herself. The pithy phrase 'the guided reinvention of culture' has been advanced to recognize that society — the adults and institutions in the child's environment — can and will guide the process of learning and enculturation but that in the end, it is an active and not a passive achievement.

But waiting for cultural mutations is slow and uncertain. The main motor of relativism and freethought, as we have seen, is the encounter with the Other. The Other — whether it is the foreign compared to the familiar, the remote compared to the local, the female compared to the male, the gay compared to the straight, the nonbeliever compared to the believer, and so on — compels us to consider alternatives. The initial resistance to and castigation of alternatives is only too natural and predictable; in fact, the Other is not an alternative at first but an exception, a deviant, a monster, a non-human. The Other does not represent competing values and truths, let alone alternative ones, but rather the absence of values and truths — only immorality and falsehood. But sustained contact, with a particular predisposition toward curiosity about otherness, leads to the inevitable acknowledgment of the humanity of the Other and to the appreciation of their different (if still unpalatable) values and truths.

Then comes the epiphanal moment, when the realization strikes that if the Other could be so, then potentially we ourselves could be so. If they have a culture, then we have a culture. And if culture is man-made, then *my* culture is man-made too. Certainty evaporates, skepticism pervades. What is the truth of truth, the value of values? Why should we do, think, or believe *this* instead of *that*? And if a society can make its own culture and reality, why cannot I, individually, make mine? So appears the threat of radical subjectivism, of value-solipsism, that runs through Western civilization: if values, morals, truths, *etc.* are human products, then I can produce any value or moral or truth that I see fit. If I think it — or even worse, if I *feel* it — it is just as true and good as anything that any society has ever created. Each individual becomes the arbiter of reality.

This is not the message or goal of anthropology, any more than of freethought, but it is a potential consequence. Anthropology of course teaches that human groups — societies — create their cultural realities together; after all, culture is shared, and if it is not shared, it is not culture. Beyond that, societies do not create their cultures self-consciously or suddenly but rather gradually and invisibly even to themselves; this is perhaps one element of the distinction between 'authentic' and 'inauthentic' cultures that anthropologists and others have spoken about over the years. We will have more to say about this issue in a later chapter, but it is a real and serious concern.

Theists will be the first and main party to argue that values, morals, and truths are not relative and to reject, vilify, and demonize those who suggest otherwise, including not only Atheists and freethinkers but practitioners of other religions and even heretics within their own religion. And that is fully understandable: the initial reaction to confrontation with the Other is denial, followed by assimilation (in the form of 'yes, the Other exists, but he is a heathen, blasphemer, sinner, subhuman, *etc.*'). This is why, as I maintained above, debating Theists or belittling them will have no effect or perhaps even a reverse effect, strengthening their sense of community if not their mental faculties and causing them to cling to their beliefs against the satanic insults of the world. Rather, Theists will have to learn the reality of relativism and the socially constructed nature of their own religion and beliefs the way that anthropologists have had to learn it — the hard way, by the sustained and inescapable confrontation with those who differ yet still deserve their humanity. This means, again, not just displaying ourselves as Atheists and freethinkers but drawing their attention to the other religions that cohabit their neighborhoods, schools, and workplaces. Insularity is the foundation of ethnocentrism and intolerance; when you only know of those like yourself, it is easy to imagine that you are alone in the world or alone in being good and right in the world. Exposure to diversity, on the contrary, is the basis for relativism and tolerance; when you are forced to face and accept the Other as real, unavoidable, and ultimately valuable, you cannot help but see yourself and your 'truths' in a new — and troubling — way.

PART II

The Concepts

CHAPTER FIVE

Knowing Is Not Believing

In theistic and even atheistic literature, in everyday language, and even in professional science and philosophy, it is common to hear 'belief' and 'knowledge' discussed in ways that make them appear to be almost interchangeable or at the very least intimately related. Naturally, Theists will ordinarily assert that their faith is either a source of knowledge or that their faith is knowledge — knowledge of the existence of a god, knowledge of the nature of that god, and knowledge of the will and plan of that god. Atheists too employ the b-word with facility; let me remind the reader of George Smith's use of the word from an earlier quote: "A belief based on reason is a belief that has been examined for evidence, internal coherence, and consistency with previously established knowledge ...." To advocate that a belief be accepted without reason is to advocate that a belief be accepted without thought and without verification.' But what exactly is a 'belief based on reason'? Is there really any such thing?

The standard answer to this question appears to be 'yes.' Theists and Atheists alike seem to have accepted the position that there are 'reasonable beliefs' and 'unreasonable beliefs,' that is, beliefs arrived at or sustainable by reason and beliefs that are not. It is even worse than this: not only in popular discourse but even in professional circles, it is common to hear of 'knowledge' being brought into the family of belief. This is partly due to some of the acidic contemporary work on 'science as a culture' which suggests that science is nothing more than another belief system — no more objective, no more true than any other. Scientific truths therefore, in this view, have no special privilege over other truths, other ways of knowing, than religion, personal opinion, or wishful thinking. At the extreme, alternative truth systems have been argued to be all simultaneously true; this can be true for you while that is true for me.

The present work is not the place to do a thorough analysis and refutation of this stance, which has been done at high and popular levels elsewhere. And the appeal of the stance, at least to those who hold unscientific and irrational views, is undeniable; if they can drag down real knowledge to their level and erase any distinctions between the true and the false, the known and the merely felt or believed or guessed, they can rest comfortably in their own undeserved self-certainty.

At any rate, the problem is that even those who ought to know, the arbiters of knowledge and the meaning of language, the philosophers and epistemologists, have been party to this great misunderstanding. In philosophy, there is a long tradition of defining knowledge in terms of belief, as 'true belief' or perhaps 'justified true belief.' Therefore, the only difference between knowledge and belief would be the truth status of the claim (what that means for belief — nothing good — will be discussed below). One implication of this position is that knowledge is not fundamentally different, logically and psychologically, from belief, or worse yet that it is a kind of belief or at the very least entails belief in some crucial way — that knowledge is not possible without belief. At the same time, faith is defined to be either a form of belief or to *be* belief. Then, in a simple commutative way (*i.e.*, if A=B and B=C then A=C), knowledge would be a form of or the same thing as faith.

This will not do, and it does not do. George Smith, who like most Atheists still uses and respects the term 'belief,' also states unequivocally that faith and knowledge, or faith and reason, are incompatible, polar opposites.

> The conflict between reason and faith is not primarily a conflict between the propositions of reason and the propositions of faith: it is a more basic conflict between epistemological requirements of reason and the nature of faith as a claim to nonrational knowledge. *I am arguing that faith as such, faith as an alleged method of acquiring knowledge, is totally invalid — and as a consequence, all propositions of faith, because they lack rational demonstration, must conflict with reason.* (120, emphasis in the original)

With this I totally agree, and I have hopefully demonstrated as much in the previous chapter on reason. But Smith, like most Atheists, freethinkers, and skeptics (such as Michael Shermer), still gives belief entirely too much latitude. Three pages after the above quote, Smith writes that "reason and faith cannot simultaneously be offered as grounds for belief. A belief can be based on reason *or* faith, but not both" (123). I strongly disagree: it is not that a belief cannot be based on reason or faith interchangeably but that a belief cannot be based on reason at all. Reason leads to conclusions and to knowledge, not to belief. Therefore I will be taking and defending the position, against all Theists, most philosophers, and many Atheists and freethinkers, that knowledge is not 'true belief' or 'true justified belief' or any kind of belief at all but that knowledge is about reason and that belief is about faith, and the two are logically and psychologically utterly different and even incompatible. In the end, I will advocate for an extremely constrained range of application of the term 'belief' and for its virtual eradication from the vocabulary of the freethinker.

To Know Is to Believe?

For those who take seriously the idea that knowledge is true belief or justified true belief, to *know* is to *believe* in some way; in other words, every 'knowing' either is or entails a 'believing.' It is possible to identify three ways in which knowledge is claimed to be or to entail belief. We will call these the 'sequential,' the 'dimensional,' and the 'foundational' relations between knowledge and belief.

The 'sequential' relation asserts that knowledge is a *kind* of belief — the *verified* kind. Human cognition, according to this view, follows a sequence: all knowledge, the argument goes, starts out as belief that, if verified, becomes knowledge. Knowledge then is a *subset* of belief — true or justified true belief. The 'dimensional' relation, as the name suggests, conceives that belief is an additional and necessary dimension to knowledge. In this interpretation, everything that is 'known' is also 'believed.' For example, if you say, 'I know that the earth is round,' you would also have to say, 'And I believe that the earth is round.' The third or 'foundational' relation is subtler, arguing that knowledge is founded on a belief or set of beliefs which could not be considered knowledge because it could never be tested or proven. A good example of this notion is geometry; geometrical knowledge builds on a base of unverified and impossible-to-verify axioms and postulates like 'Two parallel lines will never intersect.' But even everyday life is filled with such foundation-beliefs, such as 'The sun will come up tomorrow' or 'The ground will stay solid beneath my feet.' These axioms and postulates are beliefs, says the foundational view, and knowledge (or even life) could not proceed without them.

Hopefully it is already apparent that each of these relationships is logically confused, internally inconsistent, and psychologically inaccurate. In regard to the sequential argument, it is simply empirically untrue that we approach our cognitive process as if we had two boxes, the 'belief' box and the 'knowledge' box, and that we put our ideas first in the belief box and then move them to the knowledge box if and when they are verified. For one thing, some cognitions (we must here avoid using 'knowledge' or 'belief' as the general and 'raw' term for unverified mental contents, so I have chosen the clumsy word 'cognitions' to stand for either before it runs the gamut of 'verification') start out as knowledge without passing through the 'stage' of belief. When I look down at my foot and see it at the end of my leg, I do not first 'believe' I have a foot and then, upon verifying it, decide that I 'know' I have a foot. The knowledge is direct and 'immediate' (in the sense of being 'unmediated' either by a belief-process or a verification-process). The observation *is* the knowledge, and no belief is implicated at all.

The problem is much worse than this, however, especially for the defenders and apologists of belief. Let us imagine, against all sense, that there are two cognitive boxes, one for belief and one for knowledge, and that the ordinary sequence is belief, then verification, then knowledge. We agree to define knowledge as verified and therefore justified 'true' belief. What about the beliefs that are not verified — not yet verified, unverifiable, or actually falsified? Do they stay in the belief box? There are, if we use the two criteria of 'true' and 'justified/verified,' four possible combinations of the criteria: (1) true and justified, (2) untrue and justified, (3) true and unjustified, and (4) untrue and unjustified. We have agreed that (1) is the criterion of knowledge. What are the other three, and do they even exist? I would argue that they do but that this is not a meritorious thing for belief.

An example of an untrue but justified belief would be my assessment of someone's personality; I see a person acting unpleasant and difficult, and I determine that he or she is not a nice person. That seems justified on the basis of my experience. However, what I do not know is that he or she is having a bad day — just got in a car wreck, lost his or her job, *etc.* — and that the behavior I witness is atypical. He or she is actually quite a nice person; my assessment is false, but I believe it. An example of a true but unjustified belief would be my belief that a certain sports team is going to win the championship. I have no evidence for this — I may not even know the sport — but I have lighted upon an opinion that they will win, perhaps on the basis of their team name, city of origin, or uniform color. Sure enough, they win the championship. My belief turned out to be true, but was it in any way justified? Was it in any way 'knowledge'? Finally, an untrue and unjustified belief would be one like a belief that ducks created the universe and will take us to another dimension of eternal life and bliss someday; there is absolutely no basis for the belief whatsoever, and it is almost certainly false, but it might be this or that person's belief.

What are we to make of these three situations? Primarily, they are not knowledge — not any of them. Even when they are true, they are lucky guesses or something else short of knowledge. They are even perhaps arrived at by 'reason' (except maybe the duck one), but as we noted in the chapter on reason, there is reason and there is good reason; each of these 'reasonings' illustrates either evidential or logical fallacies or both. But beyond that, they are all three still beliefs — they are something that somebody believes. Thus, if (and I say *if*) knowledge is justified true belief, then what are unjustified true belief, justified untrue belief, and unjustified untrue belief? Are they anything other than *belief*? Is not the definition of 'belief' then either unjustified true belief or justified untrue belief or unjustified untrue belief — that is, all the stuff left over in the belief box when the verification process is finished? I do not think this is where believers want the argument to go.

In other words, contrary to the presumptions of the sequential relation between belief and knowledge, (1) this is not an accurate depiction of the psychological process of acquiring or testing knowledge, and (2) it is insufficient as a characterization or definition of knowledge. Simply stated, the truth-status of a statement is not sufficient to distinguish it as knowledge in opposition to belief. Truth or justification, alone or in combination, are not enough to separate knowledge from belief — and the leftovers would not be satisfactory to believers as all that legitimately can be called belief.

Let us turn to the dimensional argument. It is actually a rather silly fallacy based on the preposterous premise that no one would say he *disbelieves* what he knows. But that is a spurious dichotomy and an example of the fallacy of interrogation or of presupposition that we discussed in the chapter on reason: it would be as if our questioner were to ask us, 'you say you know that Mars has two moons, but don't you also believe that Mars has two moons?' You could not say that you do not believe it, as that would appear to contradict your knowledge claim. So you might feel compelled to admit that you do believe it too. But you would merely have been the victim of the 'fallacy of the leading question.'

In fact, knowledge in most cases has nothing to do with belief, either prior to or simultaneous with the knowledge. The knowledge that Mars has two moons may have been acquired in a number of ways, only one of them completely rational and sound — direct observation. If I look through a telescope and observe two moons revolving around Mars, there is no belief involved here whatsoever. I know it from empirical evidence. One might also claim to know about the moons of Mars on the basis of authority (some professor or astronomer said so) or from 'common knowledge' ('oh, everyone knows that'). We often take these sources of information on face value, assuming that someone somewhere back there made an actual observation and that we too could make the observation, with the right opportunity and equipment.

There is perhaps one sense in which the knowledge that Mars has two moons could co-occur with or be based on a belief. Say, if you had an intuition that Mars has two moons, or a strong feeling, or an ancient sacred text that said so, or had made a personal astral journey to Mars, these would all serve as grounds of commitment rather than reason for claiming the knowledge of the satellites of Mars. It might turn out, accidentally, that you have the 'correct' knowledge of this case, but none of these bases alone would ever be sufficient justification for the alleged knowledge (unless we discover that astral projection really exists, which we have not done so far). Looking at another case will illustrate the problem. Assume that a person was on trial for being a Mafia kingpin. If the jury members themselves had observed the defendant engaging in criminal activities, that would be enough to ensure a conviction (within the limits of the dependability of human acuity and memory). If the jury heard other eyewitness or expert testimony, that would be weighty but still in need of corroboration, but they might sensibly claim to 'know' that he is guilty. But if the prosecution merely argued that "everyone knows he's the godfather" or that it "just had a feeling" he was guilty or "had received a vision from god" that he was guilty or "had had a psychic experience" that he was guilty, the jury (hopefully) would not call that evidence and would not say that it now had knowledge that he was guilty. Of course, the serious and dangerous difference between 'knowing' and 'being convinced' makes the human world a much more complicated place.

So, as we discussed in the chapter on reason, knowledge is based on evidence and logic, not on belief, and certainly not on any of the fallacious forms of argument. When someone — usually a Theist — asks us that old have-you-stopped-beating-your-wife type of question of "Don't you also believe it?" our proper response is not to answer affirmatively or negatively but to dismiss the question — "Belief has nothing to do with it." One interesting twist on the dimensional relation is that it could be argued that every belief is accompanied by or depends on a dimension of knowledge, so that knowledge is primary and belief derivative. After all, you cannot believe in a god unless you think you have some knowledge of what a god is. We should probe the Theist with this tool when he or she makes a simple statement like "I believe in god." "How do you know what a god is?" we can ask. Often the answer will be either that they have had a personal experience or accept scriptural authority — both invalid bases for knowledge — or that they do not know, they believe. At that point, the distinction between knowledge and belief becomes all too clear.

Finally, the foundational relation, which maintains that there are unproven or unprovable assumptions underneath our knowledge, actually refers to an important and true phenomenon but one that has nothing to do with belief. In most if not all fields of human thought, reasoning begins from certain 'givens' or 'takens-for-granted.' But we do well to refer to them as *axioms* and *postulates*, not beliefs. It is wrong and ridiculous to call axioms or postulates 'beliefs.' They are definitions, first principles, stipulations, assumptions, extrapolations, or other such statements that are either taken as axiomatic for purposes of argument and analysis (and therefore perhaps neither true nor false in the conventional sense) or reasonable conclusions based on available observation. The fundamental assumption of Euclidean geometry, that space is flat and uniform, is an axiom which need neither be true nor false for that geometry to succeed; in fact, rather than arguing that space is flat and uniform, it proposes that space is such, and the correct formulation of the axiom would be something like 'Assuming that space is flat and uniform, then ... ' or 'If space is flat and uniform, then ....' On the grounds of that first principle, a geometry can be built. But we could start and have started alternate geometries on other first principles, like curved space, not because they are 'truer' than the Euclidean assumption but because they yield other interesting and useful results.

No one, I think, would claim that Euclidean geometry or Boolean geometry or any other geometry is true or false; each is rather a game, with certain 'rules' and certain 'moves' based on those rules. It may turn out some day that we discover that space really is flat or curved or polka-dotted, but that has nothing to do with the rules of geometry and will not be settled by geometry but by physics and cosmology. Furthermore, while they are doing geometry, mathematicians are not 'believing in' their axioms and postulates (unless they 'go native' and lose themselves in their discipline) but rather exploring the implications of certain geometrical principles. Every other science and philosophy that starts from first principles — and most if not all do — approaches or should approach them in the same way; they are man-made constructs or tentative proposals, whose consequences are being fleshed out. And one other key difference exists between such concepts and 'beliefs': if the constructs or proposals prove to be false or useless or unproductive, the mathematician or scientist or philosopher will generally jettison them and try something else, while the believer will cling to the belief no matter how much it fails.

Lest the Theist think that we are privileging science in some way, the same analysis fits everyday or commonsense knowledge, like the knowledge that the sun rises every morning in the east. Some apologists for belief like to subsume this knowledge under belief, as nothing more than or equally dependent on belief. But of course, the knowledge of the sun's behavior is based on (millennia of) observation in which the exact same facts have been obtained every time. In fact, that the sun rises every morning in the east is a pure case of inductive knowledge, and the prediction that the sun will rise tomorrow in the east is a pure case of the extrapolation of inductive knowledge. There is no possibility of falsifying the induction itself, since there is not one single disconfirming case that we know of, and the validity of the prediction is very high given that nothing changes between now and tomorrow morning. But if, as we argued above, the sun dies out or a meteor knocks the earth out of its orbit, the prediction will be disconfirmed but on totally empirical and factual grounds; it would not be the case that we were 'right' before but 'wrong' now since the circumstances are not the same anymore. Thus, the layperson watching the sun rise does not 'believe' anything about the sun, any more than the mathematician doing geometry 'believes' anything about space. In fact, you could do geometry as an exercise even if you disbelieved everything about Euclidean space. Again, it is the believer, such as the Theist, who has the real problem, since the conventional 'knowledge' that the sun rises is founded securely on thousands or millions of dependable and mutually-confirming observations, while a theistic belief is founded on few or no observations at all. Here perhaps is the real essence of the knowledge-versus-belief distinction.

The Language of Belief

How then are we to think about this thing called belief, especially in comparison to knowledge? One way to approach this problem is in terms of the actual usage of the term and concept of 'belief.' When we use the word 'belief' or 'believe' in normal contexts, does the word 'knowledge' or 'know' apply equally well? In the final analysis, a word or concept *is* its usage and its referents. We have already seen above that the word *belief* is sometimes used to express concepts or cognitions that would best be expressed otherwise. The philosopher Ludwig Wittgenstein said that every word or concept in natural language is really a 'family' of words or concepts, unified only by usage. Let us look then at how English speakers use the word/concept and how this usage actually jumbles together a variety of quite different processes and predicates (a predicate being the verb of a sentence and the modifiers or clauses that follow it), few if any of them having anything to do with knowledge.

Let us look at some examples.

(1)   I believe in god.
(2)   I believe in dragons.
(3)   I believe in love.
(4)   I believe that it will rain tomorrow.
(5)   I believe that he is innocent of the crime.
(6)   I believe that the sun will rise tomorrow.
(7)   I believe that liver tastes awful.
(8)   I believe that the earth is round.
(9)   I believe that two parallel lines do not intersect.
(10)   I believe that the 1972 Miami Dolphins were the
          greatest football team in history.
(11)   I believe that the universe began in a big bang.

Hopefully, this list covers most if not all of the semantic range of the word 'believe.'

Notice first and foremost that there are two distinctly different predicates in use in the above list — 'believe in' and 'believe that.' (Often, in normal speech, we omit the 'that' — for example, 'I believe it will rain tomorrow,' thus obscuring this distinction.) It is common to use the predicate 'know that,' but I cannot think of one instance in which we would say 'know in.' Setting aside this distinction for the moment, think about sentences (4) through (11). What are they really saying?

Sentence (4) is not a belief at all. It would more appropriately be called a prediction. It is either a good prediction or a bad prediction, depending on what happens with the weather tomorrow. It is verifiable in the sense that tomorrow we will see whether it was accurate or not. But no one in her right mind would say — or substitute for this sentence — that she 'knows' it will rain tomorrow. Predictions are not knowledge.

We often hear something like sentence (5) when family members are interviewed at trials, even when the evidence is overwhelming against the defendant. What they are really expressing is a refusal to accept the facts, an emotional commitment to their family member, or a cognitive dissonance between the person with whom they are familiar and the person portrayed in court. In fact, they will often enhance this sentence by saying something like 'I believe in my heart that ... ' which often also takes the spoken form of 'I *know* in my heart that ....' I think it is quite likely that someone would believe something in his or her heart, since that is often where believing is situated, but you cannot know in your heart, since the heart is not a cognitive organ. So it would be wrong to substitute 'I know that he is innocent' for 'I believe that he is innocent,' as any right-thinking court would insist. If one said 'I know that he is innocent,' one would have to produce some evidence (like 'he was home with me at the time'), but if one said 'I believe that he is innocent,' one could and usually would be saying little more than 'I hope' or 'I trust' or 'I desire' that he is innocent — not grounds for a verdict or a rational conclusion.

Sentence (6), which we have encountered before, is not a belief but an extrapolation of an induction. The sun has risen every day so far, so we can induce fairly confidently that there is a general tendency for the sun to rise and can extrapolate that it will rise tomorrow too. Inductions are rational and they are knowledge, depending upon the amount and quality of observation and the similarity of the observations to each other and to any future situation into which they are being extrapolated. Therefore, the extrapolation is rational, but it is not a belief. It might be better, although awkward, if we were to say, 'I induce that the sun rises daily, and I extrapolate that induction to predict that the sun will rise tomorrow.' There is nothing belief-oriented about any of this.

Sentence (7) is not a belief and it is not even a truth claim; it is a taste or preference. The word *belief* could and should be substituted with another word like 'opine,' or the entire grammar of the sentence should be altered. What the sentence is asserting is that I do not like the taste of liver. Does that mean that it is 'true' that liver tastes bad? But some people (I guess) like the taste of liver, so there is neither knowledge (neither truth nor falseness) nor belief in this statement. Of course, it may be 'true' that I dislike the taste of liver (or I might be lying, for instance, to not hurt your feelings for being a really bad cook), but that has nothing to do with knowledge or belief about the qualities of liver.

Sentence (8) is a restatement of knowledge based on observation and interpretation of observation and does not reflect real language usage or a psychological process. It is an example of the fallacious dimensional relation that we treated above. No one believes that the earth is round, because it is a primary or very-nearly primary phenomenon; of course, there may be those who 'believe' that it is not round, but therein again lies the difference between knowledge and belief.

Sentence (9) is a definition or stipulation, and it is also not the way real mathematicians practicing geometry talk. In fact, for those who remember their school geometry, 'proofs' of geometrical problems usually state very clearly what they are up to; they may start out with a proposition like 'Let two parallel lines never intersect out to infinity' or 'Let the angles of a triangle sum to 180 degrees.' This is explicitly not making a truth claim but setting up a definition or establishing a boundary condition. The definition may, in some cases, be true or false, but in others it may be neither true nor false but merely operational. In none of the cases, however, is it a belief nor does it depend on belief. In fact, as we put it above, one can still do geometry without any commitment to, any 'belief' in, the axioms of geometry — just as one can do theology without any 'belief' in the dogmas of theology. However, it is hard to imagine doing religion in any meaningful sense without believing in the doctrines of religion.

Sentence (10) is an opinion at worst, an assessment at best. It may be an opinion or assessment based on study and analysis of statistics and historical comparison. It may be an opinion based on loyalty to your team. Or it may be nothing more than talking through your hat — the kind of ignorant bar-talk that gets people excited and occasionally injured. But it could never constitute knowledge since, based on the same history and statistics, another analyst or fan could arrive at a completely different conclusion, and it is impossible that two contradictory 'knowledge claims' could both be true. It is subjective in the end, since even the criteria for the judgment are not specified.

Sentence (11) is a statement of acceptance of a reigning theory as the best available explanation for an observed phenomenon. This is one of the traps that Theists like to set for scientists and Atheists: 'Well, you believe in the big bang' or 'You believe in evolution.' When Theists trot out the b-word in situations like this, I respond that I do not 'believe' in evolution but that I accept evolution as the best explanation that we have right now. A key difference between acceptance and belief is this: tell the Theist that you would gladly terminate your acceptance of the theory of evolution if another superior theory were to be proposed, and then ask them if they would gladly drop their religious belief if another superior religion were to be presented to them. Their answer shows all the difference you will ever need to see.

So, clearly, most of the time when we say that we 'believe that' something, we are really engaging in some other activity than belief. We really mean that we 'predict,' 'induce,' 'extrapolate,' 'opine,' 'prefer,' 'feel,' 'hope,' 'desire,' 'accept/refuse to accept,' 'define/stipulate,' 'hypothesize,' *etc.* Some of these are truth claims and thus potentially knowledge, while others are not claims about the truth at all. 'Belief that' often has nothing to do with knowledge whatsoever, and when it does — as in (4), (6), (8), and (11) — it seems to have nothing to do with belief whatsoever.

What about 'belief in'? Looking at sentence (3), to say 'I believe in love' is surely not a truth claim; in fact, it is not quite saying the same thing as 'I believe that there is such a thing as love.' Of course, it seems to presuppose the latter statement, but it is not simply reiterating it. This sentence can and probably must be broken down into two constituent sentences — 'I believe that there is such a thing as love' and something like 'I believe in the goodness or power or value, *etc.*, of love.' Now, the first sentence is making a roundabout truth claim: there is such a thing as love. If there is (metaphysical considerations aside), then my 'belief' makes no difference whatsoever — there is such a thing as love, just as there is such a thing as my foot, whether I 'believe in it' or not. The real thrust of the original sentence is the second constituent part of it — that I believe that love has some quality or power that will aid me or change you or enhance me in some way. That is a truth claim also; either it has this power or it doesn't. My belief is peripheral to the claim and its ultimate truth. And obviously, the second question will be settled automatically if the first question is settled negatively: if there is no such thing as love, then there is no saving or transforming power of love. But the questions can be settled.

That only leaves sentences (1) and (2) — belief in god and belief in dragons. What does it mean to say that I 'believe in' purported beings of these sorts? Clearly, again, these sentences can and must be deconstructed into at least two constituent sentences, for example, in the case of sentence (1), that 'I believe that there is such a thing as god' and that 'I believe that this god has certain qualities or powers that affect me in some way.' There is perhaps a third essential sentence to be added here as well, to the effect that 'I am emotionally committed to this god in some way.' 'Belief in,' whether in love or god, seems to entail some kind of personal commitment to the phenomenon; this is probably the case with dragons too, although the commitment is less obvious and less analytically important for our purposes. But if we were to add such sentences as 'I believe in UFOs' or 'I believe in past lives' or 'I believe in talking to the dead,' the pattern of personal commitment would begin to emerge.

What then does it even mean to say 'believe in' as opposed to 'believe that'? 'Belief in' does not simply substitute for 'belief that': for instance, one would not normally say that one 'believes in' the taste of liver or the '72 Miami Dolphins. There are other forces at work in addition to a putative knowledge claim. However, we must recognize the critical fact that *every 'belief in' entails one or more 'beliefs that,' and each 'belief that' is a truth claim and is therefore ultimately verifiable or falsifiable, at least in principle.* But beyond that, 'belief in' includes or entails a dimension of personal or emotional commitment that is absent in many if not most 'beliefs that' as well as most or all knowledge.

To expand on this point, to assert that one *believes in* a god necessarily implies that one *believes that* there is such a thing (although it does not unfortunately necessarily imply a particularly lucid notion of what that god is); however, one could, I suppose, claim that one 'believes that' there is such a thing as a god without the 'belief in' — that is, without the personal commitment or hope that this god's existence or actions have any implications for me. It would be an unusual position to adopt, but it is at least conceivable. Therefore, the two dimensions of the 'belief in' are at least theoretically detachable.

If the above statement — that every 'belief in' entails one or more 'beliefs that,' each of which is a verifiable or falsifiable truth claim — is the first conclusion of the analysis of belief, then the second and more radical conclusion is that *only this usage of 'belief' represents belief in any distinctive and serious way.* Only in sentences like 'I believe in god' or 'I believe in dragons' can 'believe' not be substituted with another predicate such as 'predict,' 'induce,' 'prefer,' *etc.* Go ahead and try: 'I predict that there is a god,' 'I induce that there is a god,' 'I prefer god,' 'I opine that there is a god,' and so forth do not capture the meaning of the sentence 'I believe in god.' If there is still any doubt about this position, then try responding to each sentence above with the question 'why?' and notice the results. Why do you predict there is a god? Why do you induce? Why do you prefer? Why do you opine? Why do you believe in god? The first four questions ask for and will only accept answers in the form of reason, and even more so in the form of observation: I predict god on the basis of past experience, I induce god on the basis of past observation, I prefer god on the basis of comparison with something else, I opine god on the basis of weighed judgment. But why 'believe in' god? There are myriad other answers, but none of them have to do with reason.

The four related questions above make no sense without the presumption that there is trustworthy evidence at hand (what experience? what observation?). Besides, nobody actually talks that way. The point is that 'believe in god' is the ordinary way of talking about belief and god, and it does not depend on trustworthy evidence. Theists can and do answer the question 'why?' with such things as scriptural authority, moral necessity, tradition, popular opinion, wishful thinking, and putative personal experience — all of which we have previously rejected as sufficient reason to take a position. In fact, a Theist need not have had any experience with god whatsoever to maintain belief: "God has never manifested in my life in any way, but I believe that he exists and that he will someday." This is a perfectly consistent, if not perfectly rational, attitude.

This brings me to my third and most radical conclusion from this analysis. Sentences like 'I believe in a god' or 'I believe in dragons' are not only prototypically and exclusively 'belief' statements, but they make or depend on one or more truth claims that have not been demonstrated and perhaps cannot be demonstrated to be true. Sentence (1) on its own is a vacuous statement; you cannot 'believe in god' but must believe in some specific god with specific attributes, goals, and demands. When a Christian, for instance, utters sentence (1), what he or she is really saying is (a) 'I believe that a god exists,' (b) 'I believe that this god is an invisible creator-person in heaven,' (c) 'I believe that this god made rules for us to live by,' (d) 'I believe that this god died for the sins of humanity,' and an indefinite set of others including beliefs about heaven and sin. The one thing that is certain about all of these statements is that they are uncertain. They are unverified and potentially unverifiable. There is no good evidence or argument for them, and there is even some good evidence and argument against them. This fact does not prevent people from believing them. Each statement is a belief; none of these statements is knowledge.

Thus, I posit that the only accurate and useful definition of 'belief' is the definition that thoroughly and exclusively characterizes the type of belief evinced in such statements as 'I believe in god' and its corollaries. This definition must be something along the lines of *acceptance of a statement as true without supporting evidence or argument or in the face of contradictory evidence and argument.* It is necessarily not only *not* knowledge but is the very *antithesis* of knowledge. Where there is knowledge, there is no need for belief, and where there is no knowledge, only belief in the strict sense can abide.

Knowledge and Certainty

From the analysis just completed, from the analysis of knowledge and belief earlier in the chapter, and from the previous chapter on reason, I think we can formulate the distinction between knowledge and belief in terms of the source and the product of knowledge. **Knowledge consists of a statement or set of statements arrived at by the consideration of evidence and the application of logic that we can with a high degree of certainty certify as true.** More simply, knowledge is *acceptance of a statement as true on the basis of the evidence or on arguments or interpretations grounded on the evidence.* This is what separates it from belief. Belief, in the proper sense, does not stand on evidence or even bend to disconfirming evidence. Belief persists — even thrives — in spite of lack of evidence; knowledge evaporates in the absence of evidence.

Knowledge is necessarily a humanly acquired thing; it takes an active participation in observation and interpretation to arrive at anything more than the most superficial sense-data. Apologists of belief see this as its greatest weakness: since knowledge is almost inevitably inductive and interpretive, they emphasize the uncertainty inherent in human knowledge. They distrust human powers of knowing and place their 'faith' in what they consider not only different but superior 'ways of knowing,' including revelation, 'apostolic' authority (that is, information passed from those who 'ought to know,' whether they are actually apostles or not), and personal subjective experiences. And they point all too often to the convolutions and failures of science as proof that mere human knowing is suspect at best and fatally flawed at worst.

In fact, they will often accuse rationalists of possessing no greater certainty than Theists or of overestimating their own certainty; 'how can you be certain that there is no god?' is one common rejoinder. This demonstrates a profound lack of understanding of the nature of certainty and of its significance in assessing truth and knowledge. There is almost no one more 'certain' than a convinced Theist; certainty in this sense is a psychological attitude toward one's proposition, not a quality of that proposition itself. Lots of people feel certain about lots of things, often diametrically opposed to each other and patently false. In actuality, certainty of the important kind — that is, the reliability and validity of one's conclusions — has absolutely nothing to do with the level of subjective confidence and self-assurance toward the conclusion. One can be — and often is — dead certain and dead wrong.

So certainty is as much misunderstood as it is maligned. First of all, certainty is not an all-or-nothing commodity. We have aptly referred frequently to the 'degree of certainty,' and the failure to appreciate the gravity of this concept is a major handicap. Certainty depends primarily on the quantity and quality of evidence upon which it is founded; secondarily, it depends on the appropriate interpretation of that evidence and the application of logic to its processing, but it is much easier to spot faults in interpretation and logic than in evidence itself.

Being in essence inductive, knowledge does have a certain margin of error; a conclusion as apparently self-evident as 'all men are mortal' depends on the accurate observation that all men known so far have been mortal and that no immortal men have been overlooked. In the end, we could not even call this knowledge 'certain,' but would we call it any the less 'knowledge'? In other words, does knowledge require certainty — is it part of the definition of knowledge to be certain of its truth?

The answer is quite simply no. Knowledge has a higher or lower degree of certainty, but it need not and perhaps theoretically cannot attain perfect certainty. I would say with confidence approaching 100% that I have a foot at the end of my leg, but I recognize that there is a diminishingly small chance that I am mistaken — that what I thought was a foot was something else or that it is not really where I thought. But does this diminishingly small chance really matter? No. And even more to the point, those who are committed to the path of knowledge rather than belief realize from the outset that knowledge is tentative and changeable — some more so than others. For instance, there is a diminishingly small chance that we might discover tomorrow that the earth really is flat, or oval, or hexagonal, but I think we can rest fairly comfortably that this will not occur. And what if it does? Does that mean that all human knowing is futile, that radical epistemological skepticism is justified? No, it means little more than that we will have to reprint some textbooks. We will return to this matter below when we discuss the relation between science and religion.

Of course, the fact that human knowing is tentative and changeable, even if not futile, is frustrating and infuriating to many people, especially Theists. They would cling to the 'rock of ages' against the tide of evidence, interpretation, and conclusion. But this is a nonexistent rock, and even if it did exist, it would really be no more secure than any other man-made mooring. For has religion not also changed over time? Does the certainty of Christians make the certainty of Muslims less real? Does the certainty of modern Christians make the certainty of ancient Christians or pre-Christians, who often believed quite different things, less real? If so, then why does the certainty of Muslims or ancient Christians or pre-Christians not make modern Christian certainty less real? Again, certainty is not the key factor in separating the wheat of truth from the chaff of error.

In the end, it may be that certainty of the type called for by Theists — not statistical certainty, not reasonable certainty, but absolute certainty — is not possible from looking at the evidence but *only from not looking at the evidence*. Perhaps *knowledge is inherently uncertain while belief is inherently certain* ... and therein lies all the difference. The world appears to be a 'statistical' world (physics has learned that it is a 'quantum' world, where events cannot be predicted with complete accuracy even with a complete knowledge of initial conditions), a world of 'fuzzy logic,' a place where some things happen with more regularity and some with less regularity but nothing with perfect regularity. If that is the kind of world we live in, then human knowledge could not help but reflect that fact; thus, the less-than-perfect certainty immanent in human knowledge would not be a flaw at all but an accurate characterization of the world we are struggling to know.

Conclusion: The Venality of Conflating Knowledge and Belief

Knowledge is not belief. Knowledge is not belief logically or psychologically. Knowledge does not originate in belief, it does not co-occur with belief, and it does not depend on belief. Then why do so many people, not only Theists but Atheists as well, subscribe to the view that it is or does? For the Atheists and freethinkers, the only reason I can see is that they have not thought through the implications of the concepts all the way to the end. Besides, if the whole world, including the professional concept-analyzers, agree that knowledge is 'justified true belief' or some other kind of belief, then it must be so. And our whole language drips with belief, even if it is no more belief-related than my belief that liver tastes bad.

I hope to accomplish two things in this chapter. The first is to make the case for eradicating belief-talk — maybe even the b-word itself — from the discourse of Atheists and free-thinkers. It is somewhat more cumbersome to use the proper descriptive predicates that we sorted out above, but it is worth the effort: most of the time, when I would carelessly say that I 'believe' A or B, what I mean is that I 'induce' A and I 'opine' B, *etc.* I have already started in my life to try to examine and reject every instance of belief that is not really belief — and since, if my analysis is correct, that only applies to unsubstantiated and potentially unsubstantiatable beliefs, this has not been as hard as it sounds, since I discover that I have few or none of them. I would call on all Atheists and freethinkers to eschew the word except when it really means what it means — and I hope we have few cases of it among us — and to reject it in our debates, especially when it is applied to us. Atheism is not a belief, doubting the existence of god is not a belief, reason is not a belief, science is not a belief. In the process, we can do two things: (1) educate believers as to the true nature of belief, and (2) demonstrate the truly limited range of the term, down to the few irrational views held by a (disappointingly) large proportion of humanity. In this way, we can isolate real 'beliefs' and perhaps even stigmatize them in the way they deserve.

To fail this is to let the 'believing' majority control the terms of language and thought. And why would they want to conflate knowledge and belief in the end? The answer is too apparent and too dismal. Knowledge, as much as they look down on it, is a good thing, a powerful thing, a prestigious thing. By claiming that belief is akin to knowledge, they attempt to acquire some of the prestige of knowledge for belief. This elevates belief in a social setting where 'mere belief,' 'mere subjectivity,' while enough for some people, earns them and their views a stake in the truth: if something is knowledge, then it must be true, and therefore anything that contradicts it must be false. By claiming, conversely, that knowledge is belief, they attempt to stain knowledge with the blights that afflict belief; if knowledge is 'belief too' or 'just belief,' then it is not superior to belief in any way, and when it contradicts belief, it has no special privilege to the truth. This denigrates knowledge by painting it as no more good or true or valuable than belief; if belief is nothing more than subjectivity and wishful thinking, then so is knowledge. It is nothing special.

I have developed a habit that I practice when I hear a Theist say something venal like "science is a religion" or "Atheism is a belief." I respond, "Do you mean that as a compliment or an insult?"

CHAPTER SIX

Positive Atheism, Negative Atheism, and Agnosticism

In the introduction we discussed the meaning of Atheism and some of the confusions — incidental and intentional — about what Atheism is and what Atheists are. In the present chapter, I would like to expand on the discussion of Atheism and another related concept, Agnosticism. My goal will be to expose what I consider to be a misconception about each — that there are two versions or 'degrees' of Atheism, commonly referred to as 'positive' and 'negative' or 'strong' and 'weak' or 'explicit' and 'implicit,' and that Agnosticism is an alternative to Atheism and Theism, a self-sufficient 'position' or waypoint between the two 'extremes' of Atheism and Theism.

These are surprisingly unconventional views to take, it seems. Why do I hold these views, and why do I consider them important? The answer is that I think both misconceptions obscure the true nature of Atheism and both attempt to minimize or sanitize the message or impact of the reality of Atheism. This sanitization occurs first through the isolation of 'fanatic' or 'fundamentalist' Atheists from the more 'moderate' and 'civil' Atheists and the ascription of most Atheists to the latter camp, and second through the establishment of a polite noncommittal position of 'doubt' or 'uncertainty' or 'indeterminacy' that nonreligious types can hold without declaring themselves Atheists. Perhaps this sanitization makes it easier to be nontheistic by not having to declare oneself an Atheist, with all the stigma attached. But it simultaneously marginalizes the 'positive Atheists,' even from other Atheists, and perpetuates the stigma against that group while creating specious distinctions within the world of non-Theism and inviting people to take a nonexistent position without thinking the implications all the way through.

Atheism: Positive and Negative

Different Atheisms?

Atheists are a headstrong lot, as would be expected from a constituency that distinguishes itself for freethinking; where thought is free, consensus is elusive. One of the most consistent character traits of Atheists is their refusal to accept authority, and most Atheists — being fairly highly educated, at least in the field of religion — esteem themselves as their own authority and expert. Yet, the one thing that Atheists agree on is a lack of belief in a god — any god, or else they would not be Atheists but Theists. (Theists too lack a belief in most gods, possessing a belief or 'faith' in only their particular chosen god, but that is another story and certainly does not qualify them as Atheists!) Atheism, then, means in essence what the Greek root of the word means: *a-the-ism*, or 'no god belief.'

What Atheism means beyond this simple formulation is a matter of contention. One way to look at the problem involves exactly how we reconstitute the word roots — whether as *a-theism* or 'no god-belief' or as *athe-ism* or 'no-god belief.' This distinction has been variously designated as 'weak/strong' or 'negative/positive' or 'implicit/explicit' Atheism, respectively. The divergence between the two positions in each set is presumably based on whether the Atheist is making a claim or merely refuting a claim (to which we will return shortly). Fundamentally, it revolves around the contrast between 'not believing' and 'believing not.' Michael Martin, in his *Atheism: A Philosophical Justification,* develops this theme, with his book roughly divided in half between negative and positive Atheism. For him, negative Atheists "are not making any claim to knowledge and the believers are," and when believers present their reasons and arguments for the existence of god, negative Atheists "must show that these reasons and arguments are inadequate" (30). Having first built his case for negative Atheism, he turns in the second half of the book to the question of "whether positive Atheism is justified — whether one is justified in disbelieving that such a being exists" (281). Happily, he succeeds at this task.

But the issue goes much deeper than this, for some have maintained Atheism is *really* only one or the other of these two positions or that Atheists only practice one or the other. George H Smith, for example, states: "An atheist is not primarily a person who *believes* that a god does *not* exist; rather, he does *not believe* in the existence of a god" (7). In other words, he holds that Atheism *really* is negative or weak or implicit Atheism (*a-theism*) — the lack of a belief in a god — and not positive Atheism. According to him, no or few Atheists adopt positive or strong or explicit Atheism (*athe-ism*) or the actual position that there is no god. This opinion has penetrated the Atheist community, such that the Internet Infidels could post on their Web site this warning to those who would understand Atheism: "Please do not fall into the trap of assuming that all Atheists are 'strong Atheists.' There is a qualitative difference in the 'strong' and 'weak' positions; it's not just a matter of degree" (http://www.infidels.org/news/atheism/intro.html#-atheisms).

I do not know for a fact that most Atheists consider themselves weak or negative Atheists rather than strong or positive Atheists, although they may. And I have never seen any figures to suggest how many consider themselves positive as opposed to negative. I do not even know for a fact that most Atheists make this distinction for themselves, although given the amount of attention to it in the literature, I suppose it is fairly likely that many do. I am certain that all Atheists are *at the very least* deliberately and self-consciously negative Atheists in the sense that they do not believe in any god(s) and would, as far as they are able, refute any evidence or argument otherwise. If they were not minimally negative or weak Atheists, they would not be Atheists at all. But why discriminate between negative and positive, strong and weak?

One obvious answer to this question is that the terms refer to actual 'qualitative' differences in how different Atheists think or identify themselves. Some may actually reject positive or strong Atheism while still considering themselves Atheists; again, I have never seen statistics on this issue, but it is conceivable. Another answer is that Atheists may be trying to be gentle or polite or acceptable in their position by saying, 'Oh, I don't believe that your god does not exist,

I just do not share your belief in him/her/it.' If this is the case, and such Atheists actually are positive or strong Atheists, they are doing themselves and their community a disservice by being intellectually dishonest. A more insidious possibility, however, is that the positive/negative dichotomy is actually a false dichotomy, founded on a false premise that Atheists should recognize and reject.

If there is a false dichotomy within Atheism, it may be because positive Atheism, as the name suggests, has been misconstrued as advancing a *positive claim* — or even worse, stating a *belief* of its own. Negative Atheism clearly is not making any claim or advancing any belief but simply rejecting the positive claim or belief of a Theist: the Theist says, "I believe in god X" and the negative Atheist says, "I do not believe in god X." As we all know, in general the burden of proof in any dispute falls on the party who advances a truth claim; if I say "X is true" or "There is X," it is incumbent upon me to justify the claim with evidence or argument (if I want to be taken seriously; I have met Theists who say "I do not have/want to prove anything," and that is of course true, but the discussion necessarily dies right there). The negative Atheist obviously is making no claim and bears little or no burden of proof; he or she is only saying, 'I see no proof of that claim, so I do not accept it.' As Martin asserts, the negative Atheist still has a job to do — to demonstrate the inadequacy of Theist arguments — but he or she does not have a 'case' to make as such; simply showing the flaws of evidence and logic, as presented in a previous chapter, will suffice.

However, the positive Atheist is interpreted as going further — all the way to making a truth claim or even advocating a belief. The positive Atheist's statement 'I believe that there is no X' resembles grammatically the Theist's claim 'I believe that there is an X.' However, this resemblance is merely superficial, merely grammatical. *In fact, the positive Atheist's declaration is nothing more than a restatement of the negative Atheist's position.* It could be reformulated in the following way: "In the absence of evidence or argument, I see no reason to conclude that there is an X, so I maintain the position that there is no X." In this version, the positive Atheist bears no more burden of proof than the negative Atheist; instead, he accepts the "null hypothesis" or the "presumption of atheism" (as Antony Flew termed it) *precisely because the Theist has not met his burden of proof.*

Another way that positive Atheism differs from negative Atheism is that, supposedly, the former is making a claim of *knowledge* that there is no god — that it has absolute certainty of the nonexistence of god(s). This, though, is also a mischaracterization, since by definition the position of positive Atheists is that they *believe* that there are no gods, not that they *know* so. No claim to knowledge is being made at all; in fact, I would argue that Atheism — positive or negative — is based precisely on the *lack* of god-knowledge: Atheists have no knowledge of a god, and neither do Theists. Therefore, it is only rational to conclude that something about which there is no knowledge does not exist. On what possible basis could we conclude otherwise, and if we make that basis a general epistemological principle, then how will we ever separate the real from the imaginary, the true from the false?

Finally, as should be apparent from the previous chapter on belief and knowledge, it is not even accurate to portray positive Atheism as a belief. Even when it is forceful, strident, 'certain,' it would be more appropriately considered a *conclusion* than a belief — a reasoned conclusion from (lack of) evidence and (lack of) logic. Reason demands that those propositions and arguments that suffer from insufficiency or error of evidence or logic be deemed unsound, quite possibly false, and definitely not demonstrably true. Positive Atheism is nothing more than the application of reason to the god question.

If, as I reason, positive Atheism has been inappropriately put on the defensive by these (deliberate?) distortions of its position, then by eliminating the distortions we can show that positive Atheism is a perfectly reasonable and consistent position. The speciousness of the attempt (1) to shift the burden of proof, which is a well-established fallacy, and (2) to misrepresent it as constituting a truth claim or worse yet a claim of certainty (the 'straw man' fallacy), frees positive Atheism from any logical stigma (although it may still suffer the social stigma of not just refusing to share but thoroughly rejecting the beliefs of the Theist). But the bigger question awaits: are there really two Atheisms?

Possible and Impossible Beliefs

Having shown that there is no logical reason why Atheists should be ashamed of their positivity, and having introduced the suggestion that positive Atheism is nothing more than a restatement of negative Atheism, let me proceed to make my case that positive and negative Atheism are indeed one and the same. We have here two 'variables' — belief in god and belief that there is a god — each with two 'values' — yes and no. It is easy to see that there are four conceivable combinations of the two variables.

1. Believe in god and believe that there is a god.
2. Do not believe in god and believe that there is a god.
3. Believe in god and believe that there is not a god.
4. Do not believe in god and believe that there is not a god.

Now, obviously combination (1) is the classic statement of Theism; even more, as we stated in the last chapter, the belief 'in' god actually includes the belief 'that' there is a god. In fact, if anything it is redundant, since why would anyone believe in god if they believed there was no god?

Yet that is precisely what combination (3) amounts to. The person who claims to hold simultaneously the belief in god but no belief that there is a god is either insane, talking nonsense, or messing with us. Belief in god, as we proved in the previous chapter, necessitates and entails belief that there is a god, or else the 'belief in' has no reference. And what would it mean to say that a person believes that there is a god but does not believe in that god, which is the meaning of (2)? There is one possible interpretation of this otherwise contradictory position: that the person believes that a god exists but does not have the personal commitment or trust in that god that we discussed previously as a concomitant of 'belief in.' It is imaginable to think of a disappointed Theist saying "I believe there is a god but I do not believe in god (anymore)." Thus, belief combination (3), if it is serious, is incoherent, and belief combination (2), while logically possible, is atypical of Theism and is certainly not Atheism.

Meanwhile, combination (4) is recognizable as positive Atheism: positive Atheists declare that they do not believe in god and do not believe that a god exists. So, where is negative Atheism? If negative Atheists do not believe in god, then their only choices are (2) and (4). Does negative Atheism hold the strange position of (2) by claiming that it does not believe *in* god but that it believes that there *is* a god anyhow? Naturally not. Therefore, in the final analysis, I propose the following: *only (1) and (4) are consistent and coherent, and (1) equals Theism, and (4) equals Atheism.*

One objection might be raised to this interpretation. The remaining purely negative Atheists, if there are any — or the Theists who want to discredit positive Atheism — may respond that negative Atheism is not really combination (2); it does not really say 'I do not believe in god and I believe that there is a god' but rather says 'I do not believe in god but there may be a god.' This is a logically possible position, but what would be the point of it? It is true that there *may be* a god; there also may be a Santa Claus. But 'maybes' are not beliefs and they are not reasoned conclusions; they are capitulations to the uncertainty of knowledge, a way of intellectually throwing your hands in the air. There also 'may be' leprechauns and unicorns — so what? And one important point of this 'position' is missed: the 'maybe'-believer still bears a burden of proof, for if one says that there may be X, one must demonstrate that there is reason to suspect there is X. If I say that I do not believe in Santa Claus but there may be a Santa Claus, I am at least making the claim that Santa Claus' existence is possible and rational, and I need a reason to suggest this. Without a good reason, this statement is moot at best and silly at worst. And finally, in practice, every Atheist (I think) — even the most hard-core positive Atheist like myself — admits that there may be a god (or a Santa or a leprechaun or a unicorn) but that there is little or no good reason to conclude so. If someone or something can establish the existence of a god tomorrow, any good rationalist would accept that because facts are facts (however, it is astronomically unlikely). If this is so, if even positive Atheists accept that there may be a god, then this criterion cannot be used to distinguish them from negative Atheists.

Only One Atheism

I conclude, therefore, that there is only one Atheism. Call it positive if you like. It goes beyond merely lacking the belief in some god or another; it goes on to — truly, it *entails* — the 'belief' that there is no such god in which to believe in the first place. The credo of positive Atheism ('I believe that there is no god') is exactly akin to the credo of negative Atheism ('I do not believe in god') and not to the credo of Theism ('I believe that there is a god'), although it appears superficially to resemble the last. The reason why negative and positive Atheism concur at the deeper level is that each entails the same implicit clause, seldom stated but always present. For example, 'I do not believe in god' is logically completed by the implicit clause 'because there is no good reason to.' Positive Atheism should be read in precisely the same way: 'I believe that there is no god (because there is no good reason to believe there is).' The difference between these two and Theism is the latter's implicit clause: 'I believe in god (because of this or that evidence or argument or feeling or personal experience, *etc.*).'

The case might be stated in another way. In the previous chapter, I argued that every 'belief in' is actually a set of 'beliefs that.' When one 'believes in' a god, one necessarily 'believes that' this god exists, as well as that he/she/it has some particular qualities. Accordingly, when one 'does not believe in' a god or anything else, one necessarily 'does not believe that' this god or other thing exists and/or has the avowed qualities. The only other possibility would be to believe that the god exists but not to believe the avowals of its qualities — that it will save you or love you or do whatever it is purportedly claimed to do. But this variation seems bankrupt to me, and I would be extremely surprised if any Atheist actually holds it.

Let me go one step further and clean up the language. We have still been following the old habit of speaking about Atheism, positive or negative, as 'believing' or 'not believing' this or that, and in the light of our discussion of belief and knowledge this is improper. Atheists of whatever sort do not 'believe in' any god(s), nor do they 'not believe in' any god(s). Atheism is not a belief but an absence of belief, just as someone who has lost his olfactory sense does not smell odors but does not thereby smell other odors. A foolish commentator on the loss of the olfactory sense might say that the non-smeller smells an alternate smell, a non-smell, the absence of smell. This is silly. No smell is no smell. And no belief is no belief, not an alternate belief and not a belief in nonbelief. Rather, negative Atheism, if there is such a thing, is a nonbelief, and positive Atheism has nothing to do with belief at all but is a rational conclusion (recall our earlier discussion of the predicates that masquerade as belief). The statement 'I do not believe in god' should and must be recast as *'I do not have any such thing as a belief in god,'* and the statement 'I believe that there is no god' should and must be recast as *'I conclude rationally that there is no god.'* Only by perfecting our language can we see what we really mean and why we mean it.

There is one conceivably useful distinction between positive and negative Atheism, made by Michael Martin in his philosophical treatise on Atheism. To paraphrase Martin, negative Atheism concerns itself with demonstrating that there are no good reasons to accept god-claims (*i.e.,* it sets out to refute theistic evidence and arguments), while positive Atheism is about demonstrating that there are good reasons to accept no-god-claims (*i.e.,* it sets out to present its own evidence and arguments in favor of Atheism). This is a procedural distinction, however, in regard to how we want to construct our arguments and whether we want to accept voluntarily any burden of proof. This is perhaps what actual negative Atheists mean by their position: that they see no need to or are unwilling to mount their own campaign of evidence and argument, being content to knock down invalid theistic ones. In this sense they are justified, for that is all that is required of an Atheist.

But Atheism is more than procedural; it is logical and epistemological. It is about truth and factuality. Whether any particular Atheist wants to employ 'positive' procedures *à la* Martin is irrelevant to what Atheism is. Atheism rejects the belief in god *because* there is no good reason (and arguably, good reason not) to conclude that such an entity even exists. In this final sense, there is no such thing as negative and positive Atheism, only incomplete (not grasping or accepting the full implications) and complete Atheism.

Atheism and Agnosticism

What is Agnosticism?

Having hopefully established that there is only one fully thought-out form of Atheism, regardless of what tactics individual Atheists care to employ in their arguments or whether they care to get into arguments at all, we can turn our attention to an even more common and troublesome distinction, the one between Atheism and Agnosticism. We frequently hear Agnosticism and Atheism contrasted as alternatives and even rivals, both by Agnostics/Atheists and by Theists — a kind of third choice between believing and not believing. There are people who call themselves Agnostics and stop there; they maintain that they are neither Theists nor Atheists. In fact, it is even possible to find people who consider themselves 'Agnostic Theists.' Normally, though, Agnostics are people who claim to be 'undecided' about religious questions or possibly uninterested in them. They are 'not sure,' they do not have 'enough information,' and hypothetically they are waiting, actively or passively, for some basis on which to adjudicate the two 'claims' of Theism and Atheism. The Agnostic — the person who declares herself to be an Agnostic — says "I don't know."

However, this will not do. First, I will argue that Agnosticism and Atheism are completely different kinds of things, different kinds of logical and empirical problems and claims and not simply different positions on the same continuum. Agnosticism is not a 'position' at all but a method for arriving at a position. Second, I will posit that Agnosticism is the only possible solution to the particular problem it addresses — the epistemological problem, the problem of knowledge — and that as such it is not only compatible with Atheism but is actually a foundation, *the best foundation*, for Atheism.

Agnosticism is a recent concept, introduced by Thomas Huxley, the famous Darwinist, in 1869 to describe his own doubts and misgivings about knowledge and belief. His original formulation of the *concept* goes as follows:

Agnosticism is not a creed but a method, the essence of which lies in the vigorous application of a single principle. Positively the principle may be expressed as, in matters of the intellect, follow your reason as far as it can carry you without other considerations. And negatively, in matters of the intellect, do not pretend the conclusions are certain that are not demonstrated or demonstrable. It is wrong for a man to say he is certain of the objective truth of a proposition unless he can produce evidence which logically justifies that certainty. (Essay "Agnosticism," 1889)

In this version, which I think we can take as decisive since Huxley was the creator of the whole notion, there is nothing specifically addressed to belief in general or religion in particular. Rather, this is a comprehensive epistemological position, addressing what we should claim to know. It is akin to skepticism in the less extreme sense: not that it is impossible to have knowledge (radical skepticism), but that we should not claim to have knowledge without some reasonable justification for our claim.

Agnosticism and the Possibility of Religious Knowledge

Agnosticism, then, is about knowledge — what it is possible to say that we know with some acceptable degree of certainty. More particularly, it is a method in regard to knowledge — a method for separating out what we can justifiably claim we know from what we cannot justifiably claim we know. The question for us is, do we have religious knowledge? *Can* we have religious knowledge? I would argue that we do not have it and that it is quite possible that we cannot have it.

What exactly is religious knowledge? It would be, from our characterization of knowledge in an earlier chapter, propositions about religious topics — in particular, the existence of god(s) and the nature of god(s) — that are accepted as true on the basis of evidence and interpretation of evidence, with the requirement that such evidence and interpretation lead soundly to the conclusion that these propositions are true. Is there anyone who actually has such knowledge? It seems astronomically unlikely. The myriad of beliefs out there about god(s), contradictory and mutually exclusive as they are, makes it just short of inconceivable that one of them could have the 'true knowledge' of god(s) while all the others have it wrong. Furthermore, there is no way imaginable that we could ever determine which was the 'true knowledge' and which was worshipping 'false gods.' There is no criterion for judging the truth of justification of a religious claim other than one that is itself part of the same religious system. For example, Christians sometimes argue the veracity of their religion on the grounds of fulfillment of biblical prophecy or the special nature of Jesus. However, if you do not accept the authority of the Bible or see its 'prophecies' as fulfilled, or if you do not accept the divinity — let alone the existence — of Jesus, then this argument means nothing. No doubt Muslims argue the veracity of their religion on the grounds of the immediate words of Allah in the Qur'an and the special mission and success of Muhammad. Similarly, if you do not already accept the Qur'an as Allah's words, or even the existence of Allah, or any unique attributes of Muhammad, the argument is in vain.

There are two problems with any claims as to possessing religious knowledge. The first is the possible source of such knowledge; the second is the satisfaction of the rules of knowledge as we have developed them previously. Let us consider the source of knowledge first. There are, in the end, only two sources of knowledge. These sources are authority and experience. In other words, if I know something, I either learned it from someone who already knew or I experienced it for myself firsthand. If I claim to have religious knowledge, I could only have received it from an authority (a priest, a theologian, a sacred text, *etc.*) or from my own personal experience. If I got it from an authority, where could my religious authority have gotten his knowledge? Either from a prior authority or from his own experience. And where could his prior authority have gotten his knowledge? Either from an even more prior authority or from his own experience. We can therefore recognize the possibility of an indefinite succession of authorities passing 'knowledge' on from one to the other, without any means of verifying the truth or accuracy of that transmission. Authority, then, amounts to little more than hearsay, and we can reject it out of court as a source of knowledge — as a way to certify that our knowledge is sound.

That only leaves experience as a source of religious knowledge. This is perhaps the fountain of all things religious and the last refuge from rationalistic criticism. If I had a personal experience, how can you argue with that? Well, there are a number of ways to argue with that. The first is that, in all fields except religion, personal experience is not accepted as a dependable source of knowledge. If a lawyer brought a psychic into court who said that she had had a personal vision of the defendant committing a crime, both would be laughed out of the building. Second, since this experience is subjective or 'internal,' there is no possible means of verification — I cannot even be sure that you *had* the experience, and I certainly cannot be sure that you had the experience you think you had or that it refers to anything in external reality. You might claim to have experienced your dog talking to you, but I would have plenty of justification to be skeptical of that claim, since it is not only not supported by any other people's experience but is positively *refuted* by those other experiences. Third and perhaps most importantly, experiences are subject to interpretation and decay. An individual who has an experience of 'transcendence' (whatever that is) might interpret that as God (*e.g.*, the Christian God) in one time or culture, as nirvana in another, as a 'good trip' in another, and as a hallucination in another. In other words, even if the *experience* is real, the *meaning* or *referent* of the experience is questionable and ultimately 'unknowable.'

But if this is the case, then experience cannot be a source of religious knowledge either. According to Agnosticism as defined above, or to skepticism as generally understood, we should not leap to conclusions without sufficient grounds. *Experience is not a sufficient ground for the conclusion that a god exists, let alone that a particular god like the Christian god exists.* There is no reason to accept that the experience of a voice or a transcendent moment or even a vision is any specific religious being or object, other than the preconceived notions that we bring to the experience. If this is the case, then religious knowledge — knowledge that there is indeed a spiritual being of some definite sort — is impossible. *And if that is true, then we are all Agnostics.*

Before we move on, it might be argued that the same criticism could be leveled against science and therefore all human knowledge. But on closer inspection this is not so. In science, if I gain some knowledge from an authority, I can be confident that this knowledge is at least in principle testable and verifiable, or more critically, falsifiable. I can even assume with some confidence that the information has already been tested and verified, by the authority himself or herself or by reviewers and peers. Sometimes bad facts and bad conclusions slip through the process, especially if they are not submitted to the process at all but are leaked directly to the media and the public, but, as has happened several times in the recent past, such facts and conclusions will not escape the grinder of peer review for long. Even if they are not probed and verified before dissemination, they will be afterwards. And, happily, each time fantastic or ludicrous claims have been made, they were eventually falsified and trashed. This speaks to the second point, the point of 'personal' versus public observation or experience: since scientific (or more aptly, rational) knowledge is based on public, objective sources rather than private, subjective ones, there is the possibility — and normally the reality — of testing and rejecting false claims.

The second problem with religious knowledge is that it does not conform to the rules of evidence and logic. Even if we might, for argument's sake, accept a person's 'religious experience' as a piece of evidence for the existence of some god, this evidence still fails to provide adequate conditions of falsifiability, comprehensiveness, honesty, replicability, and sufficiency. For instance, there is no way I can test your experience, either for accuracy or even for actuality; I cannot verify that you had any experience at all, let alone the one you claim. This is, of course, one of the charms of personal experience for Theists, since it is unimpeachable by 'science' or skepticism. However, as we have noted again and again, no one — not even a Theist — lives his whole life this way, taking for granted and acting on somebody's subjective claims; if someone said, 'I had a vision that chocolate bars cure cancer,' you would be a fool to stop your medical treatment and go on a regimen of candy. Precisely because personal experience is so unapproachable for purposes of falsifiability, it is untrustworthy as evidence.

Similarly, personal experience, and authority as well, are unacceptable for their lack of comprehensiveness and honesty. If people want to make a case for personal experience or authority, they must necessarily include *all* such experiences and authorities, which is patently impossible since they exclude each other. If one person experiences the Christian god as loving and another as punishing, and another experiences Allah and another Buddha and still another the kangaroo grandfather, there is no way to reconcile these experiences into a single religious account. Rather, they contradict and refute each other effectively as evidence of anything. The same holds for authority, since an appeal to authority would have to encompass the various contradictory Christian authorities as well as Muslim authorities, Hindu authorities, Taoist authorities, Sikh authorities, and a world of others. It would be like observing that water freezes at thirty-two degrees and at twenty degrees and at fifty degrees and hundreds of other temperatures — or finding scientists who claim each — and trying to organize those observations into a single evidential claim. It would be futile. And leaving out any of the 'facts' would be dishonest — you could just pick and choose the ones that fit your view — and ultimately insubstantial. Any prosecutor who introduced such contradictory witnesses to court would have his case tossed out on its ear.

Finally, such religious 'evidence' is fundamentally non-replicable and insufficient. Even Theists cannot have religious experiences just anytime they want, and one of the more vexing problems for them is (or should be) that some people — even some good Theists — never have them. Of course, they explain that fact away by pointing to the 'will to believe' or the lack of some faculty or 'talent' or 'gift' that the lucky experiencers possess. Why their god(s) would give some people an ability to experience him/her/it/them and not others is not immediately explained. And of course, the experience-claimer has a crushing burden of proof, not only to prove that he or she had an experience of this or that particular god but any experience at all. And the very fact that authority and testimony are by definition insufficient as evidence essentially damns the whole enterprise to failure from the start.

Without belaboring the point, such claims to knowledge fail logically as well. They constitute nothing more than anecdotal evidence, hasty generalization based on one or a few instances, *ad hoc* explanations for the experiences and *ad hominem* attacks for not having the experiences, denials of the consequent and affirmations of the antecedent, and circular reasoning. We can, therefore, safely say that there is no sound basis for claiming the existence, let alone the possession, of religious knowledge. As we maintained above, it is possible that one of the thousands of religions in the world has stumbled upon the 'truth' about religion, but if so (1) they did so totally inadvertently, (2) they still have no justification for calling their knowledge 'knowledge,' and (3) we have no way of knowing whether it is the Christians, the Jains, the Cheyenne, or the Raelians who got it right.

Agnosticism and Belief

We may safely conclude, then, that no one has any religious 'knowledge.' In fact, even Theists themselves often emphasize belief over knowledge; especially Christians, but all Theists to an extent, devalue knowledge as a way of approaching spirituality and privilege 'faith' instead. Even the Gospel Jesus himself reportedly said that blessed are those who have not seen and still believe. Undoubtedly many Theists think that knowledge is good and possible, and some have tried to reconcile faith and reason, but in the end reason — 'knowledge' in our sense and the only real sense — takes a back seat to faith. As Tertullian, an early church father, stated clearly, Christianity is true because it is absurd — because there is no evidence for it and nothing else like it in human experience.

So, as I have been wont to do in this book, I would like to make some radical propositions which are, nonetheless, true as far as I can see it. I will start with the proposition that *everyone is an Agnostic*. In the sense that no one has any religious knowledge, and more than likely no one could have any such knowledge, all human beings are Agnostic; there is nothing else to be. Atheists clearly do not have any knowledge of any god(s), so they are Agnostics, and Theists — whether they like it or not — do not have any knowledge of any god(s), so they are Agnostics too. Of course, the latter do not call themselves Agnostics, and sometimes they might even claim to have knowledge, but they don't.

This answers one of the age-old questions: can a person be an Agnostic Theist, such as an Agnostic Christian? The answer is yes; in fact, that is the only kind of Theist you can be. You can quite surely have no knowledge of a thing and still believe in that thing (although it is the height of irrationality), and people do it all the time. Only a handful of Christians call themselves Agnostics, and ultimately it is contradictory to say that you are a Christian but do not know if God exists (why in the world be a Christian then, except out of laziness or a kind of Pascal's-wager mentality?), but people believe all kinds of things in all kinds of weird combinations.

Agnosticism is, clearly, a philosophy or a method in regard to knowledge. People may and do believe things in absence of or in contradiction to knowledge. Knowing and believing are two qualitatively different things, as we discovered in the last chapter. Therefore, Agnosticism is in no way an intermediate point between Theism and Atheism; it is not a 'hedge' against the two 'extremes,' and it is not a terminal position itself. Agnosticism is a means to get to a conclusion.

Theism and Atheism, meanwhile, are points on an entirely different spectrum; in fact, I would go so far as to posit that they are the *only two points* on that spectrum. Either you believe in god(s) and are a Theist, or you do not believe in god(s) and are an Atheist. What position could possibly be 'in between'? If you are 'waiting' to make up your mind about god(s), you are in the meantime not being a Theist; to make the point, if there really was a Christian God, and he really demanded faith and worship, then if you died in the state of 'waiting to decide' it seems he would have to deem you a non-believer and condemn you to hell. It seems a little unfair, but I did not write the Christian rules; there is no provision for 'waiting to decide' and there is not even a provision for thinking about the matter yourself. 'Believe or else' is the message.

If, as I claim, all humans are Agnostics in reference to religion, and if Agnosticism is about knowledge claims while Theism/Atheism are about belief claims, then what is the relation between the two dimensions — knowledge and belief?

The answer should be apparent. If you have no knowledge of a thing — not of its existence, not of its characteristics — then how could you justifiably ever believe anything about it? I am an Atheist; I do not have any beliefs about any god(s). I am also an Agnostic, as all humans are; I have no knowledge about any god(s). *I am an Atheist because I am an Agnostic.* If I knew there was a god, I would be stupid not to believe that there was a god or not to 'believe in' that god (after all, my knowledge would entail that I know about the god's powers, wishes, and intentions). In fact, it would no longer be a matter of 'belief' at all; if I knew there was a god, I would not have to believe there was a god, any more than I have to believe that the earth is round or that my foot is at the end of my leg. Knowledge renders belief irrelevant and inapplicable; belief indicates the unavailability of knowledge.

Let me thereby offer another proposition, this time on the relation between Agnosticism and Atheism: *if Agnosticism is the method pertaining to religious knowledge, then the only valid conclusion from that method is Atheism.* There is, then, a natural and unavoidable connection between the two concepts. The question comes down to this: if you have no knowledge about a thing, what position should you take in regard to belief about the thing? If you said that you have no idea what a zorg is or what it does or wants but that you believe that there is such a thing as a zorg — and even worse, that you center your life around the existence and wishes of a zorg — I would think you were either pulling my leg or talking crazy. How is Theism, the belief in 'god(s),' any different, except for the fact that the word 'god' seems more familiar to us than the word 'zorg'? Familiarity does not mean truth; we can and have been familiar with a lot of imaginary, false, and foolish things during the lifetime of our species. It may be what we do best.

So I assert that if Agnosticism is the process, Atheism is the product. Of course, not all people 'practice' Agnosticism — certainly not in their religious lives — and not all, obviously, recognize their existential state as Agnostics. Those who do practice it conspicuously must inevitably concede that there is no foundation whatsoever for making any religious claims that have any force to them. People may, do, and probably will continue to believe despite the absence of evidence or in contradiction to the evidence, but that is now the only way that they *can* believe. Belief as a respectable and 'rational' position has been vanquished.

Conclusion: To Believe or Not to Believe

In this chapter I have hopefully cleared up the misconceptions about what Atheism is, what Agnosticism is, and what relation the two stand in. There is no doubt that I will get debate and criticism for these positions. There may still be those who consider themselves 'negative Atheists' only or at least those who consider that negative Atheists exist, even if they have never met one. I invite such negative Atheists to ponder their 'beliefs' and identify in what way they remain distinct from positive Atheists and for what reasons. If the reasons are not other than social or emotional, then it is time to go all the way.

Also, there may still be those who consider themselves 'Agnostics' only, who think they are not taking and do not need to take a 'religious position,' a 'belief position.' But Agnosticism does not invite you to suspend judgment; it invites you to make judgment in full light of the facts and the logic and to stand by it. And, as the old adage goes, if you are not taking a position, then you are taking a position — a position against. If you are not actively a Theist, you are passively an Atheist. If you are waiting to believe, you are not believing now. God, if he exists, will not make the distinction.

Everyone is an Agnostic, or at least should be. Agnosticism, like reason, is the only method for threshing the true from the false. In reality, Agnosticism is simply another name for reason — and probably an unfortunate name, since people are led to think that it is a particular process in its own right or, even worse, a particular position or conclusion in its own right. Agnosticism and reason are the road, and, if that road is followed carefully and fearlessly, then the only possible destination to which it can lead is Atheism.

Earlier, we asked the question whether it was possible to be an Agnostic Theist, for example an Agnostic Christian. Anything is possible, as is evidenced by the fact that people will believe any damned fool thing in any damned fool combination. The more important question is: is it justifiable and reasonable to be an Agnostic Theist? The answer is no. If there is no religious knowledge that we can claim with any certainty, then there is no justification for the 'leap of faith.' *An Agnostic Theist is a Theist in violation of Agnosticism.* A reasonable Theist is a Theist in violation of reason. After the previous chapters of this book, it should be immanently clear that there is no 'reasonable' path to Theism. Reason — evidence and logic — has been stripped as a ground for religious belief, since it has been stripped as a ground for religious knowledge. Sadly, there are other grounds — irrational but effective grounds — for religious belief that continue and will probably always continue to be enough for the determined Theist.

CHAPTER SEVEN

On Science and Religion

Science should be taught not in order to support religion and not in order to destroy religion. Science should be taught simply ignoring religion.
— Steven Weinberg, *Freethought Today,* April 2000

One of the most persistent and divisive questions of our time is the relationship between science and religion. Both scientists and religionists have tossed their views into the discourse on the subject — and not always on the side that we would first expect. Some scientists are accommodating of religion, and some religionists hardly see themselves at war with science but in fact recruit science in the service of faith. But there is no avoiding the fact that the two 'disciplines' at times contradict each other: what are we to do then? Does science abolish religious 'belief'? Does religion trump scientific 'speculation'? Can the two coexist? Do they perhaps even have no points of contact at all — as the early church father Tertullian said, "What has Jerusalem to do with Athens, the Church with the Academy, the Christian with the heretic?" (Miller 1970, 5).

But of course that was not quite what Tertullian was saying by alienating Jerusalem and Athens, religion and science — that the two may happily run in parallel without ever coming in contact. Rather, he was saying that Jerusalem has no need or use for Athens, the church no need or use for the academy, certainly the Christian no need or use for the heretic (in the original sense, I hope, of 'one who chooses'). This is proven by his comment a few words later: "After Jesus Christ we have no need of speculation, after the Gospel no need of research. When we come to believe, we have no desire to believe anything else; for we begin by believing that there is nothing else which we have to believe."

Naturally, not all Theists have been as strenuous as the good father, and not all would even agree. Some Theists are scientists, and almost all support and benefit from the researches of the 'Academy,' whether in the form of medicine, cell phones, or the latest toothpaste. But Tertullian is saying something profound and something that lurks in the heart of religion and of the question of the relationship between science and religion — that belief wants and needs nothing else, no proof, no reason, no research, no additional knowledge. Belief — *i.e.*, religion — is designed and intended to be self-contained and self-referential, and when it is done 'right,' it is so.

In this chapter we will look at several proposals for relationships between science and religion, some much more inclusive than Tertullian's. We will investigate what various scientists and religionists alike have said on the issue. We will, in the process, be called upon to define and operationalize our terms — what precisely do we mean by 'science' or 'religion' — particularly because some of the proposed solutions to the matter at hand depend on unstated or unfounded characterizations of one or the other. Finally, we will arrive at the position that science is, if not in practice in every case, then 'essentially' or at heart, atheistic — in the strictest sense, as Weinberg stated, indifferent to god(s) and proceeding without god(s). I will eventually come to the point of asking, "What has Athens to do with Jerusalem, the academy with the church, the rationalist with the believer?" After knowledge we have no need of belief, after the fact no need of faith. When we come to know, we have no desire to believe anything; for we end by knowing that there is nothing which we have to believe.

Models of Science-and-Religion Interaction

The viewpoints on the matter of science and religion have been many and varied, as are even the opinions on how many such viewpoints there are. Michael Shermer (2000), for example, from the skeptical side, resolves the debate into three basic "models," which he dubs the *same worlds*, *separate worlds*, and *conflicting worlds* models. In the *same worlds* model, science and religion are seen as accomplishing pretty much the same goals, or at least asking pretty much the same questions. From the *separate worlds* perspective, they are determined to be pursuing different goals and questions that either complement or ignore each other. And, predictably, if they occupy *conflicting worlds* then they are locked in a struggle which only one can win, a competition for truth in which the success of one is the failure of the other. Ian Barbour (1997), from a somewhat more theistic side, categorizes the relationships into four types, which he names *Conflict*, *Independence, Dialogue*, and *Integration*. The *Conflict* relation is obviously identical to Shermer's *conflicting worlds* model, and the *Integration* relation is comparable to his *same worlds* model. That leaves *Independence* and *Dialogue*, which are probably identifiable as subtypes (and often co-occurring subtypes) of the *separate worlds* model. Barbour explains that the *Independence* relation is based on the notion of contrasting methods or contrasting 'languages' in science versus religion, while *Dialogue* itself is a set of diverse solutions that go further toward reconciliation than *Independence* but not as far as *Integration*. For our present purposes, we will adopt Shermer's slightly more streamlined system, but we will make reference to Barbour's subheadings at the appropriate juncture.

Let us establish at the outset that there is no strong correlation between scientists and one particular model or Theists and another particular model. This might seem surprising at first glance, but it is really quite natural. Scientists, you might think, normally take a *conflicting worlds* approach to religion, but this is not necessarily so, and besides, what approach would religionists normally take? Many of the latter are just as adamant in their *conflicting worlds* attitude as the most hardheaded scientist, for the exact opposite reasons. And there are also scientists and religionists who take a *same worlds* stand, if for no other reason than that some scientists are religionists and want to reconcile scientific 'truth' with religious 'truth' (and sometimes succeed, at least in their own minds). Finally, *separate worlds*, as a kind of truce or 'mutual respect' or as a 'mutual avoidance' position, is also something that can appeal to scientists and Theists equally and that has in fact captivated a number of intelligent scientific minds as well as important theistic minds.

Having said this, let us examine the three models to see what they offer and who holds them for what reasons. The *same worlds* model, first of all, is one that probably many lay people have for themselves, on the basis that people can compartmentalize their experience and knowledge in ways that allow them to keep odd, and occasionally even mutually contradictory, notions in their heads at the same time. But this is by no means solely the province of the unreflective nor the uneducated. Early anthropologists, when they observed societies around the world engaged in all manner of inexplicable religious behavior, often pointed to the 'logical' if untutored nature of some of these beliefs and practices. For example, when traditional peoples perform rainmaking rituals or rub butter on their heads to keep dragons away, they are in fact engaging in 'instrumental' actions — that is, actions that are aimed at achieving some practical end. Anthropologists like Sir James Frazer and Bronislaw Malinowski looked upon their efforts, although expressed in magical form, as a kind of 'primitive science' sharing with modern science a concept of causality — if you perform the ritual or action correctly, then a desired effect will follow. The 'if-then' nature of their thinking was on target, it could be argued, but they had the wrong causal relationships in mind. In other words, 'primitive' religion was like science in that it was using causes to reach effects, but it was just 'bad science.'

Within the modern, especially American, religious camp, there are certainly those who practice a marriage of science and religion, typically for the 'validation' or 'verification' of religious belief. For instance, when Christians try to find the site of the landing of Noah's ark, they are attempting to integrate science and religion — or to enlist science to 'prove' religion. Archaeologists who excavate the Holy Land in hopes of finding Jesus' grave or some other biblical site; geologists who search through the strata for signs of the Flood; biologists who explore cellular or molecular life looking for traces of God — all of these are practicing a *same worlds* approach. However, their motivation again generally is to use science to support what religion already believes — that is, to muster the academy to buttress the church.

The embrace of the *same worlds* model within religion is more common, therefore, than you might think. Mostly this affection comes down to the design issue again, from the incredulity of many religionists that the universe could be undesigned to the appeal of beauty and order as a signal of design; as it says in Psalms 19:1, "The heavens declare the glory of God, and the firmament showeth his handiwork." In fact, Shermer finds in his survey of belief that the largest number of believers claim to believe because of the 'evidence' of design, rather than because of personal religious experience or biblical authority. In that sense, 'evidence' is a key factor in most colloquial belief.

Within the ranks of formal 'research,' two especially well-known expressions of this phenomenon are the Intelligent Design movement, which we have met already, and the "Reasons to Believe" project. Intelligent Design, or ID, which is associated with Michael Behe, Phillip Johnson, and William Dembski among others, is not always overtly theistic but is self-consciously 'scientific.' In other words, ID 'researchers,' often working under the auspices of the Discovery Institute (www.discovery.org), speak the language of science to assert certain inadequacies of science, at least mainstream science, most particularly evolutionary biology. Behe (1996), for example, marshals information from biochemistry to suggest that at least some biochemical phenomena, like the flagella (or microscopic "whip-tails") of protozoa, are so "irreducibly complex" that they could not have evolved by a series of chance mutations. This leads him to another conclusion, that these complex features must have been the result of some intelligent intervention into physical evolution. Precisely what this 'intelligence' is is not always stated, although, by some ID practitioners, it is stated, and — no big surprise — it is 'God.' Of course, how they leap from 'some intelligence' to the biblical god is a matter of real concern for a thinking person.

The second high-profile example of science in the service of religion is Hugh Ross' "Reasons to Believe" project and the general 'creation science' movement. Ross and his associates do not restrict themselves to any one area of science, nor are they ashamed to publicize their biblical agenda. "Whether you are looking for scientific support for your faith or answers to questions about God and science," they state on their Web site (www.reasons.org), this is the place for scientifically minded Christians. There, one finds scientific-sounding information about stratigraphy, biology, astronomy, and a congeries of other subjects which, like other brands of creation science, purportedly support the biblical/creationist account of the universe.

These are hardly the only efforts afoot from a theistic perspective to promote the wedding (however unhappy and 'shotgun') between science and religion, from the honorable to the dishonorable. Perhaps from a more prestigious position, the Templeton Foundation provides prizes (more lucrative even than the Nobel Prize) to scholars whose work integrates science and religion. From a more insidious and alarming position, agendas like the 'wedge strategy' of the ID camp or the musings of the Institute for Creation Research are overt examples of abduction-marriages between science and religion: as the ICR boasts, "If both are true, they must agree .... In fact, true science supports the Biblical worldview. There are many facts of science revealed in the Bible and no proven scientific errors." (Shermer, 132)

But religion and the social sciences are not the only places to find some form of *same worlds* model in action. There are, in fact, instances of the model at work in the 'hard' or natural sciences as well. At the most innocent level, it is interesting how many scientific books contain the word 'god' in the title, even if the book ultimately is not theistic or even has nothing much to do with any god; probably the motivation has more to do with book sales than anything else. For instance, there are *The Mind of God* (Davies, 1993), *God and the Astronomers* (Jastrow, 1992), *Finding Darwin's God* (Miller, 1999), and *The God Particle* (Lederman and Teresi, 1994), not to mention others that are not strictly Christian in their orientation, like *The Tao of Physics* (Capra, 1991). In such works, and like ones that do not specifically mention god(s) or religion in the title, the goal may be anything from a good old-fashioned apologetics of religion to some more idiosyncratic conclusion with 'theological' implications.

Among the former are some recent scientific publications that purport to find god(s) in various corners of the natural world. One such home of god(s) is the human nervous system — a so-called 'god spot' in the brain or some such. One example that received considerable popular attention is Newberg, d'Aquili, and Rause's *Why God Won't Go Away* (2002), a neurological study of 'mystical experiences,' which showed that there are measurable brain states associated with such 'religious' experiences. Another, wackier home is the realm of quantum uncertainty, in which William Pollard proposed that god intervenes in the world at the subatomic level to settle the uncertainty of quantum mechanics and 'collapse the wave function' in such a manner as to direct natural events. (For those unfamiliar with quantum physics, the basic idea is that subatomic events are not completely determined — they could go this way or that — until they are observed. Thus, in Pollard's view, god is the ultimate observer.) And naturally, there has been a steady flow of studies on the physical effects of prayer as scientific evidence of the existence and power of god(s).

Maybe the most intriguing and perplexing of the scientific idlings with religion is the so-called 'anthropic principle,' which has roughly to do with the notion of the universe being 'fine-tuned' for the phenomena that would subsequently emerge in it, particularly organic life and even more particularly human life. An assortment of names are associated with this idea, but the best known may be John Barrow and Frank Tipler, who coauthored *The Anthropic Cosmological Principle* (1988). The principle is usefully distinguished into its "strong" and "weak" versions, the latter of which claims that the "observed values of all physical and cosmological quantities are not equally probable, but they take on values restricted by the requirement that there exist sites where carbon-based life can evolve and by the requirement that the Universe be old enough for it to have already done so" (15). In other words, the argument asserts something like that the universe was required to have certain physical characteristics that were conducive to life-forms like our own. The strong anthropic principle goes further, demanding that the universe was intentionally fine-tuned so that humans could live in it. It approaches, if not crosses, the line into Intelligent Design.

In other works, including his *The Physics of Immortality: Modern Cosmology, God and the Resurrection of the Dead (1995)* Tipler goes beyond a mere anthropic analysis of the universe to the conclusion that God is the inevitable future of the universe. He argues, quite novelly, that life, once introduced into the universe, must eventually expand to "engulf" it, that the amount of information accumulated by the arrival at the "final state" of the universe is infinite, and therefore that at this final state — the Omega Point — all of the information that ever existed (including all of the beings who ever existed) will be stored in an infinitude which he identifies as "God." While this analysis seems unconventional and anything but Christian, he writes on his Web site that "a main reason for my identification Omega Point = God, comes from Exodus 3:14 ... best translated into English as I SHALL BE WHAT I SHALL BE. In other words, God is telling Moses that His essence is future tense."

No doubt there are other scientific dabblings in religion than the ones discussed above, but the point is hopefully sufficiently clear — the *same worlds* model is not just for anti-science types. Let us then move on and consider the *separate worlds* model. Here too, well-meaning scientists and theologians alike — up to the pope himself — can share this view, although not always concurring in every detail.

A critical element of the *separate worlds* position is a distinction between religion and science in terms of their subject matter, their methods, and what Barbour call their "language." This distinction, picked up by Stephen Jay Gould, about whom we will say more shortly, has a long heritage going back to the early church and probably beyond. For present purposes, though, we need go back no further than Descartes, whose 'dualism' divided the human world into the material and the immaterial or spiritual. Humans, unlike other material beings including animals, were of a dual nature — a material body and an immaterial soul. This was hardly a new idea (even most premodern cultures make a distinction between physical/sensible — as in *sense-able* — and the nonphysical or spiritual dimensions, and the ancient Greeks like Plato certainly made a comparable distinction), but its power in the newly emerging 'age of reason' was profound. Causality, empirical observation, and mechanistic explanation belong to the material side but not to the spiritual side. And that which cannot be decided by observation and explanation can be settled by appeal to faith, an equally certain and valid way of knowing, as Pascal would posit.

The real religious significance of the dualistic view for our purposes came in the work of Immanuel Kant, who submitted reason to his famous critique and discovered its 'limits.' Reason, he argued, is very effective at processing and deciding matters of 'phenomena,' that is, matters of sense-experience and the 'surface' of things. However, some matters cannot be decided on the basis of experience or phenomena, since they pertain to the other realm of the *'noumena'* or the 'thing-in-itself,' which cannot be experienced and therefore cannot be known. Science, then, has its province in which it is supreme, but outside of its province it is impotent. There, we must rely on other human capacities. In particular, the human capacity of 'morality' is the guiding light for Kant in the province of the spirit. He insists that the moral sense is the proof of a god and its activity in human affairs, and that since moral matters cannot be settled by 'pure reason' alone, then faith or religion or 'practical reason' is the proper course or method for such concerns. Here is the crucial identification: physical=reason and science, while moral=faith and religion.

Other philosophers (like William James) and naturally later theologians and sympathizers of religion developed this line of thinking, not the least of whom are Huston Smith and Pope John Paul II. Smith (2001), one of the great scholars and popularizers of comparative religion, holds primarily that science and religion are two discrete ways of knowing the world. Science possesses its tools of experimentation, dissection, and logical analysis, but religion possesses tools of its own, namely intuition and revelation. Science, which as for Kant is fine as far as it goes, does not have access to these religious 'methods' and therefore will always be either completely excluded from or comparatively deficient in the matters of the spirit. The pope's problem is more practical: to reconcile church doctrine and faith with the advances in science, most immediately evolution. The Catholic church has a noteworthy history of accommodationism not only with science but with other prevailing social forces (which has arguably been one of its strengths and secrets to its longevity). In fact, faced with the challenge of evolutionary science, in 1950 Pope Pius XII approved of research "with regard to the doctrine of evolution, in as far as it inquires into the origin of the human body as coming from pre-existent and living matter." John Paul II in 1996 was able to go a step further and declare research not only acceptable but fairly convincing: "The convergence, neither sought nor fabricated, of the results of the work that was conducted independently is in itself a significant argument in favor of the theory" (quoted in Shermer, 128).

How is the pontiff of the church allowed to make these concessions to science? The answer is, simply, by holding onto a separate realm which science cannot disturb. The words following those quoted above tell the tale. Pius XII continues directly after the line above by saying that "The Catholic faith obliges us to hold that souls are immediately created by God," and John Paul II (1996) proceeds to state dogmatically that

> Revelation teaches us that [man] was created in the image and likeness of God. ... if the human body takes its origin from pre-existent living matter, the spiritual soul is immediately created by God ... Consequently, theories of evolution which, in accordance with the philosophies inspiring them, consider the mind as emerging from forces of living matter, or as a mere epiphenomenon of this matter, are incompatible with the truth about man. ... With man, then, we find ourselves in the presence of an ontological difference, an ontological leap, one could say.

The solution, in other words, is the separation of the worlds, one for the body, one for the soul. Let science study the body, for religion will minister to the soul.

Lest it be thought that only religion would be inclined to this concessionist arrangement, some very respectable and influential people of science have also endorsed it. The most prominent of these is probably Stephen Jay Gould, who even coined the term "non-overlapping magisteria"' or NOMA for it. In *Rock of Ages* (1999), he advocates passionately for a peaceful, even loving, coexistence between science and religion on the basis of their noncompeting domains of interest. Science, as has become the classic answer of the *separate worlds* proponents, concerns itself with the physical nature of the world, with the questions, "What is the universe made of (fact) and why does it work this way (theory)?" Religion, on the other hand, "extends over questions of ultimate meaning and moral value." Or, as he says: "To cite the old clichés, science gets the age of rocks, and religion the rock of ages; science studies how the heavens go, religion how to go to heaven" (6).

Another leading figure in science who seems to recommend a *separate worlds* approach in Eugenie Scott, director of the National Center for Science Education, one of the essential organizations for promoting science and opposing pseudoscience in schools. However, while one might expect her to be a firm *conflicting worlds* adherent, she is not, at least from her writings and speeches. On the NCSE Web site (www.ncseweb.org), in response to the question, "What is the NCSE's religious position?" the answer is a capitalized "NONE!" It goes on to state that the organization "enthusiastically supports the right of every individual to hold, practice, and advocate their beliefs, religious and non-religious." Similarly, in a 2000 speech entitled "Why NOT Creationism in the Public Schools," she makes her usual point that there is not a simple "evolution versus creation" choice but a range of theistic positions in regard to creation and a fundamental dichotomy within science. Within the theistic camp, there are Bible literalists, young-earth creationists, old-earth creationists, *etc.*, all the way up to theistic evolutionists who accept evolution but explain it as the 'method' or vehicle of their god's design. More importantly, however, science itself is really two different things — a philosophy and a method. As a method, specifically 'methodological materialism,' natural or materialist explanations are sought because, if we accept a god as an explanation, then we stop asking questions. As a philosophy, specifically 'philosophical materialism,' though, science outruns its evidence by suggesting that matter (and energy) are all there is in the universe. Philosophical materialism would demand the exclusion of god(s) from the discussion, but since it is not scientific itself but rather a presupposition of science, it cannot be proven. Or, in more practical terms, science can tell us 'what happened' but not 'whodunit.' "Evolution is a statement of history," she states in her speech, "As to the ultimate cause of evolution, you are on your own." Or finally: "Science is an equal-opportunity methodology — you do not have to have any particular religious or non-religious belief as long as you are using the method of methodological materialism."

The last example I want to give of the *separate worlds* model comes from the very man who gave us the term, Michael Shermer. Perhaps the most prominent skeptic of our time, Shermer personifies the nontheoretical, 'live-and-let-live' attitude of the separate-worlders. Calling himself an Agnostic who does not believe in a god (review Chapter Six above for my position on that question), he expresses his tolerance-through-schism as follows:

> I am an Agnostic who has no ax to grind with believers, and I hold no grudge against religion. My only beef with believers is when they claim they can use science and reason to *prove* God's existence, or that *theirs* is the One True Belief; my only gripe with religion is when it becomes intolerant of other peoples' beliefs, or when it becomes a tool of political oppression, ideological extremism, or the cultural suppression of diversity .... My primary focus in addressing readers is not whether they believe or disbelieve, but *how* and *why* they have made their particular belief choice. (xv)

Thus, from this scientific skeptic's point of view, religion is okay as long as it *stays on its own turf* and does not claim the authority or challenge the conclusions of science — and, of course, as long as it does not bug the rest of us.

Finally, we have the *conflicting worlds* model, which we can dispatch more quickly since there are always fewer ways to fight than to get along! Again, religionists and scientists alike can take this stance, each seeing the threat of disagreement as an all-or-nothing rivalry. Some, but a diminishing number, of fundamentalist Christians (and fundamentalists of other faiths too) reject science outright, either in its specific claims like Big Bang cosmology or biological evolution or its materialistic (and therefore godless) 'secular humanist' methodology. (Few of these true believers swear off the benefits of modern science, though. A few do, for example, shunning medical treatment, often with fatal results to themselves or a loved one.) As we saw at the outset, Tertullian represents a strain in Christianity that rebukes science as irrelevant if not unconducive to faith.

On the science side, there are some voices as well that convey little time or patience for religion. Massimo Pigliucci does a nice job of representing these people, as well as the others we have discussed, on a grid of the three worlds (2000, 38). Although he places the scientific creationists in the *conflicting worlds* box whereas I have placed them in the *same worlds* box, I think that we would have to agree that the Behes and Dembskis and Rosses of our country are not hostile to science as such — since they use it intimately — as much as to certain discoveries or conclusions of mainstream science. Anyhow, Pigliucci puts Carl Sagan, Richard Dawkins, Victor Stenger, Paul Kurtz, and himself, among others, in the *conflicting worlds* camp (to which I would add Stephen Weinberg), and he further divides the camp into the "soft" and "strict" scientific rationalists, with Sagan the sole well-known member of the "soft" group.

Very seldom do these men frontally condemn religion as false and stupid; typically, they criticize or 'bracket' it as unproved or irrelevant. They are, in a word, unwilling to spare its feelings or give it any special credence or comfort. If religion disagrees with science, religion is wrong, and if that deprives the believer of some refuge, then so be it. While Sagan waxes somewhat romantic about the cosmos being all that there is or ever was or ever will be (which sounds pretty nontheistic), Dawkins, Stenger, and others pull their punches considerably less. Dawkins is one of the most unforgiving in his treatment of religion; he writes toward the end of *The Blind Watchmaker* (1986), a book intended to demonstrate the lack of need for a cosmic designer (and thus a full-on assault against conventional religion), the following in regard to the *same worlds* or *separate worlds* arguments for scientific creationism or 'divinely-guided evolution' alike:

> We cannot disprove beliefs like these, especially if it is assumed that God took the care that his interventions always closely mimicked what would be expected from evolution by natural selection. All that we can say about such beliefs is, firstly,

that they are superfluous and, secondly, that they assume the existence of the main thing we want to explain, namely organized complexity. (316)

In his *Not by Design*, Stenger (1988) takes a muscular materialist and rationalist position that "if what we see disagrees with what was written by some ancient revered master, then it is the master who is wrong and not our eyes" (34). He also rejects the *separate world* concessions of Kant and his successors: "Science is unwilling to make any assumptions about the limitations of the human mind in understanding the mysteries of the universe, including its origins and the sources of the order that is observed" (180).

Finally, while there are many other *conflicting worlds* practitioners out there, one other prong of attack I want to mention, contra those who are doing 'brain research' to find the circuit where god(s) communicate(s) with us, is being pursued by neuroscientists like Michael Persinger (1987) whose research points in exactly the opposite direction. Persinger and others interpret their results to mean that 'religious experience' is a mere epiphenomenon of brain function and not a reference (and certainly not a trustworthy reference) to a 'spiritual reality' outside the brain.

Defining Science

We have now seen the range and variety of not only answers but motivations for those answers as to the relation between science and religion. How do we proceed from here? Perhaps we should heed our own warning from an earlier chapter of this book and stop and examine our terms before we get too far along the road. We have probably gone as far as we can go without pausing to define the very words we — and so many others — have been pontificating on.

As we said about *reason* in a previous discussion, so also *science* is a subject of some mystification and reification, both by the public and by its enemies, and occasionally by its friends. There has of course been extensive discourse for many years as to what exactly science is, and I am not going to try to mediate or consummate that discourse. Rather, I want to simplify it for our purposes, so as to make the best possible and most useful distinction between it and religion. Only then can we say what their relations should be.

So what is science, and what are 'scientific data'? People often refer to 'scientific' information as if it is different from other kinds of information. But information is information, facts are facts. Maybe we should refer to 'information acquired through science' as opposed to 'information acquired through other means,' but the bigger point is that we are not in a discussion primarily about science but about information — how information is acquired and what, in the end, qualifies as information.

Let me start with a bold statement: science is not some unique or mysterious thing, any more than reason is. Just as we said earlier, reason is not one way of thinking among other ways of thinking; nor is science one way of getting information among other ways of getting information. *Reason is thinking, and science is information-gathering.* Science is, nothing more and nothing less, the systematic application of reason to studying phenomena and solving problems, together with the body of information (facts) and interpretation (theory) that results from the process. Science has identified specific methods to gather specific kinds of information and to test that information for validity, including most conspicuously the 'experiment' and statistical analysis. But science is not experimentation per se, nor is it statistical analysis *per se*. Science is reason *per se*.

Experimentation is important in 'reasonable research' because it allows the experimenter to isolate relationships between variables and to avoid certain empirical and logical errors. It is, nothing more and nothing less, a controlled situation. Where there is no control or isolation of factors, our observations can be 'confounded' so that we do not know what goes with what, what causes what. Experiment is the surest way to sort out causes and their effects. However, experimentation, while highly desirable, is not required of science, and in some cases it is impossible, as in astronomy: we cannot experiment on stars or on onetime phenomena like supernovae. Nor is experimentation always necessary: I do not need to experiment to determine if my foot is at the end of my leg. I only need to observe.

The true essence of 'science' as a particular activity is *systematic observation under the rules of reason*. We have discussed those rules thoroughly elsewhere, and we have explained why only observations under those rules yield 'knowledge.' It is almost redundant, then, to discuss the philosophy and method of science, since they are basically the philosophy and method of reason. But let us proceed nonetheless.

I

Science starts from a position of doubt, skepticism, or even distrust. If there were not doubt or skepticism about a phenomenon — if we thought we understood it thoroughly already — what would be the point of further study? Skepticism means, nothing more and nothing less, that we will not accept a bit of information into the corpus of 'knowledge' until it has passed through the tests of reason. It does not mean that we can never know anything or that we must always doubt ourselves (that is one of the greatest fallacies about science and reason in general) but only that we have standards for acceptance and that no fact or theory gains admittance into the 'canon' until it meets those standards. Science is 'Agnostic' in Huxley's original sense of the word — not that knowledge is impossible (if we really thought that, there would be no point in science) but that knowledge is not knowledge until it is sufficiently justified by evidence and logic.

II

Science, in other words, starts from the null hypothesis and therefore accepts the burden of proof. As scientists, we begin our study with an attitude like 'There is no relationship between these variables' or 'This hypothesis is untrue.' Then we test. If the observations do not significantly support a positive (non-null) result, then we accept that we were right the first time — that there is 'nothing to know' here.

III

This is why it has been said, by Popper and others, that science advances by falsification. Science is inductive, and we have discussed induction in a previous chapter. Induction — the piling-up of observations — cannot 'prove' anything; it can only additionally support conclusions. But one good observation can disprove anything. So science is not about 'absolute certainty'; rather, it is about the degrees of certainty (which we can often specify) and continuing confirmation or sudden and decisive disconfirmation of our conclusions based on the evidence.

IV

Science is therefore self-criticizing and self-correcting. This does not mean that science always quickly finds its errors and fixes them. No doubt, there are some errors in science today, maybe profound ones. But science as an occupation assumes as much from the outset, looks for those mistakes, and remorselessly replaces them. This also does not mean that science is a vain enterprise in that all human thinking is flawed. Human thinking is indeed very fallible, in every application (including religion), but only science *presupposes* this fact and provides for it.

V

Science knows no loyalty to tradition, authority, prejudice, or personal preference. If that characterization sounds familiar, then it should, because that is the definition of freethought. Science is the systematic application of freethought. If our observations and analyses disagree with tradition or authority or our prejudices or personal preferences, then it is those things that must go. Our observations are the final authority.

VI

Science is therefore naturalistic, at least methodologically if not philosophically. Science looks for facts and answers in nature because that is the only thing we can 'know.' It does not look for nonnatural or 'supernatural' answers for a variety of reasons.

1. First and foremost, the entire idea of 'supernatural' is speculative, so we cannot even know if there really is such a thing.
2. If we did posit a supernatural or extra-natural answer, we could never know if it was correct, since there is no way to observe or test it. Anyone could offer any nutty supernatural solution, and we would be stuck with it.
3. The supernatural is subjective, while our questions and our data are objective — publicly observable and the same for everyone everywhere. If this one believes in one god and that one believes in multiple nature-spirits, we cannot adjudicate that difference, so it is useless to us rationally.
4. Today's supernatural answer may and hopefully will be replaced tomorrow with a naturalistic answer. Supernatural answers have proven time and again to be 'gap' answers to fill today's ignorance. We cannot know for sure that tomorrow's naturalistic knowledge will provide a new and better solution, but it has many times so far.

For these reasons, science simply eschews supernatural answers. Instead, science takes a naturalistic view, including a number of characteristics.

1. Nature is knowable. Natural causes and phenomena leave observable traces, which we can study and understand.
2. Nature is regular. The same 'laws' or descriptions apply in all places at all times. There are no mysterious exceptions to the laws of nature, no miracles — good or bad.
3. Nature is repeatable. This follows from the characteristic above. If nature is regular, then the same causes should produce the same effects every time. There are no singular events that cannot at least in theory be reproduced. There are no 'special creations,' otherwise we could not trust the results of our experiments and other observations.

4. Nature is predictable. This follows from nature's repeatability. If we correctly understand the laws of nature and the prevailing conditions, we should be able to predict the subsequent conditions. If we cannot, then some part of our knowledge is faulty.

5. Nature is impersonal. 'Personality' indicates a certain willful deviation from lawfulness — not that personality or will is lawless, but that it has its own interests that will at times vary from a 'random' or 'natural' course. Personality introduces a dimension of unpredictability or arbitrariness that science does not observe and that would corrupt the regularity, repeatability, and predictability of nature if it did. Nature should not depend either upon the personality of the observer (facts are facts no matter who observes them) nor of some supernatural actor (who could change the rules or results of nature willy-nilly).

Having made these comments, I will now make my strongest assertion in this chapter: science is at its heart atheistic. I do not mean by this that scientists are or must be Atheists; we have seen that they often are not. I do not mean that science disproves god(s) or even denies god(s). I mean, along with Weinberg and Dawkins, that science *disregards* god(s). As the scientist Pierre Simon de Laplace famously said to Napoléon of god(s): "I have had no need of that hypothesis."

All really important and profound questions connect to other important and profound questions. The question, 'Is science at heart atheistic?' connects to the question, 'What is Atheism?' As I have tried to explain in this book, Atheism is nothing more and nothing less than a lack of belief in god(s). It is a disregard for and dismissal of god-talk. It does not say, 'There is certainly no such thing' but rather, 'I see no evidence or need for any such thing.' It says, 'God-talk makes no difference in my life, nor from all accounts your life, nor the world in general.' It says, after Dawkins, that god-talk is superfluous.

Essentially and undeniably, science says the same thing. Science does not say it can disprove god(s); it says it can prove things without god(s). It merely carries on its business without them. Clearly we have seen people sneak god(s) back into science, but evolutionary theory or big bang cosmology or what have you works just fine without it/them. In fact, like politics, it works much better without god(s), because the introduction of god-talk imposes nonanswer 'god of the gaps' kind of thinking as well as theological divisiveness. Science evacuated god(s) from the academy for a good reason: because an academy with Jesus is very different from an academy with Allah or an academy with Vishnu or an Academy with Thor, and we have no standard by which to determine which is best or truest. You can certainly be a scientist and believe in god(s) — people have done crazier things — but there is no scientific basis for that combination whatsoever. The belief part comes from another source — not science, not observation, not reason — and that is the critical point.

Same, Separate, or Conflicting Worlds?

Whoever said that enduring questions are probably asked wrong was a very wise person. I will posit that the question, 'What is the relation between science and religion?' is a wrongly asked question. So is the question that heads this section: are science and religion in the same, separate, or conflicting worlds? They are in all and none of the three. Sometimes they agree, sometimes they disagree, and sometimes they ignore each other. The correct question is, 'How are science and religion different?'

Let us look quickly again at the three models of Shermer. First, the *same worlds* model asserts that science and religion study the same reality and that they do or can support each other and come to the same conclusions. Part of this assertion is correct: science and religion do study the same reality, because there only is one reality. Science and religion inhabit the same world because there is only one world to inhabit. But this is not at all what the proponents of this position say, particularly the religionists among them like Ross or Behe or Dembski, *et al*. What they say is, 'Here is science that confirms our preexisting beliefs. Any other science is suspect or false.' This is why Pigliucci put the likes of them in the *conflicting worlds* side — because they like science when it agrees with their belief and dislike it when it disagrees. But that's not how it works.

This raises the fundamental question of what religion is. Religion and science (that is, systematic reason) can agree on details without being identical or even compatible, and they do. But religion, as we have argued throughout this book, is not about fact, not about observation, not about knowledge, certainly not about reason. It is about belief and faith. Religion says, 'This is true, because authority/tradition/scripture/personal experience says it is true.' But that is completely contrary to the spirit and practice of science, and while it is entirely possible that religion and science might coincide once and a while, such co-incidence is pure coincidence, and it proves nothing. To say religion is true because science confirms this or that detail of religion is to commit the fallacy of composition.

Another important fact to face is that there is no such thing as 'religion' but only religions. The problem with most of the 'research' of the likes of the Discovery Institute or the Institute for Creation Research is that it is exclusively Christian. Why? While I am not as familiar with the literature, I am sure that somewhere in the Islamic world there is (or at least could be) an Islamic Discovery Institute, somewhere in the Hindu world there is or could be an Institute for Hindu Creation Research, *etc.* And no doubt, when the latter finds a scientific fact that supports an ancient cyclical universe created by a dreaming Brahma sitting on a lotus flower, they proclaim the 'compatibility of science and Hinduism.' Such trivial intersections mean nothing.

Furthermore, the very fact that religionists look to science for confirmation of their religious beliefs only evinces the power and prestige of science in our modern world. Notice that no scientists (at least that I know of) use religion to try to support science! No scientist says, "Oh, the Bible says the world was created at a specific moment in time, so the big bang must be correct." Well, there might be some who think that way, but the former is no proof of the latter. And of course it could not be, because even if the former is true, the latter is merely one possible way it might have happened. The scientific theory is either true or false, whatever the scripture says.

As for the scientists who 'find god,' I'm not sure quite what to say. Some probably already believed, so it was quite likely they would find what they want to find. Some work, like the brain research of Newberg and d'Aquili, obviously does not warrant the conclusions that the scientists arrive at; the work is one big *non sequitur*. Others, like the 'anthropic principle' business, are amusing unless taken too far, in which case it becomes evident that the causation is all backwards: *the universe is not the way it is because we are here, but rather we are here because the universe is the way it is*. If the universe had other constants and qualities, either life would be different or nonexistent, or maybe even the universe itself would be nonexistent. Either way, it's okay — unless you *believe* that we had to be here exactly as we are, which is a completely unscientific position. It is a matter of faith, and rather smug faith at that. And the suggestion that god(s) work(s) by manipulating quantum events is just speculative nonsense — and it is sneaking god(s) back in through the smallest imaginable hole in nature!

What of the *separate worlds* model? Well, probably from a practical standpoint, science and religion do go about their affairs relatively indifferent to each other. Recall that my central point is that science is indifferent to religion. But the arguments that are offered for this separation — whether it be mutual indifference or loving respect and dialogue — are specious. They amount to an obfuscation of the nature of religion and a distortion of the nature of knowledge.

As regards religion, we have seen that from Kant to Gould, the basic premise of the *separate worlds* argument is that religion is essentially morality. This is not true. Religion is much more and much less than morality. It is much less than morality since it is not coterminous with morality; in other words, there is much morality and much discussion of morality outside the 'magisterium' of religion, and Gould admits as much. He says himself that "while religion anchors this magisterium in most cultural traditions, the chosen pathway need not invoke religion at all, but may ground moral discourse in other disciplines, philosophy, *e.g.*" (60). So, while religion usually anchors the religious domain, the religious domain need not invoke religion at all? Nonsense.

Religion, more importantly, is much more than morality, and this is why the moral component of religion has any impact at all. Christianity, for example, makes various moral injunctions on humans; we should not kill, for example. But why? The answer is simple: because there are certain very real aspects of the universe that ordain and enforce these injunctions. If there is no god, then the commandment could not even be real. And if there is not a god who has specific wishes, who intervenes in human affairs, and who has this or that nature, then there would be no reason to follow the injunctions. In other words, religions are about a lot more than morality. They are about metaphysics, history, and yes, even 'physics.' They are complete systems of what Geertz called the 'really real.' Detach the metaphysics from the morality and the morality falls.

But if religion makes specific factual claims about the world — that it was created in six days, or that there was a global flood, or that lions were created with teeth before there was hunting and death in the world — then it is making propositions that are either true or false and that can be evaluated by methods of reason and science. Religious claims may *come out* of a separate world, but they *come into* the same world where reason and science reside, and once they are here, they are subject to the same rules and standards.

The other main plank of the *separate worlds* model is that religion and science employ different methods and languages. I may be wrong about this, but from my investigation *religion does not have a method at all.* What precisely would be the method of religion? Huston Smith, for instance, seems to think that intuition and revelation are among the methods of religion. However, these are not methods, since (1) you cannot control or employ them whenever you want (*e.g.* you cannot say, "I am going to have an intuition now"), and (2) they do not provide knowledge in any important sense of the word. What problem has religion ever solved? Religion cannot even solve religious disputes, let alone practical ones. One of the hallmarks of science is that it gets results; another is that it permanently condemns to the rubbish heap ideas that have been disproved. Religion gets no regular and dependable results from its 'methods,' and it has never settled even a single religious dispute once and for all. That's why there are still so many different versions of Christianity today. When phlogiston was definitively debunked, no scientists continued to hold the notion into the present. But when, say, Protestantism came along, it did not decisively unseat Catholicism. Rather, they and many others coexist as 'alternative truths.' It would be as if every scientific theory that was ever hatched was still held and practiced by some bunch of scientists somewhere in the world. It would be absurd.

If religion does have a 'method,' its two elements are exegesis and mysticism. Exegesis is 'reading out' of a source — verbal, textual, and so on — the implications of that source, and mysticism roughly encompasses Smith's "intuition and revelation." But both of these 'methods' violate the standards of reason and therefore cannot yield trustworthy knowledge. Exegesis commits the fallacy of appeal to authority; why should we take that source as an authoritative source in the first place? There is and can be no rational answer to that question. Also, exegesis cannot tell us anything new about the world; it can only tell us what is already in the source (say, the scriptures). It is interpretation, nothing more, and therefore only as valid as the original source and the interpreter. That is why we find so many – and conflicting – interpretations of any original source or scripture. It is at best transmission of 'knowledge' perhaps, but never discovery of knowledge. That is why religion does not produce computers or cures for cancer. Since this can only be as reliable as the source and interpreter, how can we ever determine that reliability — other than by comparing both source and interpretation to reality, that is, by doing the science?

There are those who also suggest that religious knowledge can be discovered through a 'method,' or one or more 'methods' that we call mysticism. Mysticism is roughly a personal contact with the religious or spiritual realm (see Chapter Twelve for a discussion of 'spirituality') where new knowledge may be acquired and brought back to the world. These methods, practiced by shamans, adepts, gurus, prophets, and other 'religious specialists' throughout human history and across human cultures, are incredibly diverse. They include meditation, hallucinogenic drugs of all kinds, prayer, asceticism and self-mortification, sleep and food deprivation, chanting, yoga, divination, oracles, trance, and even electrical stimulation of the brain. However, their very diversity and diverse goals should be an alarm to us.

John Horgan, whose research on the claims of mystics illustrates just how much they disagree with each other, identifies "satori, kensho, nirvana, samadhi, the opening of the third eye" (2003, 3), not to mention revelation, realization, enlightenment, liberation, oneness, cosmic union, the Void, the Absolute, and many others. In fact, Horgan's study of mystics and scholars of mysticism, from Huston Smith to Bernard McGinn and Steven Katz to Ken Wilber to Andrew Newberg and Eugene d'Aquili to Michael Persinger to James Austin to Christian Rausch and Franz Vollenweider to Stanislav Grof to Terence McKenna (and not even including non-Western and premodern practitioners) demonstrates just how contradictory and ultimately uninformative mysticism really is.

The logical problem is that mysticism commits the fallacy of appeal to personal experience, whether it takes the form of intuition (making the 'discovery') or revelation (having the 'discovery' handed to us). How do we know a real intuition or revelation has taken place, and why should we accept one over another? A report of a mystical experience is nothing more than testimony to the rest of us nonmystics, which still needs to be verified. And that raises the even more damaging empirical problem: mysticism does not produce consistent, objective, verifiable experience. Mystical seekers like to assert that all mystical experiences are similar and converge on the same 'truth,' which is supposed to be deep, positive, ineffable, transient, and beyond our control (we are passive recipients of it). Instead, mystical experiences result in wildly inconsistent and even incompatible results: for one person, it may be positive and loving, for another negative and terrifying. For one it may seem deep, for another (and the audience) trivial. Some mystics can expound at remarkable length on their ineffable experiences! Some claim permanent vision or knowledge and control over the transient and passive experience.

In short, the 'knowledge' obtained by mystical 'methods' is (1) different for different individuals; (2) different for different cultures, that is, people in Christian cultures experience

Christ or Mary or whatever, while those in Buddhist cultures experience buddha-nature and nirvana, while those in Aboriginal Australia experience the Dreamtime and the kangaroo-grandfather, *ad infinitum*; (3) available only to a small minority of 'spiritual elite' who are highly preconditioned for their experiences; (4) subjective and outside of any possible standard for determining their 'truth' – what would we compare or refer such experiences to? – and not reproducible; (5) unproductive of any actual useful knowledge (What truth has any mystic ever returned with other than platitudes about being a better person or the wondrousness of the universe? Would you go to a doctor who had had a mystical experience about how to perform your surgery?); (6) potentially reducible to altered brain states and not some contact with 'another reality' at all; and (7) actually against the traditions and teachings of many religions, including Christianity, which maintain that the god or the spiritual is 'wholly other' and not to be approached by humans with their paltry methods. We would not tolerate such limitations and contradictions in knowledge in any other field, nor should we. Every scientist who measures the acceleration of gravity should — no must — get the same result from the same method. Otherwise, the 'knowledge' is suspect and the method futile.

In the end, as we have said before, it is not at all impossible that someone might discover a truth by mysticism or exegesis, but the discovery would be purely accidental. The 'knowledge' cannot verify itself, and not until it has passed through the gauntlet of reason can we legitimately call it knowledge. Here then is the crux of the matter: religion is not an 'alternate' way of knowing. *Religion is not a way of knowing at all.* Of course, one can have 'religious knowledge,' but such 'knowledge' is self-referential. It amounts to knowing 'what the religion says' or what the beliefs and practices of the religion are. It is knowing *about the religion*, not knowing *about the world*. As the credits on a motion picture declare, any resemblance between this 'knowledge' and the real world is purely coincidental.

Ultimately, scientific/rational knowing has no need and little use for religious 'knowing.' Eugenie Scott is too polite to say so, especially since saying so would potentially offend the folks she is trying to get to accept science in schools. I respect that agenda, but I feel no compunction to be polite. When she argues that "as to the ultimate cause of evolution, you are on your own," inviting religious interpretations of science at individual whim, she is wrong. As to any matter of fact, you are not on your own; you are beholden to the rules and standards of reason. If there is no basis for introducing an additional claim — like that god(s) work(s) through evolution — then don't introduce it. And if you see it introduced, see it for what it is: faith intruding on fact.

This is also why I take exception to Shermer's 'live-and-let-live' spirit. His only "beef" is when religion intrudes on or usurps science. But as we have seen, religion does not have a completely distinct realm of its own; it lives in the world with science. In some details it is right, in some it is wrong. But it seldom if ever accepts that evaluation. It thinks itself completely right and has only yielded ground to superior knowledge when it had no other choice — and then grudgingly. Not going into the issues of "political oppression, ideological extremism, or the cultural suppression of diversity," which, as I will discuss later are congenital to religion, one can focus on the "belief choice" but only by obscuring the fact that for the believer, it is not a choice at all. Choice is heresy. Choice is reason and science. No religion ever invites you to make a choice — other than the choice between inclusion and exclusion, heaven and hell.

This takes us to the *conflicting worlds* model. It might seem that I am a firm advocate of this position. In a way I am. However, as stated, sometimes religion and science converge, and that's fine. Sometimes they have little in common, as in matters of morality, and that's fine. And sometimes they conflict in details or deeper philosophy. In the first two cases, the course is simple. But in the third case, what do we do? The answer is actually simple too: trust science. Science, or rather its methods of observation, skepticism, statistical analysis, self-criticism, *etc.* are the only trustworthy path to knowledge. This does not mean that everything science says today is correct. It does not mean that everything that religion says today is incorrect. But it does mean that, in a dispute, *science has a better chance of being correct than religion does.*

There are, I suspect, few if any religionists who are such Luddites that they reject every breath of science. Most are modern people. Even flat-earthers still accept the law of gravity. But religion has and must have an ambivalent attitude toward science. It is sympathetic and open to scientific thinking when that thinking supports its own and hostile and closed to it when it refutes it. Science is, at heart, neither hostile nor friendly to religion; it is utterly disinterested.

Conclusion: Science Has No Friends, Only Interests.

A politician once said that countries do not have friends, they have interests. Science is that way too. Science does not care who you are or what you believe, as long as you use the method and justify your conclusions (it is, as Scott asserted, an "equal-opportunity methodology"). As such, science, as the systematic application of reason to experience, is fundamentally 'a-religious,' or I would say 'a-theistic.' It does not look for religious answers, and it does not welcome them when it hears them. It is apathetic, impassive, unimpressionable, nonchalant, impervious, inattentive, even callous toward religion. Therein lies the problem for religion.

Religion does not tolerate indifference. The one thing that religion demands, and I agree with all scholars who emphasize this, is *commitment*. Religion is, as Barbour expresses it, "not meant to be a hypothesis formulated to explain phenomena in the world in competition with scientific hypotheses. Belief in God is primarily a commitment to a way of life in response to distinctive kinds of religious experience in communities formed by historic traditions; it is not a substitute for scientific research" (81–2). The reference to community is important here, and it is probably what Gould means when he says that religion is "dedicated to a quest for consensus, or at least a clarification of assumptions and criteria, about ethical 'ought,' rather than a search for any factual 'is' about the material construction of the natural world" (55). But this consensus is purely stipulative — we all agree if we take the same persons or words as our authority — while in reality consensus is the one thing religion does not provide. The fact of religious pluralism means that there is a complete lack of consensus on the very questions that religion was reputedly sent here to answer. As the highest authority on moral matters, it fails utterly.

The rest of each of the quotes above we must reject. Religion may not be 'meant' as an explanation of phenomena or the material construction of the world, but (1) it does do those things and depends fundamentally on doing them and (2) that was exactly what it was meant to do originally. In an earlier time, religion was the only game in town; it was both morality and empirical knowledge. In many societies and for many individuals it still is. This divorce of the two is a profoundly modern phenomenon, and it is one that has occurred only under the duress of science, because religion could no longer defend its claims to perfect factual as well as moral knowledge. The one thing I agree with completely in Gould is that we "can hardly expect anyone to withdraw from so much territory without a struggle" (64). And religion has only recently abandoned its claims to complete truth in factual areas because it had no other option. The 'allegorical' or 'moral' reading of religion is a rearguard action, and a rather disingenuous and sad one at that.

Religion, then, often may be inherently hostile to science since science is so completely disinterested in religion. Science does not bow to religion's authority; instead, science often takes its authoritative claims as sufficient grounds for doubt. Science does not care what the god(s) said, and it does not care what the prophets or the church fathers said. It is, therefore, intrinsically disrespectful to religion, and that is a mortal threat. As we have seen repeatedly, and as I cannot repeat enough, authority, along with personal experience, tradition, and emotional motivation — the very bread and butter of religion — are not trustworthy bases of knowledge. In any head-to-head disagreement, we have to give the benefit of trustworthiness to science. In a fair fight on factual ground, science wins.

There are two other reasons why religion and science share an innate hostility. Since religion depends for its life on authority and subjectivity, the favoring of scientific (that is, empirical and objective) claims over religious ones does in the end cast doubt on the whole religious enterprise and forebodes to vanquish religion, by marginalizing it if nothing else. Under the glare of science, religion perhaps does contract to nothing more than ethics with no 'real' or 'objective' foundation, or perhaps it emerges as a mixed bag of truth and falsity with no other standard to distinguish the two than tradition and taste, in which case its authority is curtailed. In other words, while not setting out to assault religion, science assaults it nonetheless. The second reason why science menaces religion is that the former includes and urges a willingness (however hesitant or reluctant) to give up a position or even a fact if the situation demands it, and a scientifically literate citizenry that takes this lesson to heart is likely to apply it to religion too. Scientists can specify the facts or figures that would lead them to abandon their current position; the difference between science and religion could not be clearer than by the answer that a Ross or a Dembski or a Smith would give to the question, 'What would make you give up your position on god, and how would you feel about it?'

CHAPTER EIGHT

Toleration and Truth

We pride ourselves on our toleration in America. Other people are free, at least in principle, to think and believe what they want to think and believe, and even within limits to act on it; while we do not condone racist behavior or political violence, we still find that we must (and can, without all that much disturbance to our society) allow groups like the Ku Klux Klan or various neo-Nazi organizations to exist and to march and rally in public. Of course, we culturally condemn certain beliefs and practices, including racism and sexism, but we cannot bring ourselves to prevent or prohibit such things from being promoted and proselytized, unless someone is actually hurt in the process. Toleration of other positions ends where they come in contact with the life and limb of people who are the object of intolerance. But we feel wrong in, for example, denying the KKK a marching permit, and that is probably all to the good. If government or even society begins to decide which groups and causes may exist and function and which may not, we are all in danger. It is the small and unpopular groups and causes that always live most under the cloud of potential intolerance, but tomorrow it could be any. Every group or cause rubs somebody the wrong way.

Toleration (which I will use interchangeably with *tolerance*), like church(es)/state separation (as we will discuss in the next chapter) is good for everyone, not just the minority or fringe groups that are today's beneficiaries. But it does make for a much more cacophonous society than one that speaks with a single voice and silences opposing voices. The problem is, the facile phrase 'silences opposing voices' has real visceral consequences; you cannot usually silence opposition without someone getting hurt. Sometimes, even with people getting hurt, you still cannot silence their voice.

But there is no doubt that one of the reasons why toleration is so precious to us in America is that it is so rare in the world. Most societies in most of human history have not been tolerant. Most have attempted, if not succeeded, to establish what anthropologist W.E.H. Stanner, in a different context, called a "one-possibility" culture. In a one-possibility culture, of which he considered traditional Australian Aboriginal culture to be an instance, members simply cannot conceive that things could be any other way than they are. Opposition or heterodoxy is virtually impossible, so toleration is not an issue; society really does speak with a single voice. Alternative voices are quite literally inconceivable.

Many if not most traditional cultures present some degree of one-possibility thinking, so toleration never had any reason to develop. Society was small enough and enculturation was effective enough to bring all members into sufficient consensus on what is true and real and valuable and normal. Of course, we must be cautious about imposing our own Western slant on this matter: for example, while things are pretty much what they are and nothing else in many traditional cultures, the way things are is often very different from the way we think they are. For example, in some Plains Indian societies in the western United States, people recognized not two but three genders — a male, a female, and a 'two-spirit' or third gender commonly referred to as *berdache* for men who were inclined to perform some of the roles of women. *Berdache* were not 'tolerated' but welcomed and valued in society, often holding respected positions in society as teachers or similar roles. We have no such thing in our society, and if we did, we would probably 'tolerate' it rather than value it.

In other ways too, traditional cultures embraced difference or novelty without exactly tolerating it. For example, in Australian Aboriginal society, Christianity diffused as a novelty from Western civilization only in recent history (sometimes within the living memories of the elders). However, instead of 'tolerating' Christians in their midst, Aboriginal societies could actually incorporate Christian views and values within their cultural understanding of religious novelty, which ordinarily came from dreams. A member could introduce new religious content from dream sources, and religious specialists were always interested to enhance their repertoire of religious knowledge from their own and others' dreams.

Christianity seemed to them like any other dream revelation, which could be added as yet one more tool in their spiritual tool chest. Accordingly, I have seen Aboriginal men going to church in the morning and participating in traditional ceremonies in the evening, or dancing what looks like a traditional corroboree but with Christian themes and motifs, like crosses painted on their bodies.

But their world is not our world. In our world, innovations and heterodoxies are not so easily integrated (although they are, certainly, sometimes integrated). Perhaps because 'belief' is so fundamental to the American and Western way of thinking, 'correct' and 'incorrect' belief is an essential problem. And when we enter the realm of totalistic 'world religions,' which claim exclusive access to all truth and good, toleration becomes even more of a problem. Divergence from the established orthodoxy (from *ortho* meaning 'right' or 'straight' or 'true' and *doxa* meaning 'opinion') is necessarily and by definition false — and maybe worse than false but also perilous. False views (that is, all but the official views) are hazardous to the individuals who hold them, since they will be punished for them in some way, and even hazardous to the community, which may be lured by them or held responsible for them ultimately.

So toleration is not only a rare but a relatively (and comprehensibly) unnatural thing in 'modern,' 'civilized' totalistic belief-systems, of which the world religions are prime examples. I will offer this assertion, which I hold to be true: *there is no world-religious source that includes toleration as one of its values*. There are of course members of world religions, including many American Christians, who value toleration, but there is no authority for it in the sources and teachings of the religion. In other words, to be blunt, the Christian Bible never says anywhere that you should tolerate nonbelievers. I think this generally holds true across world religions. For example, there is a passage in the Bhagavad Gita that sounds very much like an openness to 'other faiths': "Those who worship the demigods will take birth among the demigods; those who worship the ancestors go to the ancestors; those who worship ghosts and spirits will take birth among such beings; and those who worship Me [Krishna] will live with Me" (Chapter

Nine, verse 25). However, a few lines before this statement, Krishna points out that, while you are free to worship in other ways, you are mistaken: "Those who are devotees of other gods and who worship them with faith actually worship only Me, O son of Kunti, but they do so in a wrong way" (verse 23). Later in the tale, Krishna clarifies that not only are nonbelievers in him wrong but they will pay a price for their nonconformity:

> Those who are demoniac ... say that this world is unreal, with no foundation, no God in control. They say [the world] is produced of sex desire and has no cause other than lust. Following such conclusions, the demoniac, who are lost to themselves and who have no intelligence, engage in unbeneficial, horrible works meant to destroy the world. Taking shelter of insatiable lust and absorbed in the conceit of pride and false prestige, the demoniac, thus illusioned, are always sworn to unclean work, attracted by the impermanent. They believe that to gratify the sense is the prime necessity of human civilization. Thus until the end of life their anxiety is immeasurable. Bound by a network of hundreds of thousands of desires and absorbed in lust and anger, they secure money by illegal means for sense gratification. (Chapter Sixteen, verses 4–12)
>
> Thus perplexed by various anxieties and bound by a network of illusions, they become too strongly attached to sense enjoyment and fall down into hell .... Bewildered by false ego, strength, pride, lust and anger, the demons become envious of the Supreme Personality of Godhead, who is situated in their own bodies and in the bodies of others, and blaspheme against the real religion. Those who are envious and mischievous, who are the lowest among men, I perpetually cast into the ocean of material existence, into various demoniac species of life. Attaining repeated birth amongst the species of demoniac life, O son of Kunti, such persons can never approach Me. Gradually they sink down to the most abominable type of existence. (Chapter Sixteen, verses 16–20)

The Judeo-Christian tradition definitely has no time for divergence of opinion, especially when that opinion is nonbelief. Deuteronomy 13:6–10 says clearly and unequivocally that if "thy brother, the son of thy mother, or thy son, or thy daughter, or the wife of thy bosom, or thy friend, which is as thine own soul, entice thee secretly, saying, Let us go and serve other gods, which thou hast not known, thou, nor thy fathers," then you should stone them to death. Leviticus 24:10–16 tells the story of a man who was condemned to death merely for cursing the name of his god. And of course the Old Testament is replete with accounts of war against other nations and their gods and the prophetic warnings of dire consequences for worshipping the wrong gods. Passages including II Samuel 23: 33–43, Psalms 137:8–9, and Isaiah 13:15–18 recount the pleasure of the death that is to be meted out to these idolaters, including dashing their babies against a rock. Finally, there is no uncertainty at all in the New Testament about what will befall unbelievers at the end. Of course, sensitive Theists might argue that Jesus also said to love your neighbor and your enemy, but I think it is obvious that he assumed that your neighbor and even your enemy would be a Christian too. There is nowhere, I repeat nowhere, where Jesus says to love the non-believer or to be free to be a nonbeliever yourself.

Islam is often credited with a modicum of toleration, and it is true that 'people of the book' — that is, Jews and Christians, fellow monotheists who share some of the beliefs of Islam — are to be left unmolested, providing they accept Muslim suzerainty and pay a special non-Muslim tax. But non-monotheists are considered idolaters in Islam, and of them the Qur'an speaks, for example in sura 9, verse 5: "So when the sacred months have passed away, then slay the idolaters wherever you find them, and take them captives and besiege them and lie in wait for them in every ambush." Also in sura 2,191 we find: "And kill them wherever you find them, and drive them out from whence they drove you out, and persecution is severer than slaughter, and do not fight with them at the Sacred Mosque until they fight with you in it, but if they do fight you, then slay them; such is the recompense of the unbelievers." In fact, the scripture mentions the afterworldly fire that is prepared for unbelievers (2:24), because Allah's curse is on the unbeliever (2:89).

The point is made. There is no major world tradition that allows true toleration of opinion, even the opinion that the tradition itself is wrong or irrelevant. The one near-exception is the small religion of Jainism, a faith of extreme nonviolence that originated around the time of the birth of Buddhism and shares many elements with it. One of the tenets of Jainism is *anekantvada* or 'non-absolutism,' which maintains that the limitations of human knowledge preclude absolute assertions and demand an openness or liberalism of mind. However, Jainism still posits a whole complex of specific beliefs and practices, including right knowledge, right faith, and right conduct, which are intertwined and necessary for a successful life. Right knowledge in particular must be free from "three main defects": doubt, delusion, and indefiniteness.

We can, then, conclude that no contemporary religious tradition in its source really tolerates, and emphatically does not welcome, differences. Each sets a proper or correct way to think, feel, and act. While there may be some latitude on specific points, there is absolutely no case in which the tradition says it is okay to reject the teachings of the faith or choose some other teachings or to ponder the teachings and then decide for yourself. How could it possibly do so? The faith and the scriptures claim utter truth and completeness, so allowing 'freedom to choose' would undermine the entire project. Of course, you are 'free to choose,' if by freedom we understand acceptance of the penalties and consequences of your choice.

So, if there is toleration in the world, it does not come from religious sources. Where then does it come from? And what are the implications of toleration for 'truth'? In other words, if I accept your right to believe differently from me, but I think I believe the truth and you think you believe the truth, then what has become of truth?

Toleration — An All-Too-Brief History

Toleration, as we have affirmed, is not the natural state of the major world religions nor of most societies throughout time. In the vast majority of societies, great and small, belief is truth and truth is social order. To disbelieve is to be wrong, and to be wrong is to threaten the established order of things, spiritual and political. Conformity of opinion and action is the foundation of law and order; dissidence is disruption and disorder. No wonder then that even democratic Athens charged some of its greatest citizens, including Anaxagoras, Euripides, Protagoras, and Alcibiades, with impiety for questioning the conventional religion; it is only too well-known that Socrates was condemned to death for impiety and corrupting youth by asking troubling questions and spreading doubt — the very things that toleration is intended to protect.

To focus on Europe and Christian civilization, we have already seen that the Judeo-Christian tradition has definite and rigid notions about belief and nonbelief, particularly blasphemy, generally defined as cursing or abusing the name of the god of that tradition. It is, as such, a speech act. Now, Christianity is distinct as a religion in its emphasis on beliefs as opposed to actions; it is a creed-driven religion, rather than a ritualistic or works-driven one (although the faith-versus-works problem has been a persistent one for Christianity). At any rate, since Christianity is first and foremost a belief *about* and a belief *in* the person of Jesus and his salvific mission, rather than a moral code or set of rules, belief — *correct* belief — is crucial to the religion. This had two consequences for European views on religious nonconformity. The first was that *orthodoxy* (right belief), as opposed to *orthopraxy* (right practice or behavior) or any other ortho-subject, was at the center of things, even while the right beliefs were not quite clear and very much in dispute. The second is that, on the premise of the divinity of Jesus, any blasphemy or error or sin against 'God' was extended to include Jesus as well; to curse, insult, question, doubt, or otherwise disrupt Jesus-belief was equivalent to an assault against the Christian god.

In combination, these two factors created an environment in which correct beliefs regarding Jesus were the centerpiece of the religion, and any other beliefs regarding him were outside acceptance. Alternate beliefs were 'heresy,' from the Greek *hairesis* meaning to choose or take for yourself, and practitioners were heretics. The problem, of course, was that there was, for the first few centuries, no orthodoxy but a variety of heterodoxies; there was no church but a variety of churches. Despite the work of Paul to bring local churches into line, there was a wide range of opinions on the person and significance of Jesus and therefore the meaning of Christianity. One of the most fundamental was whether Jesus was a man, a god, or both. Another was whether the god in question was exclusively 'one' or whether he was a 'multiple person' including manifestations as Jesus and the 'Holy Spirit.' Obviously, at this early stage there was no court of arbitration to settle the matters, and the Bible itself was mute or confusing on the subjects.

Orthodoxy was established by the Council of Nicaea in 325, when the first Christian Roman emperor, Constantine I, put his seal on a creed that answered the problematic questions: Jesus was wholly human and divine, and God was three-in-one (the Trinitarian solution). Having thus established an orthodoxy, and one with official government approval, all other opinions on the matter instantly became heterodoxy, dissent, and heresy. This included of course all non-Christian religions — especially Judaism (which by denying Jesus denied the Christian god) and all shades of paganism — as well as other interpretations of Christianity, of which there were legion. Docetists believed that Jesus was purely divine and not human; Gnostics believed that only they possessed the 'mysteries' of Jesus and could be one with him; Arianism taught that God was not three but one, that there was no biblical authority for the Trinity concept (replacing it with a Monarchian or Unitarian conception). These were among, and the most durable of, the wide assortment of local variations of Christian understanding. Early on, even before Nicaea, Christians were arguing with and condemning each other for false doctrine, as in Hippolytus' *The Refutation of All Heresies*, Irenaeus' *The Detection and Refutation of False Knowledge*, also known as *Against Heresies*, Tertullian's *Prescription Against Heretics*, and so on and so forth. In fact, writing treatises against heresy, defined as anything disagreeing with your or the official version of things, became something of a cottage industry and tradition of its own in Christianity.

It stands to reason that, with doctrinal disputes running rampant and the authority of the emperor authorizing one particular version, there would be a price to pay for heresy, and there was. When the state sponsors one view of religion, all other views become 'outlaw' or even 'criminal' (a strong argument for separation of church[es] and state, as we will examine in the following chapter), so once Trinitarianism and Jesus' dual nature were settled, other opinions became civil infractions, punishable by the state. Starting then with the Arian controversy, bishops who advocated Arianism were deposed, books were burned, and lives were threatened. As Leonard Levy, a scholar of the history of blasphemy and heresy, writes: "Thus, for the first time, Christians began to persecute one another for differences of opinion and faith. Constantine's edict fixed the precedent for temporal punishment of offenses against the true Christian faith" (1993, 42). In fact, temporal punishments would not take long to transform into capital punishment; the code of emperor Theodosius (380 CE) established Christianity as the sole religion of the realm and set penalties for disagreement from the official version, which came to include restriction from officeholding, fines, confiscation of property, banishment, torture, and even death for Christian heresy and prohibition of other religions altogether. In 385 Bishop Priscillian of Spain and six followers had the dubious honor of becoming the first Christians to die over theological disputes, by decapitation. They would not be the last. As Levy concludes: "Religious intolerance became a Christian principle" (44).

It should not be imagined that persecution and intolerance were attitudes that were foisted on the church by a zealous state. Founding church leaders like Tertullian, Augustine, and Aquinas saw great virtue in the elimination of schism as well. Tertullian, whom we met in the last chapter, positively salivated at the prospect of the damnation of sinners, disbelievers, and the wise and mighty:

> How shall I admire, how laugh, how rejoice, how exult, when I behold so many proud monarchs, and fancied gods, groaning in the lowest abyss of darkness; so many magistrates who persecuted the name of the Lord, liquefying in fiercer fires than they ever kindled against the Christians; so many sage philosophers blushing in red hot flames with their deluded scholars; so many celebrated poets trembling before the tribunal, not of Minos, but of Christ; so many tragedians, more tuneful in the expression of their sufferings. (Freke and Gandy 1999, 243)

While quite the stylist and polemicist, he was not the theorist that Augustine or Aquinas was. Augustine, for example, advocated the death penalty for heretics but left it to the state to carry out the punishment. For him, religious crimes were much greater threats than property or violent crimes;

rejection of the faith was much more serious than rejection of the law. Physical death as a penalty was simply not a big deal, since, as Augustine rationalized, we are all bound to die sometime; but as for heretics, he wrote, "we fear their eternal death, which can happen if we do not guard against it and can be averted if we do guard against it." In other words, executing heretics was not only doing a service to church and state by disposing of a divisive character and returning the faith to purity, but it was doing the heretic a favor by saving his soul. Therefore, he could, with a straight face, make the distinction between "an unjust persecution which the wicked inflict on the Church of Christ, and ... a just persecution which the Church of Christ inflicts on the wicked." Or again, the church could persecute "out of love ... to reclaim from error to save souls."

In fact, in Tertullian's view, and that of many who followed him, toleration was not mercy but in fact was complicity in damnation — not only damnation of the poor heretic himself but also the potential damnation of every Christian soul who might hear the heretic's message and be swayed by it. He could go so far as to assert that suffering a heretic to live extended his guilt to the church and the state for allowing him to contaminate others. And there was nothing wrong with using force to compel heretics to sit again at the table of the true faith; Augustine recommended whipping, exile, and confiscation of property over death, but he was not wholly opposed to the latter.

Several hundred years later, in the mid-1200s, Thomas Aquinas picked up the issue again, accepting the definition of heresy as an intentional choice of "false or new opinions" in regard to faith. Only the pope could determine correct faith, and any deviation from his authority constituted "a species of unbelief." He distinguished several species of unbelief, including but not limited to heresy, paganism, Judaism, apostasy, and blasphemy. He recognized that, conventionally, blasphemy referred to speaking an insult or curse against the Christian god, but this extended for him to utterances of untrue beliefs. In other words, someone who spoke something false or erroneous about 'God' also took his name in vain, and therefore heresy was a kind of unbelief and unbelief was a kind of blasphemy. All were worse than any temporal crime one might commit, and since many temporal crimes were met with capital punishment, heresy and blasphemy even more so should receive the ultimate punishment. In his own words, heretics "by right ... can be put to death and despoiled of their possessions by the secular authorities, even if they do not corrupt others, for they are blasphemers against God, because they observe a false faith. Thus they can be justly punished more than those accused of high treason" (Levy, 52). The Jews were singled out for particular attention in Aquinas' analysis. Since they especially, as God's formerly chosen people, denied the messiah-hood and divinity of Christ, they were blasphemers (they could not be heretics, since only Christians could be heretics). That left them open to persecution and discrimination too.

And persecution and discrimination they received. In 1215 the fourth Lateran Council deprived Jews of their civil rights and compelled them to wear a special mark to identify themselves in public. They could be boycotted, robbed of their property, expelled, and even murdered in great numbers — not officially by the church but unofficially by the masses of Christians filled with hate. In 1251, during the so-called Shepherd's Crusade, virtually every Jew in southern France was killed, and during the Black Plague years in the mid-1300s whole communities of Jews were massacred. Thousands of copies of the Talmud and other Jewish writings were burned over the years, and a papal bull in 1415 prohibited Jews from reading, studying, or even possessing the Talmud. As late as 1649, an Italian church leader took pride in the destruction of thousands of Jewish books.

The Jews, as non-Christians, were inherently subject to intolerance and abuse, and doubly so because of the association between them and the death of the savior in the minds of Christians. But a more ominous problem for Christianity from the 1200s through today was, as we discussed in the chapter on freethought and anthropology, the appearance and stubborn endurance of the 'Other' in their own home — the various incorrigible dissident or 'protest' sects of Christianity, even long before there was a 'Protestant' movement. Deviant Christian beliefs and sects were popping up with more and more frequency and vigor, and the church was constantly fighting such outbreaks like they were brush fires. As early as the 1200s a movement known as the Free Spirits spread across Europe. The name was appropriate, as its followers often adopted a wandering, preaching-and-ministering lifestyle. Free Spirits subscribed to a loose bundle of beliefs concerning the freedom of the soul or spirit, such that every person's soul was one with god and could be or had been perfected by that god. Sometimes they would claim that they *were* that god or that they contained that god. Since they had a direct communion with or revelation from their god, they did not need to wait for resurrection or salvation, and they did not need a religious institution to teach them about faith or to arrange for their eschatological salvation. They were free and perfect now, here on earth, and since they were perfect they could not sin anymore, so they often practiced lying, cheating, stealing, adultery or public fornication, nakedness, and other kinds of unconventional behavior generally referred to as *antinomian*. They were widely acclaimed to be insane, and some perished in prison, but most were burned for their heresy.

The Free Spirits were not alone in their fate. There was a swelling flood that would break soon in the form of the Protestant Reformation. It built up over time, producing the likes of Peter Waldo, John Wycliffe, Jerome of Prague, and Jan Hus, including many others who were themselves, or their followers, persecuted or killed. But the flood of religious deviation did not stop. Instead, it eventually crested and fell down upon the church itself, reversing the course of deviation and heresy. They and their followers were hounded, executed when possible, and even on occasion burned posthumously. But the offense of doctrinal schism and multiplication would not abate. It is no wonder at all that the Holy Inquisition first appeared in Europe around this time (early 1200s) as the anti-heretical arm of the established church. While it took many forms over the centuries before it was dismantled only in recent history, its purpose was to root out and vanquish heresy, and its very institutionalization was testimony to the level of concern felt in the church over the burgeoning protests.

The swell of protest took its crowning form in Martin Luther, who inaugurated the Protestant Reformation officially when he posted his 95 Theses or arguments against church doctrine and practice in 1517. This epoch-making action opened the door to a virtually unlimited number of new forms of Christian belief and behavior (many of which still survive today), heated up the animosity and violence within Christendom, and revived the term and charge of blasphemy in Europe. Luther himself was an adamant, even fanatical, anti-Catholic; he condemned the Church as the whore of Babylon and the pope as the Antichrist, often in the most shocking scatological language. He was naturally branded a heretic by the church, as were all 'protesters' against Catholic authority of the time. Since that term was used against him, he needed to find another term to hurl back at the Church, and 'blasphemy' was there waiting patiently to be put back into service again. To him, the Mass was blasphemy. The Pope and the papacy were blasphemies; the institution was "full of blasphemous lies" and "terrible idolatry." Catholics who did not convert to Lutheranism were committing blasphemy and should be excommunicated or exiled. Within twenty years of his original insurrection, in 1536, he called for imprisonment and execution of Catholic blasphemers.

What Protestantism, by which we mean Lutheranism, appeared to be promoting was a simplification, a 'fundamentalization,' of Christianity, a return to biblical authority and the freedom of the conscience to understand and interpret that authority. Individuals can go straight to the source, read and decide for themselves, and communicate with divinity without the assistance of a church structure. Each man could be his own priest, without the trappings and accretions of the historical church. However, this suggestion never included real toleration (Luther expected all protesters to come to his version of Christianity), and in practice — and quickly — this 'freedom' and 'tolerance' reached its limit and began to behave like any other orthodoxy — with the added problem that now, instead of one orthodoxy, there were dozens.

Luther thought that everyone who went back to the source for himself would end up sharing Luther's views and interpretations. They did not. Instead, dozens if not hundreds of new Christian sects emerged, each with a different attitude toward some aspect of the faith but each with the same attitude toward other sects — condescension or even condemnation. Arianism, which we met earlier, reared its ugly head again, still teaching that the doctrine of the Trinity was nonscriptural and that many of the church practices, like baptizing in the name of Jesus, were unprecedented and wrong. They took a Unitarian rather than a Trinitarian view of God, and they would eventually become known as the Unitarians. Perhaps the other most despised sect of the early 1500s was the Anabaptists. *Anabaptism* means 're-baptism,' and they believed that the Catholic practice of infant baptism was unscriptural and vain. Infants, being innocent, did not need baptism for salvation, and baptism prior to an individual's understanding of and commitment to the faith was pointless and wasted. For them, Christianity was a sequential call: first belief, then baptism. Anabaptism, which eventually gave rise to what we call the Baptist denomination today, appeared in the 1520s in central Europe and took a militant form in some areas, but generally it was known for its pacifism and what we might call today its 'conscientious objection.' They believed that true Christians should not bow to the state, only to their god. They refused to take any oaths of allegiance to the state, or serve in the army, accept the death penalty, or even pay tithes or church taxes. Other sects such as the Quakers, the Shakers, the Ranters, the Levellers, the Diggers, the Calvinists, the Methodists, and many more eventually took shape, and the process has not stopped nor shown any inclination to stop to this day.

It is only too predictable that the Catholic Church and the state authorities would see this as a challenge and a dangerous precedent, and accordingly Anabaptists were called heretics and often burned at the stake. The odd thing, perhaps, is that Luther joined in the condemnation of these dissidents, originally calling for their incarceration, physical mutilation (one of Europe's favorites was boring a hole through the tongue with a hot poker, to symbolize the horrible talk that the criminal engaged in), and exile. In 1530, he endorsed the government's death penalty for Anabaptists, labeling them blasphemers. The Jews too were blasphemers to him, and he recommended that their synagogues and books be burned, their homes, money, and property taken or destroyed, their rabbis prohibited from teaching, and their use of the word *God* outlawed on penalty of death. He said that he would gladly put them all to forced labor or exile, or cut their tongues out and forcibly convert them to Christianity (by which he of course meant Lutheranism).

What followed, all too predictably, were generations of religious war. The first round was fought by the dominant power, Spain under Charles V, the defender of the Catholic faith, against Protestant heresy mainly on German soil. But unlike previous schisms, this one would not die, partly for political reasons — local German princes saw religion as a means to claim and establish temporal independence in their domains, to escape the control of the centralized church. At any rate, Catholicism capitulated in 1555, in the Peace of Augsburg, in which Catholicism and Protestantism (by which we and they mean Lutheranism) agreed to 'tolerate' one another. A local prince could choose between the two faiths and establish it as the religion of his realm. Any subject unhappy with his liege's decision was at liberty to migrate to another princedom. Cities where both religions existed would tolerate both, and proselytization was forbidden; ideally, the two faiths would hold their current positions and leave each other alone. If this seemed like a reasonable settlement, and the first occasion of 'toleration under fire,' it was fatally flawed both due to the proselytizing nature of all Christianity and the obvious exclusion of any other sects from the 'peace.' All versions of Christianity besides Catholicism and Lutheranism were still identifiable as heresy and still subject to persecution. The peace held for about sixty years, awkwardly, until the Thirty Years' War (1618–48), which ravaged central Europe and cost approximately seven to eight million lives (Dunn 1970, 76). Even during the central European peace, religious wars had convulsed France (Protestant Huguenots versus Catholics) throughout the latter half of the 1500s. Anyhow, the Thirty Years' War ended with the Peace of Westphalia (1648) that guaranteed once again the right of existence to Catholicism, Lutheranism, and Calvinism at the local monarch's discretion. Greater measures were taken this time to ensure the liberties of the 'nonestablished' two religions within each territory, but other sects like the

Anabaptists were still left out of the equation and still exposed to persecution. Toleration, grudgingly won, was still applied in only a limited way: Catholics, Lutherans, and (now) Calvinists tolerated each other, but none of them tolerated anyone else.

Toleration in England and America

While continental Europe had torn itself apart and found a tentative solution in limited toleration, developments in the English-speaking world were progressing in ways more immediately consequential for modern American society. Because of its geographic isolation, schismatic sects were a little late arriving in England — although heresy was declared punishable by branding, flogging, and exposure to the elements until death as early as 1166. However, only a few individual cases resulted in such stiff penalties until 1401, when the Inquisition was extended to cover the island. Over the next 130 years, some fifty heretics were burned to death. The best known heresy was the Lollard sect based on the teachings of John Wycliffe.

As everyone knows, Henry VIII inaugurated the real Protestant Reformation in England, although for personal reasons and in a less doctrinal way than Luther. His 1534 Act of Supremacy broke the kingdom from the Catholic fold and established a local Church of England ("Anglican Ecclesia" or Anglicanism) with the head of state as the chief cleric. This touched off a royal struggle for religion that lasted for generations, as well as a hunt for heretics. Fifty-one souls were burned to death between the Act and Henry's death in 1547. However, burnings ceased after 1612 due to public sensitivities, although persecutions did not, especially of those who questioned the Trinity or the divinity of Christ. But, as in other parts of Europe, dissident groups multiplied and differentiated, many of them combining social messages with their religious nonconformity. The 1640s in particular saw the rise of Presbyterianism, Puritanism, Anabaptism, Quakerism, and the various 'social reform sects' like Ranters, Levellers, and Diggers. The response was more persecutions and more justifications for persecution. For example, Ephraim Pagitt wrote *Heresiography* in 1645 to argue in favor of death for blasphemers, and

John Bastwick championed the cause of intolerance on biblical grounds, maintaining that the Christian god himself had decreed death for "atheism, blasphemy, profanation of the Sabbath, and all manner of impiety and toleration of all religions" (Levy, 111).

A series of legal measures followed suit. The 1648 parliamentary "Ordinance for the Punishing of Blasphemies and Heresies" specified the death penalty for Atheism, Unitarianism, and the rejection of Christ's divine nature, of the authenticity of the scriptures, and of dogmas like the coming day of judgment. It also outlawed various heresies on infant baptism, salvation, free will, prayer, and such. The 1662 Act of Uniformity re-established Anglicanism as the sole religion of the state. The Test Act of 1673 ordered all officeholders or recipients of state funds to take an oath against Catholicism. These led to the Toleration Act (1689) and the Blasphemy Act (1698).

The Toleration Act, which was actually named "A Bill of Indulgence," showed just how little real toleration there still was in the land and that what little toleration there was existed not as a right but, literally, as an indulgence — that is, a grant to persist in certain limited nonconformities. While it did exempt some specific unofficial sects from persecution, it did not remove persecution as such. Baptists and Quakers were given special exemptions for some of their practices, but Catholics were still excluded (and remained so for another century) as were Unitarians, and Jews were simply ignored. The 1698 act criminalized any denial of the Trinity, of the truth of Christianity, or of the authority of the Bible. In effect, it outlawed Unitarianism, Atheism, and all non-Christian religions, and, according to Levy, it is still law today, although thankfully unenforced.

There is much more to say, and conditions waxed and waned in England throughout this time and beyond in terms of 'toleration,' but the significant point for us is that during this period the English colonization of America began, transplanting these issues and sentiments to a new land. Every school child in this country learns that the Pilgrims and the Puritans came to these shores in search of religious freedom. This is often construed, innocently or not, as implying that they came to establish religious toleration. Nothing could be further from the truth, and the settlers themselves knew it. Looking back on the first landing from a perspective of fifty years, Samuel Willard wrote in 1681: "I perceive they are mistaken in the design of our first Planters, whose business was not toleration; but were professed Enemies of it, and could leave the World professing they died not Libertines. Their business was to settle, and (as much as in them lay) secure Religion and Posterity, according to that way which they believed was of God" (Feldman 1997, 331). They came, in other words, to establish a religion — *their* religion — not religious toleration. They wanted to be in a place where they could be *tolerated*, not *tolerant*.

Their actions spoke louder than their words. Blasphemy laws were passed in Virginia as early as 1610 (the so-called Dale's Code), which set corporal punishments including death for rejecting official doctrines (essentially Anglican ones, as we will see in the following chapter). Massachusetts was even more intolerant. Nathaniel Ward, one of the early immigrants, mocked toleration by asserting that those who tolerated any religion "besides his own, unless it be in matters merely indifferent, either doubts his own, or is not sincere in it" (Levy, 240). His notion of religious freedom extended no further than this: that anyone who disputed the Puritan belief "shall have free Liberty to keep away from us, and such as will come to be gone as fast as they can, the sooner the better" (Feldman, 125). And they did not wait passively for such to eventuate. In late 1637 Anne Hutchinson and several of her followers were banished from the colony for their nonconformist views, and the year before, Roger Williams was threatened with deportation to England for advocating the separation of the Massachusetts state from the Puritan church. A 1658 law ordering banishment of Quakers and execution on their third offense led, in 1659–61, to the hanging deaths of four Quakers. Jews were naturally forbidden from inhabiting the colony as well. Blasphemy here too was a capital crime, and the story of the witch trials is already well-known.

In the rest of the colonies, things were not much different. Connecticut passed a blasphemy law in 1642, and Peter Stuyvesant of New Netherlands (later New York) wrote that

Jews should "be not allowed to further infect and trouble this new colony" (Feldman, 132). Perhaps the most famous early colonial religious act is the Maryland Toleration Act ("An Act Concerning Religion," 1649), which, much like the English Toleration Act discussed above, wasn't. It guaranteed free exercise of religion to believing Christians but created penalties for profaning the Sabbath or the Virgin Mary or the apostles, and of course for blasphemy. The act states:

> That whatsoever person or persons ... shall from henceforth blaspheme God, that is Curse him, or deny our Saviour Jesus Christ to be the son of God, or shall deny the holy Trinity the father, son, and holy Ghost, or the Godhead of any of the said Three persons of the Trinity or the Unity of the Godhead, or shall use or utter any reproachful Speeches, words or language concerning the said Holy Trinity, or any of the said three persons thereof, shall be punished with death and confiscation or forfeiture of all his or her lands and goods to the Lord Proprietary and his heirs.

Obviously no protection or toleration was offered to Unitarians, Atheists, Jews, or any other non-Christians, and accordingly in 1658 a Jew was indicted for blasphemy but escaped execution.

Why Toleration?

The next chapter will pick up the story of separation of church(es) and state from here, and it is good to remember that the founding fathers knew well what we have just discovered. So, with this ignominious history in full view, how is it that toleration ever got started, let along widely adopted and valued? As we have argued and proved, toleration is not a religious value. In fact, religious figures throughout the period reviewed above not only failed to practice toleration but conspicuously denounced it. The question for us, then, is why it evolved and where it came from.

The answers to both questions are fairly simple and related. As for why it evolved, the answer is that there was just no choice anymore, that intolerance failed and exhausted itself. No exclusivistic, totalistic religion will tolerate competition unless it has to. Religions merely learned through bitter experience that they had to.

Christianity, true to its form, tried valiantly to stamp out heterodoxy during its first millennium, with reasonable success. While it could never completely eradicate all nonconformity of thought, it did a commendable job of keeping dissent under control and marginalized for a very long time. However, the desperation of the established church was evident in the creation of the Inquisition precisely at the moment (the early 1200s) when heresies were becoming more stubborn and resistant. Economic and political changes beyond the scope of this chapter played a role too. But, whereas the church was able to extinguish or at least contain small continuous 'fires' of heresy in its early history, these fires became more and more frequent and more enormous as the 1400s and 1500s approached. Finally they were everywhere, and if one was quenched, two more broke out in its place. And gradually fewer and fewer were quenched.

Again, 'official' Christianity used every tool at its disposal to fight heresy and avoid toleration — the Inquisition, government and criminal penalties, learned argumentation, and devastating fratricidal wars. Nothing worked. Heretics kept coming, and once the flood was loosed by Luther — go to the source (the scriptures), interpret for yourself, follow your conscience — then a religious Pandora's box was opened. Where a few scattered heresies had grown before, dozens if not hundreds of sects blossomed now. They simply could not be stopped. The only other option was (grudging and gradual) acceptance of their right to life, of the possibility of co-existence without mutual genocide (or perhaps we should coin the term *deicide*). As Levy summarizes: "Theological reasons for persecution are blind to reason; secular reasons for persecution disintegrate when experience proves them to be unfounded. Religious reasons for toleration meet with prejudiced repudiation; secular reasons for toleration become acceptable when experience validates them" (211).

Put another way, religion on its own will never see the wisdom of toleration; if I am right, you must be wrong, and if I am a saint, you must be a sinner. The secular world, however, following experience and reason, understands when persecution has lost its effectiveness and when toleration is a safe and sane alternative. Before 1500 or so, no European polity had ever tried governing without an established religion, so they thought, reasonably, that religious establishment and conformity were necessary for good government and stable society. But when religious establishment and conformity simply became a vain dream, they discovered (grudgingly and gradually) that toleration (at first, indulgence) was also a sound foundation for a government and society. The American government, and the American Constitution, is the shining example of this understanding.

So the answer to the first question is 'because there was no other choice.' The answer to the second question — where did the notion of toleration come from — is 'from experience and reason,' from secular society, from an evolving liberal consciousness and consensus. 'Liberal' philosophy (in the classical 'enlightenment' sense) respects the value of the individual, the difference between thought and action, and the freedom of debate and of conscience. Religion talks about conscience but assumes (and tries to achieve) a conformity of conscience: debate all you want and then return to the fold. Religion presumes to already possess the truth, so what dissent can there be? Liberalism, experience, and reason know that truth is something we must achieve — so what use is conformity when there is work to be done?

We tolerate because it is the best response to the current situation — a situation of dizzying and unrepentant diversity of thought, opinion, and belief. In a uniform world, toleration is not only unnecessary, it is inconceivable. In a diverse world, conformity is not only inconceivable, it is unnecessary.

But the topic of toleration raises another and more troubling concern. Must we tolerate everything? *Can* we tolerate everything? Actually, based on our earlier discussions of knowledge, culture, and relativism, the problem is not quite as big or intractable as it might appear. Admittedly, we are told in America to 'be tolerant,' to 'be open-minded,' to not judge or condemn any positions or attitudes. Perhaps now is a good occasion to ask what exactly we mean by toleration. One sense of the word — the original sense historically and etymologically — is to suffer, to allow to exist, to 'put up with' despite the fact that it irritates or offends us. In other words, we refrain from killing or persecuting those with whom we disagree.

Another and stronger sense — the general American sense, hopefully — is to 'be blind or indifferent to' differences, to accept into the community of discourse on equal terms what we believe and what we do not believe. A third sense is to embrace and exhort all positions equally — for example, to take them all as equally true or to teach them all in our schools.

Now, I think we recognize the first of these as something short of toleration; it is the 'indulgence' that we saw earlier, where a majority gives permission to dissenters rather than acknowledging their equal right to their opinions. This interpretation implies that there is a correct or official reality that condescends to suffer the errors of the heretics. The second sense, which we recognized as American pluralism, does not designate a correct or official doctrine but gives free play to all in the marketplace of ideas. The third, however, is intellectually bankrupt, and I would like to demonstrate why.

At the practical level, no American tolerates everything, nor should they. We do not tolerate racism or sexism or violence or crime. We accept that such things exist, but we do not accept them as good or worthy of respect or certainly of teaching in school. Indeed, we use our public institutions to inculcate the exact opposite of these — racial and gender equality, peace and fairness, and social order. So anyone who says that we must 'tolerate everything' is talking nonsense. At a more epistemological level, our discussion of relativism sheds light on the issue. Relativism does not mean accepting everything as true or equal; in fact, *true* is either a rational conclusion or a value judgment, and in the first case it is not relative and in the second case it is not 'truth.' Some things, as we said, are either true or false, and some things are neither true nor false. As a society, we aspire to teach the true (as determined by reason) and instill the good (as defined by culture). Thus, while we do not desire to kill racists or sexists or criminals (except of the most heinous kind), neither do we have to help to promote their causes. Yet, as a 'tolerant' society we cannot deny them their public hearing.

There is a crucial distinction to be made before we can decide what must be tolerated and what need not be: there are *alternatives*, and there are *errors*. Errors are matters of propositional falseness; in the system of 'true or false,' they prove false. Alternatives are not propositional and therefore neither true nor false; they are, in a manner of speaking, parallel relativistic perspectives. For example, if someone says that women are inferior to men or that blacks are inferior to whites, they are uttering falsehood (actually, they are uttering nonsense, since 'inferior' has not been and probably cannot be defined). Racism and sexism, then, are errors, just as surely as 1+1=3 is an error or 'k-a-t' is an error or 'the sun revolves around the earth' is an error. We are under no obligation to 'tolerate' these claims and, while we do not then turn to exterminating their proponents, neither do we have to give them a forum for propounding their ideas. Rather than persecute, we educate: 1+1 in fact equals 2, cat is spelled 'c-a-t,' the earth revolves around the sun, and women/blacks are not inferior to men/whites. That is an entirely reasonable and consistent approach to such matters.

Alternatives are different. The gay lifestyle or perspective, for instance, is neither true nor false. The existence of gays does not challenge the fact of heterosexuality, nor *vice-versa*. Likewise, the female perspective (feminism) is not true or false relative to the male but is an alternative to it — and an informative alternative at that. Cultures are alternatives to each other; American culture does not make French or Japanese or Aboriginal culture false. Those who misunderstand this issue — in particular, who take their values on some point as 'truth' on the point, like fundamentalist Christians on homosexuality — will disagree, but society can make time for, can tolerate, can even teach, about these alternatives without raising questions of truth or threatening each other's alternatives. The fact of homosexuality in the world does not threaten or say anything at all about my heterosexuality, other than that it is not the only way to be. Alternatives are merely the various elements in the diversity that is human life.

Religion falls somewhere in between or straddles the error/alternative distinction. When one studies religion from a comparative-religion point of view, as do Joseph Campbell or Mircea Eliade, then religions appear to be alternatives: "Here is what Christianity says about this question, and here is what Hinduism says about it, *etc.*" As such, no truth-claim is made (unless we lie or are mistaken about our analysis of these religions, *e.g.* someone says that Jews use the blood of children in their rituals). However, devotees of a religion do not adopt this stance; from their point of view their religion is true, and so other religions are in error compared to it. Also, insofar as religions make truth-claims (about the age of the universe, *etc.*), those claims stand to be falsified by observation and logic (that is, reason and science), as we discussed previously. Thus, religion can be in error in points of fact, and we are under no obligation to perpetuate or teach those errors, like, say, creationism.

But What of Truth?

The practice of toleration, its adoption as a social value, raises one other problem that I would like to share briefly. It is this: if I believe something to be true, and I tolerate your belief that something else is true, what does that suggest about the truth of my belief? This is a subtle, almost invisible, subject in American culture, where people are at the same time tolerant and devout.

Indisputably, the original and innate intolerance of religions like Christianity is their claim to truth — they are the whole truth and the only truth, so any other claims or disagreements are automatically false. "All the great religions of the world are totalistic in essence …. It is probably an accident of history that much modern religion has become compartmentalized and respectable. 'Sects' may be more true to the essence of religion than 'churches' …. 'Churches' may be sects that have accommodated themselves to modern society" (Maloney 1988, 133). This is exactly correct, except that it is not, as we have seen, an "accident of history" but a painful lesson of history that has led religions to make peace with each other and withdraw into their respective 'magisteria.' But the more general point is well made: religions by nature do not want to make this peace, and when they are forced to, it throws some confuson on the 'truth' of the religion. Recall the four-hundred-year-old awareness of the Puritans that toleration means that one "either doubts his own [religion], or is not sincere in it."

What can it mean to say, then, that I have my belief in the truth but I tolerate you and yours? There are three main possibilities: (1) I am correct and I tolerate your 'right to be wrong,' (2) I am correct and so are you — we both have the truth, or (3) truth is not important, or there is no such thing as truth. No doubt all three of these occupy some minds or another in our society. Possibility (2) has become a popular and fashionable position, that all religions are true 'in a way' or that they all express some 'greater truth.' This is the message in the mystical/symbolic interpretations of people like Joseph Campbell or even of Stephen Jay Gould and his NOMA concept. Campbell says quite explicitly that all religions are "masks" or symbols of transcendent truths that are basically psychological in nature (the *mysterium tremendum et fascinatum*, or tremendous and fascinating mystery); people who take their specific religious forms literally are deluding themselves. Gould reasons that religion is a moral sphere but does admit that this approach does not correspond to the attitudes of many believers, who do not believe in 'morality' or 'general values' but in very particular factual claims about the natural world and the spirits that inhabit it. Both Campbell and Gould in essence tell ordinary Theists that they do not really believe what they think they believe. It is a wonder that they are as popular among the masses as they are.

So, many Americans may actually be able to entertain that their religion is true and other religions are true too — perhaps true in different ways, perhaps manifestations of a Campbellian higher truth, perhaps in a schizophrenic 'A=A and not-A' sort of way. No matter which, it evinces a curious notion of truth. Why go to your church if the other church is just as true and good? The choice becomes nothing more than a matter of taste or familiarity. It certainly shows a disregard for the exclusivity of their religion's claims and even for the idea of 'truth' altogether; Jesus did not say "no one gets to heaven except through me ... and some or all other religions too"!

Probably this perception (that my religion is true and so is yours) is some combination of civility and sloppy thinking. It is accepted as impolite to deem only yourself right and everyone else wrong, yet that is exactly what religion asks/demands that you do. Religious conviction and public civility, write Martin Marty and Frederick Greenspahn, are at odds: "Exclusivistic doctrines did not simply disappear in order to conform with the newly expected public toleration. The result was a kind of ideological schizophrenia. Inwardly, to their communicants, [religions] continue to assert that they possess the only complete version of the truth. But outwardly, in their civic relation with other churches and with the civil power, they preach and practice toleration" (1988, x–xi). This merely illustrates the ability of humans to hold two mutually contradictory ideas at the same time. James Kennedy, television evangelist and virulent anti-Atheist, echoes the sentiment for his own reasons: "From the idea of tolerance has sprung the false concept of equality. Since all religions are to be tolerated, then they must be equally valid. If they are equally valid, they must be equally good and true" (1997, 104). Of course, that is a spurious understanding of tolerance, but it highlights the central point of this chapter: "The idea of tolerance, as it's generally defined in today's culture, is neither biblical nor logical" (103). I don't know whether it is logical or not — values are not logical but nonrational, although toleration seems like a reasonable response to religious diversity — but it is definitely not biblical.

No doubt some tolerant religionists are also closet absolutists (joining Kennedy, who speaks for the intolerant religionists). They represent possibility (1) above, in that they think they are right and everyone else is wrong but are unwilling to condemn or kill them for it. In a way, this thinking is at least consistent, if impolite. As long as they stay peaceful, I suppose this is the best we can hope for from them, but we will occasionally suffer the burden of their hidden absolutism and judgmentalism when it peeks out in their evangelism or political activism. What worries me the most, though, is possibility (3), that perhaps the entire notion of truth has gotten lost or corrupted. Others worry with me, but for very different reasons. Michael Novak, whom we will see again at the end of the next chapter, who has shown himself to be no friend of Atheists, writes accurately enough:

> Tolerance used to mean that people of strong convictions would willingly bear the burden of putting up peacefully with people they regarded as plainly in error. Now it means that people of weak convictions facilely agree that others are also right, and anyway that truth of things doesn't make much difference as long as everyone is 'nice.' I don't know if 'judgmentaphobic' is a word, but it ought to be. This republic crawls with judgmentaphobes. Where conscience used to raise an eyebrow at our slips and falls, sunny non-judgmentalism winks and slaps us on the back (H. Smith, 210).

Novak is right, for the wrong reasons. Americans have demoted the concept of truth, partly because it is such a thorny and uncivil issue. It is in fact more comfortable to think that everything is true, or worse, truth does not matter, than to stand up with your minority (since every religious sect is a minority) and condemn all the rest while they do the same to you. In a way, it is intellectual surrender, and in another way it is relativism and subjectivism gone awry. Relativism, once again, does not mean that everything is true but that all judgments are made from a particular perspective. In practice, however, there is little difference — if Protestants shout down Catholics from the Protestant point of view, Catholics can shout down Protestants from the Catholic point of view. What does it get you? Radical subjectivism is a more serious problem and shows signs of penetration in our society. Whatever you think is true for you; truth is a matter of psychology or taste. But we have already elucidated this problem: rational claims, ones that are true or false, are not psychological or personal, such as whether the earth is round or flat. Nonrational claims about morals, values, norms, *etc.* are neither true nor false and should not be misconstrued as if they are. Irrational claims, such as the existence of spirits and souls and heavens and hells, should be recognized as speculative at best and false at worst, but usually just the opposite occurs. People have proven themselves particularly ready to kill each other over the nonrational and irrational sides of religion.

Conclusion: Atheism Intolerable?

Where does that leave Atheism? Certainly no contemporary world religion, if any religion ever, makes a welcoming place at the hearth for Atheists. Granted, we are not openly chased, persecuted, and killed the way we used to be, but neither are we considered completely equal and good citizens of this society. The reaction after the events of September 11, 2001, showed that beyond any question. And there are still those who do openly condemn us and others like us; Tim LaHaye, coauthor of the *Left Behind* series of Christian novels, actually expressed this sentiment: "No humanist is qualified to hold any governmental office in America — United States Senator, congressman, cabinet member, State Department employee, or any other position that requires him to think in the best interest of America .... A humanist is just not qualified to be elected to public office by patriotic, America-loving citizens" (Porteus 1991, 182). The fact that an avowed Atheist or Humanist could not get elected in this country testifies to the fact that his is not a fringe opinion.

Yet here we are, somewhere between 2% and 14% of the population, and we tend to have normal lives and careers, as long as we do not make our Atheism too conspicuous. We are tolerated in the first sense that I explained above: we are not killed for our position, although we are often shouted at and down. We are certainly not tolerated in the third sense, that is, in being esteemed as good and being, say, taught in school. In fact, as we will see again in the next chapter, there are many who think we have already taken control of government and education in this country and are not happy about it one bit (they of course confuse Atheism and religious neutrality). Whether we are tolerated in the second sense, that of indifference to us as one patch in the American quilt, is a matter of conjecture and dispute. I would say that we are not quite yet that well received.

And I will go further. Perhaps we will never be completely 'tolerable' to the majority of Christian Americans. It is sometimes said that the American Atheist movement in the early twenty-first century is about where the American gay and lesbian movement was in the 1970s or the black civil

rights movement was in the 1950s and 1960s. That is probably correct: you could still get away with a slur or a prejudice
against those groups then and against us today. It is also true
that we must probably follow the same course as those groups
if we want to change anything: make ourselves seen in society, raise a stink, demand our rights, go to court, march and
picket and demand that we be treated like any other citizen of
the republic (see Chapter Ten for more on Atheist activism).
We must at once show that we are good people like everyone
else and that we are here, now and forever, whether we are
good people or not — like it (and us) or not. After all, blacks
and gays and other discriminated minorities did not protest
for the right to be loved, only for the right to be equal.

But we face a challenge that these other groups did not,
and this is why we may always remain intolerable. Black or
gay or female or disabled or whatever — this is, in our language above, an *alternative*. I do not mean that people choose
whether they will be black or white, gay or straight, female or
male; of course they don't. What I mean is that gayness does
not challenge straightness, nor femaleness maleness, nor
blackness whiteness. Gay is another way to be in addition to
straight; female is another way to be in addition to male; black
is another way to be in addition to white. We can have both
and all in the world and nobody need get upset by it (although,
of course, some fundamentalists get very upset by homosexuality, some chauvinists get very upset about feminism, and
some bigots get very upset by civil rights). But at least there
is no sense that blacks are trying to 'convert' or refute red-
necks.

Atheism is not an alternative. In the pantheon of religions, neither is it another religion. But if it were, it would still
not be an alternative. As an analogy, Atheism is to all Theism,
not just Christianity, as Protestantism under Luther was to
Catholicism in his day: if we are right, they are wrong.
Atheism means, whether we face it (and publicize it) or not,
that Theism is at best unmerited and at worst that it is without merit. So Atheism is not to Theism as black civil rights is
to white society. We do not ask to be given a seat at the interfaith council. Philosophically, epistemologically, we ask that the
interfaith council disband. While we do not seek to persecute

PART III

The Applications

CHAPTER NINE

Separation of State and Churches — The Best Protection of Everyone's Freedoms

Congress shall make no law respecting an establishment of religion, or prohibiting the free exercise thereof ...
— from the First Amendment to the U.S. Constitution

Believing with you that religion is a matter which lies solely between man and his God, that he owes account to none other for his faith or his worship, that the legislative powers of government reach actions only, and not opinions, I contemplate with sovereign reverence that act of the whole American people which declared that their legislature should "make no law respecting an establishment of religion, or prohibiting the free exercise thereof," thus building a wall of separation between church and state.
— Thomas Jefferson, letter to Danbury Baptists, 1802

The legitimate powers of government extend to such acts only as are injurious to others. But it does me no injury for my neighbor to say there are twenty gods, or no God. It neither picks my pocket nor breaks my leg.
— Thomas Jefferson, *Notes on the State of Virginia*, 1781–2

In the summer of 2002, the passions of the American citizens were enflamed when the federal Ninth Circuit Court of Appeals, based in California, ruled that the words "under God" in the Pledge of Allegiance were unconstitutional according to the First Amendment because they violated the separation of church(es) and state. It probably did not help any that the suit was brought by an Atheist, Michael Newdow. It often seems, at least to proponents of civic if not official religion, together with many well-meaning pious Christians, that it is always Atheists starting this kind of ruckus, starting with Madalyn Murray O'Hair. This is of course a misconception, and many of the key First Amendment challenges have in fact been raised by Theists such as Jews, Jehovah's Witnesses, and Mormons to secure their religious rights against the government and the religious majority. This truth is easily overlooked by Theist critics of separation, who equate separation with official secularism and godlessness.

Following hotly after our discussion of religious tolerance, the present chapter will investigate the so-called "wall of separation between church and state," first referred to as such by Thomas Jefferson in his letter to the Danbury Baptists Association on New Year's Day, 1802. The guarantee of official religious freedom, of the non-interference of government in religious affairs and of the noninterference of religion in governmental affairs, in the United States is obviously the First Amendment to the Constitution, quoted at the top of this chapter. The amendment, which goes on to specify other rights including free speech, freedom of the press, and freedom of association and of petition to the government nevertheless opens with a detailed expression of freedom of religion. Jurisprudence has analyzed the text into two distinct and equally essential clauses — the 'establishment clause' ("Congress shall make no law respecting an establishment of religion"), which prevents the government from endorsing or supporting any particular religion or religion in general, and the 'free exercise' clause ("or prohibiting the free exercise thereof"), which denies the government the power to infringe on the practice of one's religious beliefs.

The prominence of this language indicates something important about the role of religious freedom in a free and democratic society, namely that they saw it as the cornerstone of all the other freedoms of Americans. Notably, in contradiction to those who opine that the United States is a Christian country founded on Christian principles, not one word occurs in the Constitution that would indicate ours to be a Christian or any other religious kind of government. The preamble refers to our seeking "the blessings of *liberty*," not of a god. Article II specifies the presidential oath to be taken without the phrase "so help me God." There is also the negative injunction in Article VI that says "but no religious Test shall ever be required as a Qualification to any Office or public Trust under the United States." Two incidental mentions of Christian-like practices, a reference to not working on Sundays and the characterization of the date as "the Year of our Lord 1787," hardly constitute a serious suggestion of Christian governance and certainly create no Christian political institutions but rather merely echo the fact that most early Americans were Christians and that many Christian habits had diffused into social practice. But then again, Sunday is a nonworking day in Japan, but that obviously does not make them a Christian people or theirs a Christian government!

Therefore, whatever the populace of the early United States, including the founding fathers themselves, may have held as religious convictions, no religion is advocated or established by the founding document of the new country and absolutely no religious (Christian or otherwise) government is designated. This chapter, then, will contemplate the role of separation of church(es) and state in the United States. We say 'church(es)' instead of 'church' throughout because there is no such thing as a single unified religion in this country (or any country) but a plethora of religions and churches. We will look at the foundations and motivations for making this striking decision, compare the words and deeds of the founders on the issue, and scan the history of the principle in American legal practice. Ultimately we will assess that the nonestablishment of official religion or the disestablishment of existing official religion is the best option not only for the state but for the churches too.

Separation — An All-Too-Brief History

The relationship between religion and politics is a complex subject, even within Christianity and more so in the perspective of comparative religion. Some religions have welcomed fusion of faith and government, seeing them as essentially the same thing, and others have had a more ambivalent attitude including, curiously, Christianity. The issue here, as we have already noted in passing, is 'establishment,' which means the adoption of one or more particular religions as official religions of the realm. Official or favored religions receive support from and provide support to the state apparatus. In the former case, this support might consist of funding, tax exemptions, grants of land, laws enforcing religious conformity, and perhaps even military aid; in the latter, religion provides legitimacy, advice, in some cases financial aid, and a parallel set of institutions for purposes of social control. 'Disestablishment' refers to the breakup of this (often incestuous) marriage between the two, withdrawing political assistance and power from religion and withdrawing religious doctrines and values from politics.

Some religions have been almost unable to conceive of anything approaching separation of church(es) and state. Religion is simply seen as part of the social order of society, along with politics and economics and even kinship. This is the case in many traditional and ancient societies. In Islam, partly because of the historical career of the prophet Muhammad, who was an administrator and lawgiver in Medina and Mecca, governance and faith have always been closely allied if not indistinguishable. Islam offers a set of religious laws known as *shariah* that forms the basis of politics and jurisprudence in formally Islamic states. This is why Islamic states are more prone to what we might call 'theocracy' than Western states, since Islam is an all-encompassing way of life — political and religious — in at least some interpretations of the creed.

Old Testament Judaism had a more ambivalent attitude toward mixing religion and politics premised not on a respect for but a disparagement of politics. Earthly rulers were seen as a threat to or corruption of Yahweh's government of the world, and all of the rules for social life were supposedly provided in the scriptures. Furthermore, prophets were continuously railing against kings whose worldly strivings and petty self-interests led them and their kingdoms astray from the path of righteousness. While there was never a thought that the 'politics' of Israel should be anything other than biblical and Jewish, still the arrival of the 'kingdom' of Israel quite late in Old Testament history was a traumatic event. For millennia the Hebrews had survived and thrived without a king or real 'government' in the modern sense, taking their leadership from prophets and judges. However, around 1000 BCE, as told in I Samuel, the people for the first time are supposed to have asked for a king, and the prophet Samuel warned them of the dire consequences of a temporal order distinct from the spiritual order:

> And [the people] said unto [Samuel], Behold, thou art old, and thy sons walk not in thy ways: now make us a king to judge us like all the nations. But the thing displeased Samuel, when they said, Give us a king to judge us. And Samuel prayed unto the LORD. And the LORD said unto Samuel, Hearken unto the voice of the people in all that they say unto thee: for they have not rejected thee, but they have rejected me, that I should not reign over them. According to all the works which they have done since the day that I brought them up out of Egypt even unto this day, wherewith they have forsaken me, and served other gods, so do they also unto thee. Now therefore hearken unto their voice: howbeit yet protest solemnly unto them, and shew them the manner of the king that shall reign over them. (I Samuel 8:5–9)

In the verses that follow, Samuel informs the people of all the unpleasant things that a king will do to them, yet they persist and demand and finally receive their king. But the precedent of tension and opposition between the worldly and the godly is made.

Christianity follows in this tradition of ambivalence between government and religion, temporal and spiritual, the domain of flesh and the domain of God. Christians particularly point to Jesus' admonition to "render unto Caesar" as a clear message of the fundamental schism between politics and piety, recognizing two worlds that function on different principles. That Jesus' kingdom is "not of this world" is another mighty suggestion. Of course, it was relatively easy for early Christians to avoid the entanglement of church and state for the first few centuries, since they were totally out of power and even out of favor for that time. The tradition of distance from if not disdain for temporal authority — of detachment from participation in politics, the military, *etc.* — was at once a natural growth from religious beliefs and an actual expression of their social position. However, as Christianity began to accumulate status and power in the Roman Empire, all of that had to change.

As described previously, the church evolved quickly in the 300s from a persecuted minority to a tolerated one to the religion of the Emperor Constantine I himself (324 CE) to the established religion of the state. The Edict of Emperors Gratian, Valentinian II, and Theodosius I in 380 raised Christianity to the official Roman religion. However, the wording of the Edict also raised the specter of the implications of the establishment of a single religion — Christianity or any other — as the one true faith of the realm:

> We desire all people, whom the benign influence of our clemency rules, to turn to the religion which tradition from Peter to the present day declares to have been delivered to the Romans .... We order those who follow this doctrine to receive the title of Catholic Christians, but others we judge to be mad and raving and worthy of incurring the disgrace of heretical teaching, nor are their assemblies to receive the name of churches. They are to be punished not only in Divine retribution but also by our own measures, which we have decided in accordance with Divine inspiration. (Feldman, 22).

So we see the inherent danger of an official religion: all other religions are either to be discouraged and even punished or to be denied the very status of a religion. Diversity and nonconformity become heresy and crime.

However, an established religion of the empire does not a religious empire make, and Augustine, one of the great early church fathers, voiced this view in a way that would become familiar in later Christianity. Writing not long after the Edict, his *City of God* describes two irreconcilable worlds or 'cities,' the city of God and the city of man or of the earth. The godly city is variously identified as the community of Christians that "still lives by faith in this fleeting course of time, and sojourns as a stranger in the midst of the ungodly" but also as that host that "shall dwell in the fixed stability of its eternal seat, which it now with patience waits for, expecting until 'righteousness shall return unto judgment,' and it obtain, by virtue of its excellence, final victory and perfect peace." So the city of God is in a sense recognizable in this world but also refers to a future heavenly world. Either way, though, it is separate from the worldly city or the city of the worldly, "which, though it be mistress of the nations, is itself ruled by its lust of rule." In the earthly city, humans pursue earthly interests, including their own creature comfort, their greater power and domination, their "private privileges," and naturally their false gods. Thus, the state is 'separate' by nature from the church in that the state does not seek heavenly goals and the church does not seek material goals.

So, from the beginning of Christianity's political history, there was a conception of separation of church and state, though not of course identical to our modern conception. Rather, there were two intrinsically separate dimensions of reality that could not become one even by the establishment of a church by the state — as much as church might appreciate that establishment in achieving its non-state purposes. And, inevitably, church officers deemed the religious character and mission of the church to be preeminent over the political character and mission of the state. As Pope Gelasius I wrote to the emperor himself in the 490s:

> There are indeed ... two powers by which this world is chiefly ruled: the sacred authority of the Popes and the royal power. Of these the priestly power is much more important, because it has to render account for the kings of men themselves at the Divine tribunal. For you know, our very clement son, that although you have the chief place in dignity over the human race, yet you must submit yourself faithfully to those who have charge of Divine things, and look to them for the means of your salvation. [But] in matters pertaining to the administration of public discipline, the bishops of the Church [know] that the Empire has been conferred on you by Divine instrumentality ... (Feldman 28).

In other words, not only does the church claim an exclusive existence and charter from the state, but in a sense, it maintains that *the church has established the state rather than vice-versa!*

This sacerdotal view of the world led quite inevitably to the concepts and conflicts that shaped medieval and eventually modern Western politics and religion. Temporal kings struggled with spiritual pontiffs for ultimate authority over Christendom, with popes for a time dominating the contest. For example, perhaps at the high point of the reign of priests, Pope Gregory VII (1073–85) formulated such principles as that the bishop of Rome (the 'pope') alone could select or depose church officers; that he "is the only one whose feet are to be kissed by all princes"; that he may even depose emperors; and of course that none should be called a Christian who does not conform to the traditions of the Roman church.

For a time, then, the church enjoyed a theoretical if not always practical hegemony over the state, all the while sustaining an ideology of radical otherness between the church world and the state world. In the end, though, the two were very much in collusion, kings claiming their divine right to rule and popes depending on the legal and military arm of the state to defend the faith and to enforce religious conformity. For instance, the church tended to rely on the state to mete out punishments such as during the Inquisition. And, as we learned in the last chapter, nonconformity, labeled as heresy, was mercilessly persecuted.

Still, the tension between kings and popes did not abate but only grew, as kings sought increased power within their domains, including power to invest priests and finally even to observe their own non-Catholic faith. The turning point in this history was the Protestant Reformation, when a Christian, Martin Luther, successfully resisted the word and force of the Catholic monopoly. Luther is important for the separation of church and state for two reasons: first, because he too reiterated the dual-world view of church and state, and second because he gave princes and kings the wedge they needed to break free of (Catholic) church domination. On the first count, in his 1523 treatise *Temporal Authority: To What Extent it Should be Obeyed*, he developed Augustine's dichotomy of two worlds or kingdoms, each with its own government — the religious kingdom "by which the Holy Spirit produces Christians and righteous people under Christ" and the political kingdom "which restrains the un-Christian and wicked" (Feldman, 59). Notice that, again or maybe more so, the political realm is not just associated with the flesh and its failings but specifically with non-Christians, who are tossed in among the wicked.

A significant departure of Luther was to identify secular power with the body and property of citizens and spiritual power with the *conscience*: faith, he wrote, "is a matter for the conscience of each individual .... For faith is a free act, to which no one can be forced. Indeed, it is a work of God in the spirit, not something which outward authority should compel or create" (60). While this proposition might sound as if it offered freedom of conscience, of course it is well known that Luther considered only his own version of Protestantism true and valid and that all other forms, as well as Catholicism and without equivocation all non-Christian religions, were blasphemy and heresy and punishable as such. So what he was arguing for was freedom to choose *his* religion — freedom for *his* conscience — but not to choose any other. Conscience, he concluded, ought to choose Lutheranism.

Anyhow, on the second count, princes, especially in Germany, used the Protestant schism to break themselves and their realms free from Catholic power and authority. Without Catholicism, there was no need to answer to any priests about filling political or religious offices, paying dues and tithes, and bowing to papal mandate. The violent conflict that ended (in its opening round, at least) with the Peace of Augsburg in 1555 gave the political rulers what they wanted — the right to choose, and establish, the religion for their territory. Individual subjects who did not accept the choice were free to 'follow their conscience' between either Catholicism or Lutheranism. However, the net effect was not more church-state separation but the substitution of one establishment for another.

That is precisely what happened in England, which is the most important location for the American story. As is well known, Henry VIII, a former stalwart of the Catholic church, broke from it for his own personal and political reasons (as did many a prince) and organized his own 'Church of England,' which became known as Anglican. This was clearly a case of an alternative establishment, since not only was the Anglican church the only official one in the state but the king himself was the head of the church. While it differed doctrinally and ritually little from Catholicism, the fact that it was a true 'state church' made it unique and consequential. Of course, England swung back and forth between Anglicanism and Catholicism under various rulers for about a century, but its religious character was settled sufficiently by the early 1600s that, as it embarked on its initial colonial project, it had a definite religion to carry with it.

Churches and State in Early America

The contemporary United States of America, being originally a transplant of English society onto new soil, predictably evinced its patterns in its earliest days. The first successful English colony in the Americas, Jamestown (1607 in present-day Virginia), an undertaking of English businessmen, of course would establish Anglicanism as its official religion. Settlers would be members of the Anglican church, and penalties would obtain for those who violated Anglican rules; even failing to attend services was punishable.

The colonies that formed later to the north had a different character but not an altogether different philosophy. As we told in the previous chapter, the Massachusetts colonies were settled by dissenters from the Anglican church (who were unwelcome in England, understandably enough), so they did not establish an Anglican society. However, this is not to say that they did not establish a religious society. Rather, their very status as dissenters and 'Separatists' (not in the sense of church/state separation but of separation from the doctrines and rituals of Anglicanism) made them more devout and excitable, not less. They fully expected and intended that they would design a society in conformity with their religious beliefs, one which would not tolerate differences, as the tales of Roger Williams and Anne Hutchinson among many others demonstrate. At first, admittedly, they did not attempt to use the arm of the law to enforce Puritan orthodoxy — partly out of their Christian suspicion of state power — but rather relied on "unofficial or non-governmental means: church attendance, sermons, public censure of heresy, social stigmatization, participation in (or owning) the covenant," and so on (Feldman, 123). However, by the 1640s, quite possibly under the pressure of such heresy and heterodoxy, religion began to be codified into law; the 1648 code, for instance, stipulated mandatory church attendance, obligatory taxes to support the church, and penalties for those who condemned or violated Puritan beliefs and regulations. We discussed some of the results in the last chapter.

The Cambridge Platform of the Massachusetts Bay Colony (also 1648) went further in defining the relation between church(es) and state in such a way as to free religion from the state but implicate the state in supporting the church(es):

> The power and authority of Magistrates is not for the restraining of churches, or any other good works, but for helping in and furthering thereof, and therefore the consent and countenance of Magistrates when it may be had, is not to be sleighted [*sic*], or lightly esteemed; but on the contrary; it is part of that honour due to Christian Magistrates to desire and crave their consent and approbation therein; which being obtained, the churches may then proceed in their way with much more encouragement, and comfort .... It is not in the power of Magistrates to compel their subjects to become church members, and to partake at the Lord's table: for the priests are reproved, that brought unworthy ones into the sanctuary: then, as it was unlawful for the priests, so it is unlawful to be done by civil Magistrates .... The object of the power of the Magistrate are not things merely inward, and so not subject to his cognisance [*sic*] and view, as unbelief, hardness of heart, erronious [*sic*] opinions not vented; but only such things as are acted by the outward man .... Idolatry, Blasphemy, Heresy, venting corrupt and pernicious opinions, that destroy the foundation, open contempt of the word preached, prophanation [*sic*] of the Lords [*sic*] day, disturbing the peaceable administration and exercise of the worship and holy things of God, and the like, are to be restrained, and punished by civil authority. (Feldman 126-7)

Notice that, as in conventional Christian theory, secular and spiritual affairs are separated but mutually supportive, that nevertheless spiritual outrank secular, and that, while 'conscience' or inward affairs are distinguished from 'outward' or behavioral ones and granted a certain independence from politics, yet it is specifically religious behaviors — blasphemy, heresy, and such — that the arm of the state is enjoined to control.

Two other facts are worth mentioning. The first is that, while these events were unfolding in the colonies, back in Europe the mainland, especially Germany, was tearing itself apart in the Thirty Years' War (1618–48) that followed the failure of the Peace of Augsburg, as well as other religious confrontations such as the Huguenot affair in France or in fact the Puritan affair (and revolution) in England. It was glaringly apparent to any intelligent observer that religion was a source of much conflict and bloodshed. The second is that, even as a revolution approached in the colonies themselves, the establishment of religion was still alive and well. For example, in late eighteenth-century Massachusetts the state constitution provided that "No man can take a seat in our legislature till he solemnly declares, 'I believe the Christian religion and have a firm persuasion of its truth'" (Feldman, 148). South Carolina's 1776 constitution left Anglican establishment in place, and even when the particular church was disestablished in 1778, Christianity and specifically Protestantism were established in its place. It said explicitly that "the Christian religion is the true religion" and went on as follows:

> That all persons and religious societies who acknowledge that there is one God, and a future state of rewards and punishments, and that God is publicly to be worshipped, shall be freely tolerated. The Christian Protestant religion shall be deemed, and is hereby constituted and declared to be, the established religion of this State. That all denominations of Christian Protestants in this State, demeaning themselves peaceably and faithfully, shall enjoy equal religious and civil privileges. (Feldman, 149)

Around this time, the Declaration of Independence was being drafted, presenting the colonies' reasons for seceding from England. Despite that document's reference to "Nature's God," the "Creator," and the "Supreme Judge of the world," it is important to understand that (1) it in no way lays out a plan for postrevolutionary American politics and is not the founding document of the United States government, (2) it was written thirteen years before the Constitution and therefore cannot be expected to conform to the later document, and (3) it assiduously avoids using familiar terms like *Jesus* or *Christianity*; in fact, even *Nature's God* is an atypical characterization of deity, more in line with Deism than mainstream Christianity.

Only after the Revolutionary War, and after a first unsuccessful attempt at government under the Articles of

Confederation, was the Constitution written and ratified. That document, as we know, contains even less religious language than the Declaration of Independence, and it prominently adds the First Amendment to clinch the disestablishment of church(es) from state. The intent and temper of the time is illustrated by contemporaneous acts of the various states, where much of the real sovereignty still resided: state-level disestablishment, while halting and not commanded by the First Amendment (which names only Congress as its focus), was advancing. North Carolina's 1776 constitution ended its official religious establishment, even if it retained (until 1868) a restriction of officeholders to those who profess "the truth of the Protestant religion." Virginia in 1779 repealed a law imposing taxes to support religious organizations. The 1790 South Carolina constitution also ended public tax subsidies to churches, although it allowed the state to incorporate churches. Georgia in 1798 completely did away with its multiple religious establishments (as some states tried to sidestep the thorny issue of church establishment by establishing more than one church simultaneously). Some other states were slower to get onboard the disestablishment train. Maryland and Pennsylvania still had constitutional provisions in 1776 for an oath of office that included declaring one's Christianity. Massachusetts, one of the first states to establish a church, was the last to disestablish in 1833.

Principles and Professions:
What the Founding Fathers Really Said

Much of the current debate in America on the subject of church(es)/state separation turns on what the founding fathers said, intended, and personally professed in the area of religion and politics. This is a legitimate and serious line of inquiry, but it is not the complete basis for evaluating — and certainly for rejecting — the principle of separation for three reasons: first, because while they often mentioned the term 'God' in their speeches and writings, many of them were anything but conventional Christians; second, because the founding fathers said and did contradictory things in regard to religion; and third, because what is important is not their personal religious beliefs but their public political philosophy.

One of the main arguments that Theists, particularly Christians, use in denouncing or weakening the separation of church(es) and state is that America is a Christian country and its founders were Christians who envisioned a Christian government and society. This is clearly and undeniably false. Jefferson, one of the main architects and arguably the most intellectual of the founders, was not a Christian at all but a Deist — that is, someone who does not believe in a personal god that intervenes in the affairs of the world but rather in an impersonal kind of 'clock-maker' god that creates and vanishes. In fact, the *Times Almanac 2001* lists Jefferson officially as a Deist, and James Kennedy, the televangelist who is often extremely critical of Atheists, characterizes him as "closer to an atheist" (Kennedy, 31). Incredibly enough, Jefferson's religious views were part of his 1800 presidential campaign, such that a newspaper of the day expressed the choice between John Adams and him as one between "God — and a religious president" and "Jefferson and no God" (Gaustad 1999, 50). Incidentally, Jefferson won and was reelected in 1804.

Other prominent members of the founding generation of American leaders were also unconventional Christians or non-Christians. Thomas Paine was definitely no Christian, being a conspicuous Deist as well. James Madison, arguably the prime mover in the drafting of the Constitution, spoke and wrote against religious establishment repeatedly and was Jefferson's successor in the fight to keep religion out of Virginia politics. As president in 1811, he vetoed a bill to incorporate an Episcopalian church in the District of Columbia, reasoning that it would blur "the essential distinction between civil and religious functions" (Gaustad, 51). And others like the venerable old Benjamin Franklin were at least ambiguous in their religious commitments. George Washington, probably the greatest leader but also the weakest theorist of the Revolution, was the only one who seemed genuinely pious in his words and deeds.

This takes us to the contradictory messages that the founders left in their statements and actions regarding religion. Taking Franklin as a prime example, he is noted for stating at the Constitutional Convention that "the longer I live, the more convincing proofs I see of this truth — that God governs in the affairs of men" as an urge to include prayers in the proceedings. (By the way, few of the conventioneers followed his suggestion, and Alexander Hamilton criticized the idea.) However, elsewhere Franklin had much less kind things to say of religion in general and Christianity in particular, such as the following:

- I have found Christian dogma unintelligible. Early in life I absented myself from Christian assemblies. (*Toward the Mystery*)
- Religion I found to be without any tendency to inspire, promote, or confirm morality, serves principally to divide us and make us unfriendly to one another.
- The way to see by faith is to shut the eye of reason. (*Poor Richard's Almanac*, 1758)
- When a religion is good, I conceive it will support itself; and when it does not support itself, and God does not take care to support it so that its professors are obliged to call for help of the civil power, 'tis a sign, I apprehend, of its being a bad one. (letter to Richard Price, October 9, 1780)
- If we look back into history for the character of the present sects of Christianity, we shall find few that have not in turns been persecutors and complainers of persecution. The primitive Christians thought persecution extremely wrong in Pagans, but practiced it on one another. The first Protestants of the Church of England blamed persecution on the Roman church, but practiced it on the Puritans. They found it wrong in Bishops, but fell into the practice both here (England) and in New England. ("An Essay on Toleration")

Notice how he not only refers to the irrational quality of faith as such and Christian doctrine in particular but clearly perceives the propriety of separating "civil power" from religion and the recurrent danger of religious persecution.

Thomas Paine, whom you would not expect to have many nice things to say about Christian-type religion, did not; among his many writings, such as *Age of Reason*, is this statement: "The most detestable wickedness, the most horrid cruelties, and the greatest miseries that have afflicted the human race have had their origin in this thing called revelation, revealed religion."

The considerably milder Jefferson wrote lines like these:

- Question with boldness even the existence of God; because if there be one, He must approve the homage of Reason rather than that of blindfolded Fear. (letter to Peter Carr, August 10, 1787)
- Christianity ... [has become] the most perverted system that ever shone on man. ... Rogueries, absurdities and untruths were perpetrated upon the teachings of Jesus by a large band of dupes and imposters [sic] led by Paul, the first great corrupter of the teaching of Jesus. (source unknown)
- I have recently been examining all the known superstitions of the world, and do not find in our particular superstition [Christianity] one redeeming feature. They are all alike, founded on fables and mythology. (letter to Dr. Woods, undated)
- Millions of innocent men, women, and children, since the introduction of Christianity, have been burnt, tortured, fined, imprisoned, yet we have not advanced one inch towards uniformity [of opinion]. What has been the effect of coercion? To make one half the world fools, and the other half hypocrites. (*Notes on the State of Virginia*, 1781–82)

Even the relatively pious John Adams is the author of these words: "I almost shudder at the thought of alluding to the most fatal example of the abuses of grief which the history of mankind has preserved — the Cross. Consider what calamities that engine of grief has produced!" (letter to Thomas Jefferson, undated).

Let us be charitable and accept that the evidence is at least inconclusive on the personal beliefs of the founding generation. Some used the term 'God' in documents or from their offices, but how they understood this god is unclear and probably not capable of clarification. This is just as well, because *the religious beliefs of the founding fathers are completely irrelevant to their politics*. Even if they were all screaming fundamentalist Christians, the point is that they knew the importance of separating their personal beliefs from the government of the state. Whatever they personally ascribed to in terms of religion, they could comprehend that they, and any other future rulers, should not impose those convictions on the citizens or the institutions of the state. Personal beliefs are personal and must remain so, even if they are the personal beliefs of the elected leader of the country, *because not everyone in the country shares them*.

Jefferson was the most articulate spokesman for this philosophy, and we will quote from his draft for a bill for establishing religious freedom in Virginia extensively below in relation to the benefits of the separation of church(es) and state. Here, let us remember other words of his, such as the ones at the top of this chapter, or these:"I am for freedom of religion and against all maneuvers to bring about a legal ascendancy of one sect over another." James Madison was perhaps second in grandeur in his arguments against established religion. In fact, when the debate came up over the Anglican establishment in Virginia, Patrick Henry, the great patriot and orator, proposed a 'compromise' between the existing establishment and Jefferson's suggestion for complete disestablishment. His "Bill for Establishing a Provision for Teachers of the Christian Religion" substituted a narrow establishment with a wider one — not Anglicanism exclusively but Christianity as a whole. The bill provided that "the Christian religion shall in all times coming be deemed and held to be the established religion of this Commonwealth" and that "all denominations of Christians demeaning themselves peaceably and faithfully shall enjoy equal privileges, civil and religious" (Gaustad, 38).

In response, Madison composed his rightly-famous "A Memorial and Remonstrance" to oppose the bill. In his remonstrance he makes fifteen numbered objections to Henry's proposal, the chief of which are:

- The Religion then of every man must be left to the conviction and conscience of every man; and it is the right of every man to exercise it as these may dictate.
- If establishment is allowed then "the majority may trespass on the rights of the minority."
- Who does not see that the same authority which can establish Christianity, in exclusion of all other Religions, may establish with the same ease any particular sect of Christians, in exclusion of all other Sects?
- The Bill implies either that the Civil Magistrate is a competent Judge of Religious Truth; or that he may employ Religion as an engine of Civil policy.
- During almost fifteen centuries has the legal establishment of Christianity been on trial. What have been its fruits? More or less, in all places, pride and indolence in the clergy; ignorance and servility in the laity; in both, superstition, bigotry and persecution.

- It will destroy that moderation and harmony which the forbearance of our laws to intermeddle with Religion had produced among its several Sects.

Finally, whether ironically or not, he raises the ugly issue of the comparative truth of religions by maintaining that "the policy of the Bill is adverse to the diffusion of the light of Christianity" to the large number "still remaining under the dominion of false Religions." Is government going to be the arbiter of this impossible question? At any rate, Henry's bill was tabled, and a modified version of Jefferson's original draft was approved. Jefferson wrote of that experience decades later in his autobiography:

> It still met with opposition; but, with some mutilations in the preamble, it was finally passed; and a singular proposition proved that its protections of opinion was meant to be universal. Where the preamble declares, that coercion is a departure from the plan of the holy author of our religion, an amendment was proposed by inserting "Jesus Christ," so that it would read "A departure from the plan of Jesus Christ, the holy author of our religion"; the insertion was rejected by the great majority, in proof that they meant to comprehend, within the mantel of its protection, the Jew and the Gentile, the Christian and Mohametan, the Hindoo and Infidel of every denomination.

So, indisputably, if the founders themselves or the majority of American citizens were Christians, the point is that they had the wisdom and vision to realize that they were not the only community of believers in America — even way back then — and that all religions should feel at home in America, not just Christianity. America was, and is, not a Christian country but a free and diverse country.

Religion and the Courts

Having laid down the principle of separation of church(es) and state (a phrase as we know coined by Jefferson but not used only by him; Madison also employed it when he wrote that "the Civil Government, though bereft of everything like an associated hierarchy, possesses the requisite stability and performs its functions with complete success, whilst the number, the industry, and the morality of the priesthood, and the devotion of the people have been manifestly increased by the total separation of the church from the state"), the issue of its implementation became a matter of interpretation and application — that is, a matter for the courts. Many anti-separationists, even when they must surrender the claim that America was founded as a Christian country, still cling to the true fact that, even after the First Amendment, there was pervasive religion in public institutions like schools and the government itself. This is, however, a moot argument. Anyone who understands the nature of revolutions knows that a policy stated is not a policy enacted; a revolution does not end when the shooting stops but it merely begins then. In other words, the First Amendment did not make church(es) and state separate; it provided the legal grounds for pursuing and accomplishing this separation. To suggest that continuing entanglements of religion and politics after the Constitution are an endorsement of establishment or a precedent we must honor would be to suggest that the perpetuation of slavery after that document is an endorsement of slavery or that slavery is 'an American tradition.' Some founding fathers still mixed their politics with religion, and some mixed their discourse of freedom with slave ownership. This merely proves their inconsistency as humans and the necessity of achieving the ideals that have been stated but not yet realized; it would take many decades and many conflicts before the ideal was approached, either in race relations or church(es)/state relations.

Again, the battleground for much of the struggle, in both cases, has been the federal court system, and the path was not straight in either case, as students of rulings on race issues (like the *Dred Scott* case) surely know. And it is probably no accident that the breakthroughs in both areas came in the 1950s and 1960s, when real progress toward the achievement of American ideals was made — a hundred years late for African-Americans and two hundred years late for American Atheists.

The history of religious decisions by the federal courts is too long and convoluted to tell thoroughly here, and there are excellent resources that do justice to the subject. Two points bear mentioning at the moment, though. The first is that First Amendment cases were slow to reach their way to the Supreme Court, and most cases in the early part of the nineteenth century had more to do with settlements of church property than the entanglement of church(es) and state. The second, which partially explains the first, is that the First Amendment as written expressly limits the power of Congress in regard to religion but makes no mention of state governments, so that the latter were not explicitly enjoined from mixing their politics with religion. In fact, this question seemed settled in 1845 when the Supreme Court ruled in *Permoli v. City of New Orleans* that the First Amendment did not apply to state legislatures.

However, a new era of judicial activism and church(es)/state controversy dawned with the ratification of the Fourteenth Amendment in 1868. Written with slavery rather than religion in mind, it provides among other things that "No State shall make or enforce any law which shall abridge the privileges or immunities of citizens of the United States; nor shall any State deprive any person of life, liberty, or property, without due process of law; nor deny to any person within its jurisdiction the equal protection of the laws." Gradually it was realized that this language effectively extended First Amendment and other federal protections — "the privileges or immunities of citizens of the United States" — to the state level. More cases involving religion began to find their way to the federal courts, but it was only in 1940 in the landmark *Cantwell v. Connecticut* decision that the Supreme Court formalized the relationship between the Fourteenth and First Amendments.

A few of the key steps between 1868 and today are worth reviewing, as they create the atmosphere and precedents within which contemporary church(es)/state cases are adjudicated. Interestingly although not surprisingly, many of the early disputes involved non-mainstream religious groups like the Mormons or the Jehovah's Witnesses, were concerned with 'free exercise' rather than 'establishment,' and pitted specific religious practices against civil law and authority. For example, *Reynolds v. United States* (1879) concerned the Mormon practice of polygamy. This was a particularly informative case, since a religious tenet violating a criminal statute (polygamy being illegal) was at stake. The Court affirmed Congress' right to legislate on matters of marriage law and then asked whether a religious exception could be made from such laws. The answer was no, on the basis of (1) fairness, (2) the traditional distinction between beliefs and actions, and (3) the principle of higher law and morality than religion. As the decision put it, if religions are given exemptions from civil law,

> then those who do not make polygamy a part of their religious belief may be found guilty and punished, while those who do, must be acquitted and go free. This would be introducing a new element into criminal law. Laws are made for the government of actions, and while they cannot interfere with mere religious belief and opinions, they may with practices. Suppose one believed that human sacrifices were a necessary part of religious worship, would it be seriously contended that the civil government under which he lived could not interfere to prevent a sacrifice? Or if a wife religiously believed it was her duty to burn herself upon the funeral pile of her dead husband, would it be beyond the power of civil government to prevent her carrying her belief into practice? (Alley 1999, 418)

Notwithstanding that some governments do not prevent such behavior but actually positively condone and encourage it, the Court ruled against religion and in favor of law in this circumstance. *Davis v. Beason* (1890) took up the same general question and came to the same conclusion: "While legislation for the establishment of a religion is forbidden, and its free exercise permitted, it does not follow that everything which may be so called can be tolerated. Crime is not the less odious because sanctioned by what any particular sect may designate as religion."

Into the early twentieth century, most of the cases continued to be 'free exercise' ones, with varying outcomes. The aforementioned *Cantwell v. Connecticut* brought the proselytizing activities of the Jehovah's Witnesses before the Court. Newton Cantwell and his sons were distributing literature, soliciting donations, and playing recordings in a predominantly Catholic neighborhood in New Haven. The recording was openly critical of Catholicism. Yet, the Court ruled that the Cantwells had a constitutional right to engage in this behavior on the basis that, in religion and politics alike, strong differences of opinion exist, and in both areas "the tenets of one man may seem the rankest error to his neighbor .... But the people of this nation have ordained in the light of history, that, in spite of the probability of excesses and abuses, these liberties are, in the long view, essential to enlightened opinion and right conduct on the part of the citizens of a democracy." Also in 1940, the Court decided *Minersville School District v. Gobitis*, in which Jehovah's Witnesses were denied their freedom to dissent from reciting the Pledge of Allegiance; however, it reversed itself shortly thereafter in *West Virginia State Board of Education v. Barnette* (1943), with Justice Robert Jackson making this classic expression of religious freedom: "If there is any fixed star in our constitutional constellation, it is that no official, high or petty, can prescribe what shall be orthodox in politics, nationalism, religion, or other matters of opinion, or force citizens to confess by word or act their faith therein." This is wisdom that is very appropriate to the more recent Pledge of Allegiance controversy.

Other cases relating to other religious groups followed these decisions logically:

- *Braunfeld v. Brown* (1961): Jewish businessmen who were compelled by their religion to close their shop on Saturday challenged Pennsylvania's 'blue law' requiring no business to be done on Sunday. The state law was upheld.
- *Sherbert v. Verner* (1963): A Seventh-Day Adventist was fired and denied unemployment benefits because she would not work on Saturday, her Sabbath. Although only three years after *Braunfeld*, the Court ruled in her favor and made some comments about the dissimilarities between the two cases.
- *Wisconsin v. Yoder* (1972): Amish parents objected to sending their children to public school past the eighth grade, for religious reasons. The Court ruled in favor of the parents.
- *Oregon Employment Division v. Smith* (1990): Two Klamath Indian men were fired and refused unemployment benefits for using peyote as part of the their Native

American church ritual. The Oregon Supreme Court agreed that the men's religious freedom had been violated, but the U.S. Supreme Court reversed them, on the same basis as the *Cantwell* decision — that the state had a right to regulate or criminalize such behavior. This ruling sent a shockwave through the American religious community, resulting in the 1993 Religious Freedom Restoration Act, which was also subsequently struck down by the Court (in *Boerne v. P. F. Flores* [1997]).

- *Church of the Lukumi Babalu Aye v. City of Hialeah* (1993): The Santeria practice of animal sacrifice was upheld unanimously (possibly because the Hialeah city ordinances came after Santeria rituals were already known in town).

There are other cases, of course, but this sampling indicates the range of problems and the range of responses.

Meanwhile, the other and potentially more contentious clause of the First Amendment, the 'establishment' clause, began to receive its share of attention and challenge. I say more contentious because, while 'free exercise' almost by definition relates to minority religions, 'establishment' strikes to the heart of the majority's religious sentiments, practices, and identity. Here the cases are far too many and far too idiosyncratic to discuss in much detail. Let us merely select a few of the turning-point decisions and the logic enlisted to arrive at them. For better or for worse, the issues tend to congregate around schools, both public and private.

- *Everson v. Board of Education of Ewing Township* (1947): By a 5-to-4 majority, the Court concluded that it was constitutional for this New Jersey town to provide public bus service for students attending parochial schools, on the premises of "child benefit" and of "non-exclusion" of people from services on the basis of their faith.
- *McCollum v. Board of Education* (1948): This was the first major school-facilities decision, over what is called released time. An Illinois law permitting religious groups to use public school facilities during school hours to teach religion classes was ruled unconstitutional by an 8-to-1

vote. "This is beyond all question a utilization of the tax-established and tax-supported public school system to aid religious groups to spread their faith."

- *Zorach v. Clausen* (1952): As opposed to released time, New York public schools granted dismissed-time, during which students could leave school premises to attend 'church school.' The practice was upheld, with the 6-to-3 majority stating that to do otherwise would be to express a "philosophy of hostility to religion." The minority mocked this logic, arguing that dismissed time does not differ significantly from released time.

- *Torcaso v. Watkins* (1961): In a case unrelated to education, the Court found that a Maryland law that required an oath of belief in God was unconstitutional.

- *Engel v. Vitale* (1962): This was the first major school-prayer decision. The Court annulled a New York school prayer, despite its attempts to be "non-denominational." The prayer was: "Almighty God, we acknowledge our dependence upon Thee, and we beg Thy blessings upon us, our parents, our teachers, and our Country." Although non-denominational, it was ruled an unconstitutional establishment of a religious belief.

- *School District of Abington Township v. Schempp* and *Murray v. Curlett* (1963): In two separate cases adjudicated together, Unitarian Edward Schempp and Atheist Madalyn Murray (later O'Hair) objected to religious exercises in the schools, including prayers and Bible readings. Although the exercises were voluntary, the Court outlawed them, evoking the "neutrality" of the state in religion as the reason for the finding: the 'free exercise' clause blocks the state from denying religious freedoms, but "it has never meant that a majority could use the machinery of the State to practice its beliefs."

- *Epperson v. Arkansas* (1968): An Arkansas law forbidding the teaching of evolution was vacated.

- *Lemon v. Kurtzman* (1971): This is one of the seminal decisions in First Amendment history. It threw out programs in Pennsylvania and Rhode Island that provided direct aid to nonpublic schools in the form of books, materials, and teachers' salaries. More enduringly, it articulated a three-part test to be applied to such legislation to adduce its conformity to First Amendment principles. Known as the "Lemon test," the three questions (usually referred to as "prongs") that make up the test are (1) whether the law or practice serves any secular purpose or is purely religious in nature, (2) whether it neither advances nor inhibits religion, and (3) whether it creates any "excessive entanglement" of government in religious matters.

- *Stone v. Graham* (1980): Using the Lemon test's first prong (secular purpose), a Kentucky law requiring the posting of the Ten Commandments in school classrooms was tossed out.
- *Lynch v. Donelly* (1984): In one of its 'religious display' cases, the Court approved by a bare majority (5-to-4) a Christmas crèche in Pawtucket, Rhode Island. The majority opined that the manger scene in the display "depicts the historical origins of this traditional event long recognized as a National Holiday," somehow missing its sole meaning as a Christian event.
- *Wallace v. Jaffree* (1985): Recognizing it as a ploy to reintroduce prayer into schools in another guise, the Court shot down Alabama's 'moment of silence' policy.
- *County of Allegheny v. ACLU* (1989): The Court struck down a nativity scene and cross on public property in Pittsburgh but let stand a menorah.
- *Lee v. Weisman* (1992): The majority of the Court found the participation of a clergyman in public school graduation ceremonies unconstitutional. The majority decision referred to constitutional principle, while the dissent emphasized tradition.

And so on.

While the controversy persists and will persist forever, these examples at least should give some sense of the magnitude and ambiguity of the issue. But the real question is not what we have done in the past but what we will do in the future, and why.

Why Separation Is a Good Thing for Everyone

Precedent is a valuable thing, depending on the principle behind the precedent. We most emphatically do not want to recreate everything that happened in our checkered national or species past. So the fact that the founding fathers separated church(es) from state over two centuries ago, or the fact that the courts have (not altogether consistently) upheld this separation, is only part of the argument for preserving the philosophy and practice. The other and still more compelling reason for maintaining a high wall between state and church(es) is that it is *good, for everyone — today*.

It would be possible to list all of the benefits that flow from the disestablishment of religion, but no one has done so more thoroughly or cogently than Thomas Jefferson, so we should let him have the word on this issue. In his draft bill for religious freedom of 1779, he offered the following reasons why a society should recognize and respect the complete and unadulterated freedom of religion. He argued

> that all attempts to influence [religious convictions] by temporal punishments, or burdens, or by civil incapacitations, tend only to beget habits of hypocrisy and meanness; that the impious presumption of legislators and rulers, civil as well as ecclesiastical, who, being themselves but fallible and uninspired men, have assumed dominion over the faith of others, setting up their own opinions and modes of thinking as the only true and infallible, and as such endeavoring to impose them on others, hath established and maintained false religions over the greatest part of the world and through all time; that to compel a man to furnish contributions of money for the propagation of opinions which he disbelieves and abhors, is sinful and tyrannical; that even the forcing him to support this or that teacher of his own religious persuasion, is depriving him of the comfortable liberty of giving his contributions to the particular pastor whose morals he would make his pattern, and whose powers he feels most persuasive to righteousness; and is withdrawing from the ministry those temporary rewards, which proceeding from an approbation of their personal conduct, are an additional incitement to earnest and unremitting labours for the instruction of mankind; that our civil rights have no dependence on our religious opinions, any more than our opinions in physics or geometry; that therefore the

proscribing any citizen as unworthy of the public confidence by laying upon him an incapacity of being called to offices of trust and emolument, unless he profess or renounce this or that religious opinion, is depriving him injuriously of those privileges and advantages to which, in common with his fellow citizens, he has a natural right; that it tends also to corrupt the principles of that very religion it is meant to encourage, by bribing, with a monopoly of worldly honours and emoluments, those who will externally profess and conform to it; that though indeed these are criminal who do not withstand such temptation, yet neither are those innocent who lay the bait in their way; that the opinions of men are not the object of civil government, nor under its jurisdiction; that to suffer the civil magistrate to intrude his powers into the field of opinion and to restrain the profession or propagation of principles on supposition of their ill tendency is a dangerous fallacy, which at once destroys all religious liberty, because he being of course judge of that tendency will make his opinions the rule of judgment, and approve or condemn the sentiments of others only as they shall square with or differ from his own; that it is time enough for the rightful purposes of civil government for its officers to interfere when principles break out into overt acts against peace and good order; and finally, that truth is great and will prevail if left to herself; that she is the proper and sufficient antagonist to error, and has nothing to fear from the conflict unless by human interposition disarmed of her natural weapons, free argument and debate; errors ceasing to be dangerous when it is permitted freely to contradict them.

A more complete or poetic statement of the case would be difficult to make.

So, then, the separation of church(es) and state is good not only for the state but also for the church(es), as well as for the third and often-overlooked interest group in the situation, the citizenry itself. Official disestablishment is good for the state (that is, the government) in a variety of ways. First and foremost, it keeps politics above or outside of the fray of religious controversy. The state is not dragged into doctrinal or sectarian disputes, which have proven throughout time to be divisive and intractable; particularly, it is not required to take sides with the official religion against other religions. It is neither compelled nor allowed to make laws that disadvantage one religion or sect. It is left to say and do things that all of the populace can agree on — or at least that they can debate on, since religious issues are not resolvable by debate the way political ones are. It is not forced to attempt to define or regulate religion, which is not the expertise of civil magistrates; would you want the government telling you what is a religion and what is not, what is acceptable prayer or ritual or so on and what is not? It is not corrupted by the wealth or interests of religious factions. And it is not called upon to spend its limited public funds on religious projects that would be fractiously argued over in Congress (although current actions by the administration jeopardize this). For example, if the government were to provide support to religious schools, it would either have to support all schools equally — including Protestant Bible schools, Muslim madrasas, Wiccan coven-schools, and every other — or give good reasons why it was including some and excluding others. It would be exceedingly difficult to do so without demonstrating preferential religious values itself.

Disestablishment is actually good for the church(es) too, although that might be a little less obvious. It is a historical fact that American religion entered a kind of Golden Age immediately after disestablishment, when new sects flourished and the general level of religious engagement rose. While as an Atheist I am hardly excited about the expansion of religion, it is a truth that by not favoring any single religion, society in effect supports all religions — at least, supports them to go out there and do what they can and succeed or fail on their own. A few of the more enlightened or experienced religious sects today understand this; some of the minority religious sects also understand the converse danger. If a religion is established, it will probably not be theirs. That is one reason why Jews, Mormons, Jehovah's Witnesses, Seventh-Day Adventists, and other like groups have often been champions of disestablishment (although some, like the Mormons, turn around and effect a virtual establishment in their own territories). In other words, establishment might be good for one religion, but it would be bad for all the rest.

Furthermore, there are practical difficulties with establishment, even for the churches. In America, official state sponsorship comes with state regulations, about hiring and benefits and other nondiscrimination practices. Religions that disfavor, for example, gays or nonbelievers would suddenly come under federal laws demanding equal treatment of such people. In other words, government would have a much stronger voice in what churches do and say and ultimately believe. Also, the acceptance of public money would mean an opening of church ledgers to show how that money was spent. Putting churches on the public dole would in some ways threaten their uniquely religious mission, as they would become more like every other public institution or program. Leaving them to their own devices, in a market-based society like ours, means that they will have to compete more effectively and give the people something of value to them — or else fail. Finally, as history too has illustrated, making civil servants out of the clergy has tended to degrade the clergy itself by implicating them in worldly pursuits of wealth and power. By being constrained within the religious sphere, they can (more easily if not completely) resist the temptations and intrigues of political life.

The state and the church(es) are important in the discussion of church(es)/state separation, but neither is the real central point of disestablishment; rather, the real point and the real benefactor of religious freedom is the citizenry. Religion, when it is not established, supported, or advocated by the government is a true matter of conscience and not of compulsion; if churches mean what they say about the personal character of faith and about conscience, then they should welcome disestablishment. Also, members of minority religions will be free from the predatory practices of official and favored religion. In an honestly free-market religious environment, niche religions can survive, and people will be able to choose the religion that suits them most. Of course, not all religions — especially the larger and powerful ones — want a level playing field, any more than all large corporations want one. But that's precisely the point: no church could sit back on its past successes and continue to water at the public trough.

Other benefits of disestablishment for the people are cultural and financial. No one can be, at least legally, persecuted or disbarred for his or her personal convictions. Inevitably, if there is an orthodoxy, then everything else is heterodoxy and discrimination follows. If religion is really voluntary, then opting out is and must be an acceptable possibility. Contrary to what some critics think, the First Amendment, in promoting freedom *of* religion also grants freedom *from* religion. Freedom is not freedom if it only entails a choice between a set of options and not a freedom from choosing any of those options at all. And finally, there is the money side of things. If the state establishes all religions or some religions or one religion, then tax-payers are being obliged to support religious positions that they may disagree with, dislike, or even fervently despise. Some Protestants do not want their money going to Catholic institutions, some Christians do not want theirs going to non-Christian institutions, and no doubt some non-Christians do not want theirs going to Christians. Better to avoid the entire problem and let those who believe support their own, and let churches undertake only such projects as they can afford from their religious sources.

Conclusion: An Atheist Agenda?

Despite the fact that the separation of church(es) and state is good for everyone, Atheists included, opponents of disestablishment often see an Atheist conspiracy in First Amendment cases and in the very principle of separation. They are misguided and uninformed. Dramatically, of the many First Amendment cases we reviewed above, few were — in fact perhaps only one or two were — brought by Atheists. Rather, it was Jews, Mormons, Jehovah's Witnesses, Unitarians, Santerians, and others who protested specific practices and laws. And that is the whole point: America is a religiously diverse society, and disestablishment protects religious diversity.

For, you see, it is impossible to establish 'religion' because, as we have repeatedly warned, there is no such thing as 'religion.' *Religion* is a general term for all the various religious denominations and sects in the country and the world. It is nearly impossible to establish 'Christianity,' because that too is a term for a widely divergent set of sects. It is of limited usefulness even to establish one flavor of Christianity, like 'Protestantism,' since there are so many different Protestant denominations, some with strongly differing beliefs and practices. In other words, whatever 'church' you choose to establish, an awful lot of churches are left out of the establishment.

The word *sect* is an informative one in this context, since it reminds us that each 'church' is a sect that represents only a *section* of the population. No matter what sect you establish, support, promote, encourage, *etc.* not only other sections but the *majority* of the population is disenfranchised. That is problem number one. Problem number two is that established religions almost always use their favored status as a weapon against other religions; it is a law of nature. A particularly glaring example at the present moment emerges from the voucher debate, with a number (thirty-six to be precise) of states discovering that they have constitutional language that prohibits public support of religious schools. These so-called 'Blaine Amendments' (named after nineteenth-century politician James G. Blaine) were explicit efforts by the Protestant majority to block aid to Catholic academies. They have been recognized as such by twentieth-century lawmakers; the Arizona Supreme Court in 1999 addressed them as part of a greater plan "to institute a general war against the Catholic Church," adding that "we would be hard pressed to divorce the amendment's language from the insidious discriminatory intent that prompted it."

The fact of the matter is that religions are, almost universally, monopolistic, expansionist, and predatory. Each wants to be the sole truth and the sole law, and each, given the opportunity and power, will attempt to drive others to extinction. In the process, as we saw in the previous chapter, persecution, discrimination, and worse will prevail. The memory of this truth was still fresh with our founding generation, even while religious diversity in America was not very advanced in their time — there were few Jews, no Muslims, and hardly anybody had even heard of Hindus, Buddhists, and hundreds of other religions. Jefferson was remarkably prescient in including in his vision of religious freedom "the Jew and the Gentile, the Christian and Mohametan, the Hindoo and Infidel of every denomination."

When the Ninth Circuit Court of Appeals decision on the Pledge of Allegiance came down in June 2002, the logic of the decision was articulate and unimpeachable: "A profession that we are a nation 'under God' is identical, for Establishment Clause purposes, to a profession that we are a nation 'under Jesus,' a nation 'under Vishnu,' a nation 'under Zeus,' or a nation 'under no god,' because none of these professions can be neutral with respect to religion" (Judge Alfred Goodwin, *Michael Newdow v. U.S. Congress et al.* 2002, 9123). Despite the foolish argument that 'God' is not religious (after all, is 'God' not a proper name for the deity of a particular religion, and don't all Christians know that piercingly clearly?), if it is intent that we want to know, as with the founding fathers, then the intent of the 1954 inclusion of "under God" is perfectly certain. The legislative record from that year states:

> At this moment of our history the principles underlying our American Government and the American way of life are under attack by a system whose philosophy is at direct odds with our own. Our American Government is founded on the concept of the individuality and the dignity of the human being. Underlying this concept is the belief that the human person is important because he was created by God and endowed by Him with certain inalienable rights which no civil authority may usurp. The inclusion of God in our pledge therefore would further acknowledge the dependence of our people and our Government upon the moral directions of the Creator. At the same time it would serve to deny the atheistic and materialistic concepts of communism with its attendant subservience of the individual (9126).

Then-president Eisenhower himself said on the occasion of authorizing the change to the pledge: "From this day forward, the millions of our school children will daily proclaim in every city and town, every village and rural schoolhouse, the dedication of our Nation and our people to the Almighty" (9125–6).

Yet politicians and pundits alike had the ignorance and audacity to condemn the *Newdow* decision as a pro-Atheism endorsement. Admittedly, the plaintiff was an Atheist, but does that principle make *Minersville School District v. Gobitis* a pro-Jehovah's Witness case or *Sherbert v. Verner* a pro-Seventh-Day Adventist case? Michael Novak (2002) of the *National Review* wrote that *Newdow v. U.S. Congress* is part of the Atheist agenda "to make the United States in all her public manifestations reflect an atheist's view ... [that this] nation must so thoroughly appear to be atheist in public as to be, in fact, and for all practical purposes, atheist in all public spheres." Bob Just of *WorldNetDaily* (2002) similarly fretted that by increments in the courts Atheism "is thus able to rise to a legal dominance never seen before in America, never even imagined," where " 'disbelief' is considered to be on an equal footing with 'belief,' " resulting in a situation where "not only will faith find itself unwelcome in our halls of power, it will eventually be removed from the body politic like a threatening tumor." If only!

Both analysts base their opinions on the same flawed perceptions of the founding fathers and the First Amendment and of conscience as well as, perhaps most alarmingly, their certainty of the superiority of monotheism in general or Christianity in particular. They misquote and decontextualize the founders to make them sound like Christians, which we know absolutely now that they were not. They object, in self-contradictory fashion, that Atheism triumphant will constrict religious conscience until "it is totally squeezed down into private life" (Novak 2002), which is where conscience is, isn't it? But most egregiously they commit the very error that the First Amendment and (almost) all jurisprudence protects us from: presuming that theirs is the best religion and therefore deserves special status.

According to Novak,

few other world religions require that their God must be worshipped "in spirit and in truth." It is not clear, for example, that Buddhism is even to be understood as a theistic religion; and probably not Animism, either. For most world religions, such as those of ancient Greece and Rome, all that is required is external observance: bow your head, bend your knee, burn the incense, say the words. There is no personal God to see directly into your heart as in an open book. Not so, Judaism and Christianity (Novak 2002).

According to Mr. Just,

[the Ninth Circuit Court decision] revealed another established belief, that monotheism itself — the pumping heart of Western culture — is just another form of worship, essentially no different, as far as the government is concerned, than, say, worshiping [sic] ancient Greek gods like Zeus and Hera .... The bottom line? If you are someone who thinks that thunder happens "when the gods are angry," or if you burn incense to a rock you found on the beach, or if you believe in nothing at all, you've got as much potential credibility with this new government as those who believe the biblical worldview that reveals God as "love," that speaks of the struggle between good and evil, and promises hope of true freedom and eternal peace for all mankind. (Just, 2002)

Precisely, Mr. Just. From the government's point of view, they are all equal and equally protected.

Finally, both writers condescend to Atheists: "One must feel sorry for atheists," mourns Novak. "They seem so lonely. Alone not only under the vast stars of a summer's night ... [but] alone also in this religion-drenched country, most of whose public spaces reek of faith in the God of Abraham, Isaac, and Jacob." Just reminds us, as if we need reminding, that "atheists like Newdow will always feel like outsiders in a nation under God .... That's the reality of it." And it was the senior member of the Senate, Robert Byrd, who actually called us "pernicious atheists" immediately after the decision.

The real issue, and the one that only emphasizes the value of the First Amendment and the fact that the struggle for First Amendment actualization is far from complete, is that it is not only Atheists who are made to feel lonely in this "religion-drenched" society but also all non-Christians, including Jews, and even some Christians, such as Jehovah's Witnesses, Seventh-Day Adventists, Amish, Mormons, and others. They too are made to feel like outsiders in a country that supposedly prides itself on inclusiveness and equality. Please note again that most of the free-exercise and even establishment cases have had nothing to do with Atheism at all.

If Atheists have an agenda, and I think they do, it is not in defiance of the words or spirit of the founding fathers. Indeed, it is perfectly in tune with them: to realize true freedom and equality and acceptance for all convictions and opinions. The only means to this golden end is strict neutrality in religious matters on the part of the government — that is, strict separation of church(es) and state. The unforgivable, perhaps even deliberate, error on the part of antiseparationists is that neutrality somehow equates to hostility. The exact opposite is the truth: neutrality is liberation. The government cannot prevent you from practicing whatever religious belief you desire (including praying to rocks), but more importantly it cannot tell you what to believe or to believe at all. That is not government's job, and if Theists are serious about faith being a matter of conscience, they should celebrate the fact, not bemoan it. But of course they are not serious; from the beginning of religion, 'religious conscience' has meant that you should believe 'in your heart' what the establishment tells you to believe. Wise Theists would join Atheists in upholding church(es)/state separation, for as Sam Ervin writes, the assumption that the First Amendment prohibits or is hostile to religion "is without foundation. While it forbids government to teach religion, the First Amendment leaves individuals, homes, and non-governmental institutions, such as Sunday schools, churches, and private schools, free to do so. Indeed, it encourages them to do so by securing religious freedom for all" (Alley 1985, 222).

CHAPTER TEN

Spreading The Unfaith — Atheism As Good News

It appears to me (whether rightly or wrongly) that direct arguments against Christianity and theism produce hardly any effect on the public; and freedom of thought is best promoted by the gradual illumination of men's minds which follows from the advance of science.
—Charles Darwin, letter to Karl Marx, 1880

One of the more remarkable questions that we Atheists are confronted with is whether we should, or even can, 'proselytize' or 'evangelize' Atheism — that is, actively attempt to spread the position, to 'convert' other people to our viewpoint. The answer, surprisingly or not, is often negative, often from some of the most ardent Atheists. Why is this?

Part of the reason for the aversion to proselytization or evangelization is the association between these behaviors and the very religion(s) that we seek to distance ourselves from. But is this an appropriate reaction? I would say no. After all, proselytization or evangelization is not a necessarily or exclusively religious thing. *Evangelization* simply derives from the Greek for 'doing or bringing a good message' (*eu-angelos* equals 'good messenger'). As we can see, the very word *angel* does not have uniquely religious denotations but refers to a messenger. Evangelization does not, therefore, entirely evoke associations of conversion, any more than bringing any other good news does. Of course, it might be hoped that the hearer of the good news will take it to heart (and mind) in some way.

The same argument can be made for proselytization. *Proselyte* comes from the Greek for something akin to 'to go near' and generally refers to an individual who changes from one position (religion, party, or philosophy) to another. To proselyte, according to *Webster's*, is both to move from one stand to another and to seek recruits to your stand, and proselytization is nothing more than the process of changing or seeking change in others. Again, there is nothing distinctly religious about the business.

Rather, in both cases (of evangelization and proselytization), we have allowed religion to commandeer the language and to monopolize the terms. We are made to feel that religion owns those words and processes and that if we use them or practice them, we are doing religion in some way. Instead, here as in many other domains, we need to reclaim the discourse and strip religion of its allegedly exclusive ownership of these phenomena. Or, if we cannot wrest the language away from religious domination, we can at least recognize the fallacy in thinking we are acting like a religion just because we practice a few of the tactics that religion practices. This is one of the other reasons Atheists give for eschewing evangelization: "We don't want to be like religion." However, as we have established firmly several times already, sharing one aspect in common with some entity does not make us indistinguishable from that entity. To think otherwise is to commit the fallacy of composition: since we are like them in one way, we are like them in every way.

Thus, on two frequent grounds — that proselytization is impossible for Atheism since it belongs to religion, and that proselytization is unseemly for Atheism since it does not want to comport itself like a religion — the objection to aiming to spread the view is unfounded. Perhaps we still prefer to use other terms for what is essentially the same process, like *advocate* or *exhort*. Even then, some Atheists still reject the notion of becoming advocates for Atheism, on the basis that such activity is negative and critical — you cannot convert people away from their religion without speaking negatively about religion. Others think that it is undignified to do the things that are often done to advocate for a cause, like knock on doors, make telephone calls, and wear a sandwich board on a downtown street corner. But is it really necessary to be destructive to spread the news of Atheism — and is it really destructive to inform someone that their beliefs are unsound to the point of obvious falsity — and are these methods really the only means at our disposal? I seriously doubt it.

Yet other Atheists simply do not have the time to make a career out of Atheism; that is one of the major differences between Atheism and Theism — there are few if any 'full-time Atheists,' while there are legions of full-time Theists (priests, ministers, councilors, *etc.*) to keep their juggernaut going. And of course it cannot be overstated that most Atheists are timid Atheists, who do not want to advertise their Atheism to the world at large for fear of reprisals — professional, personal, and bodily — which, being a valid concern, is a sad commentary on the society of the twenty-first century. So most Atheists in America today are content (well, maybe not *content*) to visit the occasional Web-site, perhaps read an Atheist book, sometimes join an Atheist group and talk with other Atheists, or often just rail at home against the absurdity and invasiveness of religion in society.

So, what are we to do? Does all this mean, then, that Atheism *should or should not* proselytize or evangelize or advocate or whatever, or that it even *could if it wanted to*? Those are very different and much more complex questions. I will consider them now in terms of some recent dialogue that has occurred in the Atheist community, approaching the issue first through the question of whether Atheists should join Atheist organizations, or even whether such organizations actually exist (they do). Then I will discuss what an 'activist' or 'advocatory' Atheism might look like and arrive at the destination that, while Atheism as a *conclusion* of a reasoning process might not be evangelizable, the *process itself* certainly is and definitely should be. In other words, I will support a kind of Darwinian Atheism, according to the opening quotation of this chapter, that advocates reason and education, which, I hold, should and will lead to the inevitable conclusion of Atheism.

Should You Join an Atheist Group?
Is There Any Such Thing?

I was astounded to read an opinion some time ago that most Atheists will never join an Atheist group, mainly on the grounds that there are no such things. The analysis came from an article entitled, aptly enough, 'Why Most Atheists Will Never Join an Atheist Organization' (Versluys 2001). It was written by an Atheist, yet it starts out in its first paragraph to stereotype Atheists as folks who have merely had a bad personal experience with religion, as if that personal reason for rejecting religion demeans Atheism. If it is probably true that most Atheists are not 'natural Atheists' but 'born-again Atheists,' that seems irrelevant to the status of Atheism. Perhaps it was such an experience that got them thinking for the first time about the contradictory or absurd nature of their religions.

The author then goes forth to castigate Atheist organizations as nonexistent. He writes: "The very good reason why most atheists would never dream of joining an atheistic organization is because most atheistic organizations are not atheistic at all, they're shills for ideological commitments other-than-atheism." He specifically implicates liberal causes like "humanism, vegetarianism, identity politics, and all sorts of patent nonsense" including crystals and shakras and socialism. He concludes that he has found no more than one Atheist in all the world that he would even care to talk to (that happening to be the editor of the magazine the article is published in), and goes so far as to say that "I have found my repulsion for organized atheists grows in direct proportion to my exposure to them."

Well, then, here is someone who should probably not join an Atheist organization! The level of Atheist self-loathing in the discussion is fascinating, informative, and probably not singular. The contention that all Atheists are damaged and vengeful children is of course reprehensibly false and would be irrelevant if it were true. The fact that he only knows one Atheist worth his breath probably just means that he needs to get out and meet more Atheists. But there actually are two issues in the article with some merit. The first is that Atheism is not a totalistic worldview. Atheism is the conclusion (not the belief) that there are no gods. It entails or demands no claims about politics, diet, or medical practices. Now, there is no doubt whatsoever that most Atheists are liberal in their general outlook, since godlessness is the most 'liberal' of all possible positions. However, there are Atheists who are conservatives — even Republicans! — or who oppose abortion or gun control. This is not to say that the overall Atheist community is not sometimes unfriendly to such views, but Atheism is just one among the conclusions and opinions of the typical Atheist.

It would have been useful to draw the crucial distinction between Atheism and Rationalism. Atheism is a rationalistic stance, but not all Atheists arrive at Atheism by way of Rationalism, and not all Atheists practice Rationalism flawlessly in every department of their lives. I would like to think that rationality, good old-fashioned skepticism, would rule out pseudoscience like pyramid-power and astrology, and I have no place for those things in my life, but Atheism does not equal or compel extreme rationality in other parts of a person's psyche. I would prefer if it did, but that is another question. On the matter of political positions, there is again no doubt that Atheism 'goes better' with liberalism than conservatism (especially classical liberalism, with its values of individual freedom and enlightened rationalism), but conservative — especially fiscally conservative — Atheists do exist and do belong to our organizations. The point is that you cannot predict absolutely peoples' other views and commitments from their Atheism.

The second issue worth raising from the otherwise negative article is that Atheists do in fact tend to be contentious, critical (of each other as well as the religious society surrounding them), self-important, and solitary creatures. If it is actually true that most Atheists will never join groups, it is more likely to be explained by the radically individualistic nature of Atheists than the inferior qualities of the groups; in other words, if Atheists are disinclined to join Atheist groups, it is less because the latter are atheistic than because they are groups. As the ultimate freethinkers, Atheists are unwilling to accept the opinions and authority of others, making typical group dynamics difficult. They are not followers or even joiners, and it is a struggle to keep a group going if the members have their own untamed wills (as any Atheist-group organizer will attest). Many, if not most, are well-informed and well-read, so they do not quietly tolerate others telling them what to think or do. These are obstacles indeed to atheistic organization. Insurmountable obstacles? Clearly not, since there are functioning Atheist groups out there. But it threatens to keep such groups small and volatile.

A more extensive critique of Atheist organizations came recently from the editor of *Positive Atheism* magazine, Cliff Walker (2000). Walker asked the question, not whether organized Atheism is possible or currently exists, but whether it is "even a valid approach." This is a question, interestingly, that some Theists also use against Atheism: what would Atheists do in atheistic organizations other than ask each other, "Do you still disbelieve in god? Yeah, me too." Notwithstanding that the same silly and dismissive question could be directed at religion (what do you do in church every week besides ask each other, "Do you still believe in god? Yeah, me too"), Walker's criticism goes far beyond such a simplistic inquiry. He posits three possible reasons for Atheist groups, which he then sets out to discredit.

The first of his justifications for Atheist organizations is socio-political activism, which is "the only remotely valid reason I can think of for organizing as Atheists." If the goal of such activism is church(es)/state separation, then there is no reason why the groups should be exclusively or primarily atheistic; in fact, he argues, with some merit, that many Theists share this interest. Yet, atheistic groups do not welcome Theists into the club, leading him to suspect: "Something else is going on in addition to the activism."

The second possible justification is "propagating atheism to the public" or proselytizing Atheism. He rejects this avenue for one of the reasons that we considered at the outset of this chapter, namely, that propagating Atheism amounts to no more than debunking religion. He, like the skeptics and Humanists but unlike the Atheists, is untroubled by the truth-status of religious claims and is only worried by "the more destructive manifestations of religious charlatanry." Religion being private, and sometimes even positive and beneficial, there is no cause for going after religion as if it were an enemy. Further: "If I am going around trying to deconvert religionists, then I have no business complaining when they try to convert me, or even when they stage high-profile evangelism campaigns, for that matter." He calls proselytization, as we said above, undignified.

The third and final possible justification in his analysis is what he dubs "the oasis approach," that is, the argument or sentiment "that atheists make superior company ... or that congregating in a group of fellow-atheists is like an oasis in a desert of irrationality. It also suggests that we may do well to form a 'support group,' of sorts, to help one another cope with the stigma of being an atheist and the bigotry that many of us endure." However, he dismisses this notion on the bases that (1) Atheists are not superior company to Theists, (2) that living alongside Theists is no big deal, and (3) that if we do retreat to an Atheist oasis, "we'll never learn to cope with being a minority in a world that's set up to suit the needs of other people."

I acknowledge the three reasons that Walker lists as probably the three preeminent explanations for atheistic aggregation. I disagree with his evaluation of all three of them. Let's look at activism first. Activism is a prime motivation for association and mobilization, whether the cause is to advance Atheism or button-collecting. If button-collectors want to advocate for the rights and interests of button-collectors, I see no possible argument against their freedom and rightness to do so. Perhaps the question is not whether Atheists have a cause that they are within their rights to organize and act on, but what precisely that cause is. Walker can only recognize church(es)/state separation as the activist goal of Atheist collectivities, and he thinks like-minded Theists should be included as well. In fact, there are several groups in American society that do exactly that; the American Civil Liberties Union, Americans United for Separation of Church and State, and the Freedom from Religion Foundation, among others, are organizations that welcome Theists and Atheists alike in their socio-political struggles to maintain First Amendment protections. Why, the head of Americans United is a reverend, Barry Lynn. Of course, one might argue that these are not, then, 'atheistic' organizations, but that is precisely the point: a group need not be explicitly or formally atheistic to propound separationist or other religious freedom positions.

However, church(es)/state separation is not the only cause of action for Atheists. Atheists are also concerned about the civil rights of Atheists as a minority in a religious society. We are proponents of rationality and freethought, specifically but not exclusively in the form of science education. We are critics of biblical morality. We are, above all else, skeptics and truth-seekers, with little respect for the sanctity of religious 'facts.' Religionists can join us in some of these principles, but not all, as we have seen all too clearly: some recognize our right to exist as equals in American society, and some want us the hell out. Some support rationality and science, but not (as we saw in the earlier chapter on science and religion) when those forces oppose or corrode religious truths or values.

I have nothing against groups that want to and are able to integrate Theists and Atheists in the cause of certain worthwhile goals or principles. I belong to some such groups myself. And there is nothing wrong with strategic alliances between purely atheistic groups and other, non-atheistic groups when their agendas coincide. However, as we sometimes see, even the agendas of liberal groups like the ACLU do not invariably parallel those of purely atheistic groups like American Atheists. For those moments, action *as Atheists* is appropriate and desirable. Besides, in organizations like the ACLU, where the Atheist component is a minority (making us a minority of a minority), it is possible that we will once again be voted down or lost in the larger constituency. It is therefore right and appropriate that there be groups that speak with an unalloyed atheistic voice. To say otherwise would require saying as well that women or African-Americans or button-collectors or any interest group have no right to associate *as members of that group* in representing and speaking for themselves. I think no one would want to take this stand. Surely, African-Americans should work with and join with other racial groups, and women with men, when possible and advantageous, but to deny them the right to gather and meet as members of their group, in their own name and in their own interest, is unsupportable to the verge of discriminatory.

Let us turn to the propagation of Atheism, which was after all our original question for this chapter. As we saw, the three premises for rejecting advocacy of Atheism were that it is a negative activity, that religion is often positive, and that it makes us "no better than theists." In regard to the first of these, where Walker writes that the "only message atheism has for theists in this respect is to dump religion," he is wrong. Atheism actually has several messages, each more positive than the last. It teaches, for one thing, that you can think for yourself, without the authority or tradition of a scripture or sect to tell you what is good and true. It reminds that you are not the first or only individual or sect to believe that you have the keys to truth. It calls — no, demands — that you reflect critically on this and every claim to truth, querying why you hold it to be true and why anyone else should. It protects you from foolish error, which might be avoided with a simple rational investigation. And it urges on you the diversity of views in the world and the unavoidable course of tolerance as the only means of living in such a world. Potentially (and hopefully), armed with these messages, the religionist will spontaneously "dump religion." Most of us did not become Atheists by having someone yelling Atheist slogans at us or telling us our religion is stupid, but by giving us the information, methods, and perspective to ask questions — and find answers — ourselves.

The second claim is that religion is not all bad, that it can be "benign and even healthy." That is highly debatable, but it is not the point. As I have said, unlike some of my more adamant companions, I do not hold religion responsible for all the evils in the world. As Stephen Weinberg, the atheistic physicist, has said, "With or without religion, good people will do good, and evil people will do evil, but it takes religion to get good people to do evil." Religion is *a* source of morality (but not *the only* source, and not always a good or effective source) and *a* source of community (but not *the only* source). That's not the point. The problem with religion is not that it is evil or destructive but that it is irrational and authoritarian. What Atheists want — at least what I want — is not to propagate Atheism as such but to propagate rationality and antiauthoritarianism.

A subclaim to the larger claim is that religion is a private matter, and so we Atheists have no business trying to insinuate our views into their private world. This is wrong and silly. Religion is not private but very public. It is public in the sense that no child is born with it, therefore only by the public existence and indoctrination or proselytization of religion does it become a person's belief in the first place. If religionists really think religion is private, then perhaps they would refrain from teaching it to their children so as not to intrude on the child's 'private' beliefs. Religion is also very public in that it expects — and in too many places and times compels — certain behaviors and even values and attitudes. Religion is about community and consensus, the religionists tell us, but then they try to prevaricate by asserting that religion's truths or values are only 'for them' or 'for their community.' But no religion, as we discovered in a previous chapter, is meant to apply only to the current believers; rather, each makes a universal claim, which the community may or may not express publicly and militantly. And no religion teaches that it is okay not to believe what the religion says. Finally, religion is more public than at any recent time in America because politically active religionists are enjoying success at setting the agenda and controlling the discourse of society and politics. Religionists feel no compunction whatsoever at shoving god(s) into official oaths, government meetings, school curricula, and elsewhere. When Atheists, or just constitutionally aware Theists, agitate for legal separation of church and state and for individual religious liberties, religionists come down hard that they are promoting an 'atheistic society,' as if the privatization of religion equals Atheism! Then they try to retreat to the dodge that religion is private. If religion only were private, there would be much less motivation for Atheists to organize and act.

The third objection to propagating Atheism, we will recall, is that it is disrespectful and undignified and that it legitimizes the conversion activities of Theists. But that is an obtuse complaint. Theists certainly do not wait for us to invite them to conduct their conversion efforts and evangelism campaigns. No matter what we do, they are going to carry out their recruitment and indoctrination directives. Agreeing not to deconvert them does not prevent them from trying to convert us — and the rest of the world too, including native societies that need American religion the way they need American television and junk food. In a way, by refusing to enter the competition, we are guaranteed to lose the competition. If Theists would accede to a truce and 'cease-fire' of proselytism, we could afford to become passive on the issue, but in a world of encroaching and disrespectful, even predatory, Theism, passivity is death, or at the very least marginalization.

Walker's third and final possible justification for atheistic association is to form an Atheist oasis in a hostile theistic world. His reproof of this foundation for organizations is as flawed as the others. First and foremost, it is a gross caricature of what Atheist organizations are or what Atheists do when they aggregate. Atheists do not seek out each other as a 'support group,' although we do occasionally sigh the sigh that one only feels when one is among one's own kind. How can that be wrong? I'm sure African-Americans, women, and even our friends the button-collectors feel a kind of comfortable familiarity among their own that they do not feel with coin-collectors or stamp-collectors. But most of us do not join or attend groups to feel at home, but to talk, laugh, argue, learn, eat, and engage in other social pleasantries. However, the main failure of the criticism of the oasis view is that Atheist groups are not an oasis in any way. In particular, they are being portrayed as 'total communities,' as if they were a gated and locked neighborhood where Atheists retire after their hard day at religion. Atheist organizations are not ethnic enclaves where Atheists only associate with other Atheists. There are moments when I say, "Would that it were so!" But American Atheists, for example, is not a place for Atheists to eat and sleep and work and live. It is one place we go for a few short moments in our lives. In fact, on this analogy, the plaintiff would have to oppose ethnic neighborhoods or other true exclusivistic communities to be consistent in his principles. Forced desegregation it is.

But the truth is that we Atheists could not be segregated if we wanted to. All of us must and do associate with Theists every day. Why, some of my best friends are Theists! Theists are not by and large terrible people, and most keep their Theism pretty much to themselves, as do Atheists with our Atheism. Therefore, associating as an Atheist organization is hardly 'isolating oneself from society.' And the suggestion that Atheists need to learn how to cope in a theistic world is laughable; nobody knows better than Atheists how to cope in a hostile world. We live in their world because there is no other. It's not even conceivable to isolate ourselves from the general theistic world, and most of us don't have any inclination to.

What is truly amusing about this objection is that, even as I write this, Jerry Falwell is making plans for a 'total Christian community' in Virginia, where members can be born, grow, work, and eventually die without ever stepping foot outside. Probably if an Atheist proposed an atheistic condominium or town, there would be an uproar of opprobrium, calling us isolationists, rejectionists, cultists, and non-Americans. And let us not forget that when Atheists like Madalyn Murray O'Hair or Michael Newdow dare to show their faces in this country, they are invited in no uncertain terms to "get out and go back to Russia." If Atheists ever end up locked away in an all-Atheist neighborhood, like the Jews of Europe were for centuries, then, like them, it will not be at our own request or contrivance. But when I hear myself and freethinkers like me called evil, guilty of terrorism like the World Trade Center attacks, un-American for defending separation of church and state or official governmental neutrality of religion, or even nonexistent (like 'there are no Atheists in foxholes' or 'all Atheists are just disenchanted Christians), then yes, a short vacation from Theism sounds pretty appealing.

Should Atheists Promote Atheism?
Is Such a Thing Possible?

I hope I have supported the argument that there are good reasons for forming and joining Atheist organizations and that there really are such organizations alive and well in American society. Among them I would count American Atheists, the Atheist Alliance, United States Atheists, and other smaller (sometimes predominantly online) groups and communities. The bigger question now is, what should these groups be doing? Is it desirable that we Atheists, individually or in association, should be 'proselytizing' or advocating or promoting Atheism? If it is desirable, is it really possible? And, if it is really possible, how is it best to be done?

Let's start by being candid that every group or principle desires to spread itself; growth is the imperative of all existence. It is either disingenuous or unthoughtful to assert that we do not want more of ourselves, whoever we are. Variety may be the spice of life, but lambs do not aspire to have more lions in the world, and there is no reason why Atheists should aspire to perpetuating a theistic component in the world. Besides, no matter what we do, the chances of ever deconverting the entire theistic majority, or even a significant portion of it, is slim to nil. So they have little to fear from us. They will persist with or without us.

So, it would only be natural if we had an impulse to be messengers of some good Atheist news. The three questions, in order, that we must ask are: (1) should we make an effort to 'get out the message,' (2) if so, what message should it be, and (3) once we have chosen the message, what are the most effective methods for promoting it? We have already responded, I hope, to the main objections to being aggressive in promulgating our own Atheist presence in the culture and consciousness of America. Evangelization is not an exclusively religious function; someone could be, I suppose, an evangelist for button-collecting — desiring to share the joys and benefits of the hobby. Engaging in evangelization, further, does not make us like a religion, although even if it did, I would not see the problem. It would be like saying that police cannot use guns because that makes them 'like criminals.' And why single out evangelization? We use language and writing like Theists, so does that make us "like a religion"? The objection is irrelevant. In fact, religion has hardly hesitated to use the tools and language of science, as we discussed in a prior chapter — including scientific-looking journals and communications technologies such as the Internet — and that has not made religion "more like science." So I think that the worry is misplaced.

I conclude, then, that Atheists have the right to be seen and heard in the public discourse as much as any other group and that we are perfectly right to attempt to engage, sway, and attract the religious or religiously indifferent masses. Not only that, but Walker, who is antiorganization, is not antiactivism (like some Theists and crypto-Theists, he is just opposed to 'organized irreligion' but not irreligion as such); in fact, he himself has written a three-part "Introduction to Activist Atheism" (2003). If some religionists feel that this is a negative attack on them, so be it. We have certainly been the target of negative attacks in the past and present, and no doubt will be in the future. If they want religion in the 'public square,' they will have to get used to the rough-and-tumble of that venue. But it is capricious and opportunistic of Theists to condemn proselytizing by others while indulging in it themselves, and it is a case of misguided nobility for Atheists to want to hold back from it.

I would go so far as to say that this is one good reason for participating in 'proselytizing' behavior — to remind people that we are here and that we have something to say. Probably the two greatest challenges to Atheists in this society are the notion that we don't really exist or that we are an insignificant minority that only likes to complain and tear down and the impression that we are bad people who will have a poor effect on society if we are heard. If for no other reasons than these, we need to be seen and heard as we really are. And this is one strong basis for Atheist organizations being our main avenue for expression in the public domain. Other types of groups — mixed Atheist/Theist or pure Theist — do not have the same interest in portraying and promoting the voice and image of Atheists as Atheists do. We can hope to ally with groups like the ACLU or Americans United, or even liberal theistic associations whenever possible, but we need vehicles and institutions to speak for ourselves. African-Americans do not wait for whites to speak for them, nor women wait for men, nor gays wait for straights. We welcome non-Atheists to support us, but we are a distinct constituency with rights as such.

There are also, as we have seen, other important issues that concern Atheists. Separation of state and church is one of them, and again we can affiliate with non-Atheist groups in some cases, but their reasons for embracing religious freedom and ours often do not completely coincide (they may, for example, want more freedom to go door to door to market their religion, as a federal court just recently endorsed). Atheist civil rights and legalized discrimination against Atheists are other important issues. The negative stereotypes and virtual (and in some cases literal) demonization of Atheists is yet a further issue. Finally, no less pressing than the previous, is the issue of the generally low level of scientific and rational or critical thinking in this country. This threatens us all in more ways than one.

So I posit that there are plenty of sound reasons for having an active and distinctly Atheist voice in public. Can this be done? Well, it is being done, if in insufficient ways so far. The biggest obstacle to Atheist activism is the low degree of Atheist mobilization in this country. If we really are even as little as 2% of the population, that amounts to 5.5 million (out of approximately 270 million) Americans; if we are as much as 15%, then we add up to over 40 million. Of course, as with all identity-groups, only a small proportion will ever join groups or become active in the cause. Most African-Americans do not belong to the NAACP, and most women do not belong to NOW. There will always be a small activist core. But let's accept the lowest estimate, of 2% of the total population, and guess that about 2% of any category will actually join organizations. Then we should still have over 100,000 members of Atheist organizations, which we do not.

The rationale for this underrepresentation is multifaceted, as we have noted above. Atheists tend to be, by personality type, loners and nonjoiners. How many times have we been told by a fellow Atheist that he or she is 'not really a joiner' or does 'not really like groups'? Some, for various reasons, are nearly misanthropes, either preferring to spend time with their own thoughts or actually experiencing an aversion to society, often stemming from the unkind treatment of Atheists at large. And finally, Atheists, being independent and opinionated, often feel no need for a group that can teach or offer them little. But all of these factors in combination do not invalidate the cause of Atheism. To say that Atheism is not conducive to concerted action is to elevate a personality trait to a principle. Perhaps if Atheists saw the real value of organization in their personal and shared intellectual and social interests, more would rally to the cause. In other words, one last reason why Atheism ought to 'proselytize' is not so much to convert non-Atheists to Atheism but to attract existing Atheists — who we know are out there — to the groups that act on their behalf.

We have decided then that Atheism should and can 'get the message out.' What message in particular should that be? For instance, we probably do not want our non-credo to be 'religion stinks' or 'Theists are stupid.' I know that many

Atheists privately feel exactly that way, but that is not an appropriate or constructive public message. What can and should we say, as Atheists, that no one else is saying? What precisely is our good news?

Good News #1 — We Are Here and We Are Not Going Away.

The first and most critical thing we have to convey is that Atheists exist, that we are all around you, and that we have always existed and will always exist. Too many people do not even know what an Atheist is or that there are any, and too many Atheists do not realize that they have co-nonbelievers out there. Over and over I hear from new contacts to our group that they 'didn't know there were others like them' or that they 'felt alone' for the longest time. Although not primarily serving as a support group for each other, Atheists — in common with all humans — feel better knowing that they are not 'minorities of one,' not social freaks, not the only person in the world who thinks like them. And the vast theistic majority needs to understand that we are part of the American and world landscape like every other group, with the same rights and dignities as anyone else.

Good News #2 — We Are Not the Ogres or Demons That We Are Often portrayed To Be.

I have seen religious television. I have heard the talk about us from pulpits and pressrooms. Theists, if they think about us at all, think about us in negative terms, often approaching the demonic. They need to realize, and no one but us can tell them, that we are perfectly normal people. We hold jobs, raise families, own pets, keep our lawns presentable, contribute to charities, serve in the military (yes, there are Atheists in foxholes), and do everything that mainstream Americans do. Even if we did not, there would still be no grounds for discriminating against us, but we do. Why, most Theists probably know an Atheist without even being aware of it. Atheists blend well, and they are often (understandably) demure about their Atheism. Like every group that is, in a way, at the very beginning of its fight for social recognition and social justice, we must combat the unpleasant and false stereotypes that prevent people from accepting us. This will, beyond a doubt, be more difficult for us than for some groups, since their very religions tell them that we are devils or agents of the devil, threats to their salvation and to the salvation of the world. We must not kid ourselves about the sources of these unflattering prejudices: they are ignorance and religious teaching.

Good News #3 — Atheists Are Good People Too.

This, like the one above, will be hard for many Theists to accept. It also constitutes perhaps the first actual bit of 'content' to our public message. One does not have to have religion to be moral. Morality is about how you live your life, no matter what the source of that morality is. It is simply untrue — and we need to refute this from the rooftops — that Atheists are more harmful, criminal, licentious, or evil than anyone else. While evil is a purely religious concept (most Atheists, I think and hope, do not talk about or believe in 'evil') and licentiousness is relative (anyone who lives by a different code than, say, the Ten Commandments will be perceived as wicked by the standards of the Ten Commandments), there is simply no evidence at all to back up the claim that we are more inclined to crime and deviance than the general population. In fact, if anything, we are *less* inclined, since reason and critical thinking lead us to the determination that crime and vice are not desirable, healthy, or effective ways to live life. And it needs no repeating here that religion is hardly a dependable guarantee against crime and vice: most of the antisocial behaviors in America and the world are committed by Theists (because they constitute the majority), and way too many of them have been done explicitly in the name of religion for one god or another. This message will seem like an affront to some religionists, but facts are facts.

Good News #4 — Atheists Have Rights Too.

In America at least, where civil and legal rights are bestowed on the individual regardless of his or her politics, beliefs, race, gender, national origin, sexual orientation, or any other factor, Atheists are equal citizens with the same rights as Theists. We cannot be asked to leave the country when we disagree with you, no matter how deep your convictions are. We are not unpatriotic when we question the policies or practices of government or churches. We cannot be compelled to say theistic pledges or oaths, or to support with our tax money religious institutions or initiatives. Neither can any other group of believers or nonbelievers, and when we raise legal objections to such behavior, we do so not as Atheists but as constitutionalists and good Americans, concerned, as Jefferson was, about the deleterious effects on both church and state when the two become entangled. Atheists should and must enjoy the same civil rights as anyone in America, including the right to be known as an Atheist without fear of reprisal — loss of employment, loss of social status, even physical harm. And Atheists should and must be seen as just as patriotic as any other Americans — some of the firmest of all defenders of basic American rights. It should be, in the end, viewed as a kind of test of American principles whether this society can accept us fully while we differ so fundamentally on what many people deem to be the founding values of America. But our message must be that America is not a religious country, certainly not a Christian country, but a *free* country. In that sense, we concur completely on the basic premise of American identity.

Good News #5 — Atheism Is a Positive and Freeing Position.

It is widely perceived, and Atheists often contribute to this perception, that Atheism is a purely negative enterprise. It consists of nothing more than belittling and debunking religion. Cliff Walker reiterated as much. It is true that Atheists have not given sufficient attention to the positive message of Atheism and the outlines of a post-religious world (toward which I will make a humble contribution in the final chapter of this book). But it is not true that Atheists are unhappy grumbling people who enjoy merely tearing down other people's beliefs and insulting their intelligence. And, if anything, Atheists endure much more offense than Theists, but that does not make reciprocal offensiveness good or adequate. Instead, we have a set of positive messages, not the least of which is that you can live your life successfully and happily without religion. You can think for yourself and evaluate options and rival claims; in fact, you have no choice but to do so and actually do do so every day. Religion itself is not a cookbook for life but requires you to apply and interpret and evaluate. Of course, Atheism will never offer all the goodies of religion, like eternal life and guarantees of wealth, health, and happiness. But then, those religious promises are vain (in the case of wealth, health, and happiness, since many Theists have none of those) or unsubstantiated to the point of probable falsehood (we do not even know if there is such a thing as eternal life, and it is most likely that there is not). What we have to offer instead is *freedom* — freedom from authoritarianism, from guilt, from fear of a spiritual being and its arbitrary ways, from the tyranny of an intolerant community and institution, and freedom from vain hopes.

Good News #6 — You Can and Must Think For Yourself.

The ultimate piece of good news from Atheism is that it is possible and good to think for yourself. The ultimate good news is reason and freethought. Atheism can and must advocate and promote the use of reason, by teaching critical thinking, science, comparative religion and philosophy, anthropology and relativism, and all the tools and perspectives that humans have devised over history to address and understand their world. In fact, let me make this my rallying statement: *we should proselytize reason first, Atheism second.*

There, then, is a multifaceted and positive message that Atheism can take to the world. The remaining question is one of method and means — how can we best communicate this message in a spirit of goodwill and positivity? As Darwin wisely attested at the top of this chapter, "direct arguments against Christianity and theism produce hardly any effect on the public," and besides, not all of the effects we seek have to do with Christianity and Theism. So, the first thing I would warn against is arguing with Theists. While it is fun, and in some situations (like appearances on conservative talk shows, I guess) necessary, it is not going to be our best or most effective device. It tends to evoke defensiveness and often devolves into an exchange of commitments at best and a yelling match at worst. Dan Barker, who recommends atheistic evangelism, and Cliff Walker, who does not, agree on one thing: "Many attempts at evangelistic Atheism are a waste of time," writes the former, and "it is important to remember that philosophical dialogues with most theists are an exercise in futility," writes the latter.

If direct arguments are ineffective, then indirect ones will be our preferred procedure. I am not talking about deception or misdirection or any other illicit or dishonest behaviors. I am talking about Atheism as a result or conclusion as opposed to the process by which one arrives at the result. And remember, our goal is not necessarily to turn every Theist in the world into an Atheist; rather, our goals include the six parts of the message above, which basically amount to a demand for Atheist equality and a plea for reason and critical thinking.

Here, in the end, is the real point and what makes Atheist proselytization something other than proselytization in the familiar sense. We do not seek to make everyone an Atheist but rather a *thinker*. I would probably go so far as to say that you cannot, with any regularity, turn people into Atheists. You can, however, turn them into thinkers. You cannot teach Atheism, but you can teach reason and critical thinking. And critical thinking does not have the stigma that Atheism does. Instead, it is actually taught in school (mostly at the college level, and not necessarily all that well) with wide acceptance and approval.

This is what makes proselytization not proselytization at all in the case of Atheism. Talking and teaching about reason and freethought is no more proselytization of Atheism than teaching reading is proselytization of literacy. We do not refer to literacy as a "conversion from illiteracy," and we do not castigate or condescend to the illiterate. They are merely people who have not learned a skill and a subject yet, and when they master it they can do with it what they will. I take the same approach to Atheism, or more fundamentally, reason. We are not 'converting' people from irrationality to reason, and certainly not from Theism to Atheism, but teaching a thinking skill that they can employ in every aspect of their lives, from the church to the grocery store. Once they master and apply reason, I have my guess and preference where that will lead them, but we cannot force them into a conclusion but simply give them the methods and set them on their way. To demand that people 'give up' their religions and become Atheists is in fact as dogmatic and doctrinaire as any religious conversion campaign. However, to arm them with a thinking skill — one that leads them not into falsehood but delivers them from error — is already to set them on the path of independent reasoning ... and we know where that can end.

The most effective method in spreading the good news is, as Darwin suggested, education. This need not be necessarily or exclusively science education, although science should be an important part of the curriculum. This education initiative should include basic and advanced reasoning and critical thinking training, political education (what does the Constitution *really* say and what did the founding fathers *mean*), history (what has America, and the world, been through that makes separation of church and state a good idea), civics (what does it mean to be an American and to have and use rights), diversity training (why are tolerance and inclusiveness good and necessary in a multicultural, multireligious world), and so on. And I am not talking about holding actual classes that people must attend (although that might be nice). Instead, I am talking about infusing these values and principles in all of our messages. We are not out to tell people about the wonders of Atheism but about the wonders of history, civil society, tolerance and diversity, and yes, science and reason. And perhaps above all, we should make it firm and clear that our actions are not just for us but for all Americans, who are equally diverse and equally in need of the freedom and toleration that American society — so far — has afforded individuals. In another kind of society, a dictatorial and intolerant society, we will be the first to go, but we won't be the last.

The specific forms that this approach will take are various, and many of them are in action already. The courts will be a central place where this drama is played out. Like it or not, the courts — especially the federal courts — are the main scenes where public agendas are set. But, as other civil rights-oriented groups have discovered in the past, this is not where the culture of the society and the hearts and minds of the citizenry are won over. The culture war is fought in the trenches — in the workplace, in the neighborhood, in the newspapers, in the schools, and everywhere that people live and share public space. We must represent ourselves *at all times* — and then positively, constructively, and in the name of reason and American values of freedom of conscience and diversity of opinion. No one can argue against that, or if they do, they brand themselves in the same way that segregationists branded themselves by turning hoses on peaceful civil rights activists. I am not saying the process will be quick or painless — probably neither — or that it will even be successful. I am only saying that it is good and unavoidable.

Conclusion: Speak or Be Silenced

Most Atheists presumably will never join an Atheist organization, and that is fine; the fact that most African-Americans will never join the NAACP does not detract from the validity of that organization or its mission. Organizations exist primarily to be the representatives of and advocates for the 'silent majority' of any constituency — to do the work for them. And most Atheists will apparently never be proselytizers for the position of Atheism, and that is fine; not every individual has the time, inclination, or skill to be a spokesperson and activist for a cause, and after all, for many Atheists, Atheism is just one part of their personality and worldview. And as we have seen at various points in this book, many Atheists do not even know that they are Atheists, have not accepted that they are Atheists, or hide behind euphemisms for Atheism like Agnosticism, secularism, or Humanism. And many Atheists are cowed into silence by the overwhelming pressure in this society to be religious and the overwhelming disapproval of Atheism — not always explicitly stated but always present.

However, I hope I have illustrated in this chapter that Atheism, no less than racial civil rights or button-collecting, has a right to exist, to organize, to speak for and about itself, and to promote its view of the world, even attract or convert others to it. I hardly recommend, as I said early on, going door-to-door or even handing out pamphlets on street corners as either a desirable or effective way to disseminate the message, but there is a message there that is worth hearing. It is also not just a message for Atheists, but in elements at least a message of American civics, diversity and tolerance, and reason.

In short, the processes and principles implicit in the good news are as valuable as the specific atheistic content, if not more so. There may be no motivation to spread Atheism, but then there may be no need; spreading reason and freethought may and will have the consequence of putting people on their own voyage of questioning and discovery, which can (and I argue should) end in Atheism. So it is not incumbent on us to teach any 'conclusion' or 'position,' merely a skill and a habit. However, at length, the specific 'evangel' of Atheism will be heard, and it is worth hearing. It is summed up well by Dan Barker, who exhorts an evangelistic Atheism that takes the argument directly to the Theist; whoever we choose to direct our energies toward, and whatever form and medium, these positive items are part of our message to a credulous world:

> The fact that indoctrination can be eliminated ... The fact that there is no universal dictator, no sin, no cosmic guilt, and no hell ... The fact that human beings possess the potential for good ... The fact that love can be truly shared between self-respecting peers with both feet on the ground ... The fact that human reason is capable ... The fact that intellectual integrity brings the only honest peace of mind ... The fact that there is no God ... All of this is truly Good News.

CHAPTER ELEVEN

Fundamentalism and the Fight for the Future

Relativism, science, toleration, church(es)-state separation, activist Atheism — all of these things must feel to the Theist like the world is going to hell, quite literally. In fact, until a few decades ago, the general expectation in Western civilization was an increased and unabated secularization of society, that society was on a one-way and non-stop journey to the marginalization if not the eradication of religion as a significant cultural force. Other forces — scientific, ideological, ethnic perhaps — would be the defining dynamics of the future.

The religious revival caught many observers by surprise. It should not have. First, culture is cyclical; the unopposed secularization of society was a cycle, and the re-emergence of religion is probably a cycle too. As in economics, one should never take a 'boom' in any sector as a permanent future state of expansion but as the 'up' part of the wave that must inevitably come down. Second, religious revival, at least in America, is one of the perpetual characteristics of our cultural and religious landscape, and of course religion can only revive when it has become moribund. Finally, the very losses of all other certainties (what post-modernism called the loss of 'grand narratives') in the collapse of colonialism, communism, and virtually every other non-religious ideology should have been and recently has been recognized as a fertile breeding ground for the oldest, last, and grandest narrative of all.

However, in culture nothing ever quite revives the way it was 'in the old days.' How could it? Today is not 30 BCE, and too many things have happened between then and now. Any revival is a remembering, and it is a remembering by people who were not there the first time and who see the past through the eyes and interests of today. Whether the revival is religious, ethnic, or some other kind, it is about the past in a way but also very much about the present and particularly about the future. As I have examined elsewhere in the context of ethnic identity and conflict (Eller 1999), appeals to the past are always a combination of remembering, forgetting (leaving certain parts out), reinterpreting (in the light of current forces and interests), and outright inventing (that is, making things up and attributing them to the past).

So it is with today's fundamentalism. Fundamentalism is old-time religion with a distinctly contemporary spin and therefore ultimately it is not old-time religion at all but something very modern. One clear way to see this fact is that nothing quite like or by the name of fundamentalism existed until about a century ago. Another way is to compare it to what we know about the real old-time religion. And of course a third and perhaps most explosive way is to inquire: just which 'old time' do you mean? A hundred years ago? A thousand years ago? Two thousand years ago? Five thousand years ago?

In this chapter we will consider fundamentalism as a cultural phenomenon, which is the only way one can consider it (although fundamentalists naturally would complain bitterly about such treatment). We will see that, while there are many, many historical precedents for it, contemporary fundamentalism is a distinct phenomenon arising from the particular conditions of modernity. In fact, without modernity fundamentalism makes no sense, since it is a reaction to, a war against, modernity. Along the way we will see how religion provides a powerful impetus for 'inspired violence,' how fundamentalism distorts both fact and myth in its theory and practice, and how we non-religionists are involuntary but inescapable combatants in the war that fundamentalists have declared.

Religion in Reaction: The Phenomenon of Fundamentalism

What is this thing called fundamentalism? It is not simply religion, since many religious people are not fundamentalists, and fundamentalists do not consider all religious people to belong to their movement. Yet, to refer to it as a movement is to make a first insight into its nature: fundamentalism is a particular kind of religion *on the move.*

The designation 'fundamentalism' or 'fundamentalist' did not enter the American lexicon until shortly after the turn of the twentieth century. It was in 1910 that the first of a series of twelve publications entitled *The Fundamentals: A Testimony to the Truth* appeared (the series ending in 1915). Out of this effort emerged an organization, the World's Christian Fundamentals Association, founded by William B. Riley in 1919, and the terms fundamentalism and fundamentalist. In 1920 the editor of the Northern Baptist newspaper *The Watchman Examiner*, Curtis Lee Laws, actually described a fundamentalist as a person who is willing to 'do battle royal' for Christian fundamentals.

Two questions engage us at this point: what were these 'fundamentals,' and why did they become a matter of 'battle royal' at this particular historical moment? The answer to the first question is fairly simple. There are five basic points to the position, which are variously specified but generally amount to the following: (1) the absolute truth and inerrancy of the Christian scriptures, (2) the virgin birth of Jesus, (3) the atonement of sin through the substitutive sacrifice of Jesus on the cross, (4) the bodily resurrection and future second coming of Jesus, and (5) the divinity of Jesus and/or the reality of the miracles he performed. Of these, the anchor is clearly the inerrancy of the bible, which is the source (and purportedly proof) of the other four claims.

In the early twenty-first century, we are all too familiar with these articles of faith, and of course there is nothing new about them; they are, after all, the basic or 'fundamental' tenets of Christianity. So the second question is, why did people feel the need to restate and to get agitated about these articles at that moment? This is a more nuanced question. Let us first acknowledge, as we mentioned at the outset, that revivalism, that is, efforts to inspire and instill religious fervor and to "win souls for Christ," is nothing new in America. Rather, it is quite possibly the very nature of American religion. There have been various revivals or 'awakenings' in American history, and some of the most successful and respected denominations in the country, like the Methodists and the Baptists, started as energetic revivalist efforts with 'circuit riders' traveling the countryside giving ordinary people a version of the religion they could understand and imbibe. Actually, this flavor of religion suits the American personality well, which is above all individualistic and somewhat anti-authority as well as emotional and pragmatic: many Americans, in the past and the present, distrust officials and authorities, including religious ones, who condescend to the masses from their university positions and their urban parishes. Revivalism was and is a religion of the people, by the people, and for the people. It is worth noting that many religious 'authorities' were and continue to be aghast at the unsophisticated and emotionally overwrought quality of revivalism, but they cannot help but admit its appeal and success.

So old-time religion is nothing new. And the nineteenth century saw its share. William Miller, for instance, in 1831, having studied the Bible carefully, determined that Jesus would return in 1843, and his 'Millerite' followers took this prediction extremely seriously, although they were obviously wrong. John Nelson Darby also delved into the scriptures, 'discovering' the concept of the Rapture, a mainstay in current fundamentalist thinking. At the very opening of the nineteenth century, Elias Smith's group that merely called themselves "Christians" represented a kind of primitivist and individualistic church, rejecting priestcraft, inviting the common man to return to the only real authority in religion, the scriptures, and condemning all other forms of Christianity — even Protestantism — as anti-Christian. Alexander Campbell and Barton Stone also established primitivist sects which, by 1830, had amalgamated to become the Disciples of Christ who repudiated all church structure and superfluous traditions and trappings and, as Hatch puts it, "vowed to follow nothing but the Christian name and the New Testament" (1989, 70). Most extraordinarily, in 1830 Joseph Smith introduced to the world a "new revelation," the Book of Mormon, that gave the "compelling message that God was restoring the one true fold, the ancient order of things [by] revealing an up-to-date Bible" (Hatch, 120–1).

While the specifics of these and other similar movements differ, on some general points they are in major, and crucial, agreement. All invoked the purity and perfection of scripture, whether old or new. Each looked out upon not just a physical world but a spiritual world, even a Protestant world, that had gone wrong somehow; as Campbell wrote, "The stream of Christianity has become polluted" (quoted in Hatch, 168), and each saw itself as representing authentic Christianity (even if, as in Miller's case, that meant the end of the world). Each imagined itself — and *only* itself — as the *restoration* of religion. Dramatically, Campbell wrote a column called "A Restoration of the Ancient Order of Things," in which he set the agenda to "bring the christianity [sic] and the church of the present day' up to the standards of 'the state of christianity [*sic*] and of the church of the New Testament" (quoted in Hatch, 168). Other non-primitivist churches were corrupted at best, false or even satanic at worst.

In other words, the future of Christianity was the past of Christianity — a return to its original, unalloyed, and uncorrupted condition. However, there were other menaces afoot. One was the impact of science and its attendant secularization; Darwin's *On the Origin of Species*, after all, appeared in 1859. Humanistic philosophies and social sciences were also advancing, not the least of which was Nietzsche's 1882 pronouncement that God was dead. The Bible itself was increasingly being treated as literature rather than literal truth, to the point of questioning the authenticity of some of its passages or even the very historicity of a person named Jesus. Finally, on the social front, America was changing, under the forces of urbanization, industrialization, and immigration; as early as the 1840s, Roman Catholics composed the largest single Christian denomination in the U.S., which they continue to do today, unseating any single Protestant sect as the most numerous one in the country (although Protestantism in general still outnumbers Catholicism by nearly three-to-one). Even within Christianity, there were modernizing processes at work, attempting to accommodate scientific and social realities into religion.

By the late nineteenth century, while liberal Christians were making their peace with cultural change and modernity, conservatives were organizing their opposition. Charles Hodge, in his 1873 *Systematic Theology*, argued that every word of the scriptures was serious and literal, not allegorical or symbolic; he followed with *What is Darwinism?* in 1874, where he wrote that religion "has to fight for its life against a large class of scientific men." By 1875 conservative Christians in the United States were organizing Bible conferences and other such gatherings for preachers and teachers. For instance, 1875 saw the founding of the Believers' Meeting for Bible Study (which became in 1883 the Niagara Bible Conference). In 1886 what would become the Moody Bible Institute opened, followed in 1909 by the Bible Institute of Los Angeles, and any number of books, newspapers, newsletters, and magazines. That Catholicism was seen as a threat to American religion was apparent in Josiah Strong's *Our Country: Its Possible Future and Its Present Crisis*.

There were, quite prominently, many things going on that conservative American Protestants could not tolerate, and fundamentalism was the response. Fundamentalism is born to be a struggle against forces and phenomena that, to its followers' minds, threaten religion's very survival. However, as Karen Armstrong aptly observes, fundamentalism "rarely arises as a battle with an external enemy ...; it usually begins, instead, as an internal struggle in which traditionalists fight their own coreligionists who, they believe, are making too many concessions to the secular world" (2000, 79). The truth of this observation can be appreciated in Pope Pius X's statement *Pascendi Gregis* that warned of the "virus" of "Modernism" within the church — the attempt by some leaders to adapt to modern thought — as not only a heresy but as "synthesis of all heresies." This sentiment is echoed in recent times by perhaps the most influential fundamentalist in America, Jerry Falwell, who holds that fundamentalism "was born out of a doctrinal controversy with liberalism. The ultimate issue is whether Christians who have a supernatural religion are going to be overpowered by Christians who have only a humanistic philosophy of life. Fundamentalism is the affirmation of Christian belief and a distinctly Christian lifestyle as opposed to the general secular society" (Pinnock 1990, 47).

Accordingly, by the late nineteenth century, a significant stream in American Christianity had become the Social Gospel movement, which saw religion's role as more natural than supernatural, more social than spiritual — doing good work, helping the poor, reforming society, and the like. But when Charles Eliot gave his 1909 speech "The Future of Religion," outlining a radical version of the Social Gospel — a future without churches or scriptures or theology or monopoly of truth but nothing more than love of god and social action — the fundamentalists were called to arms. It is no accident that *The Fundamentals* began appearing the very next year.

To return to the first question of this section, what then is fundamentalism? It is not just Christianity, nor even just conservative Christianity, nor even just evangelical Christianity. Evangelical Christianity we could characterize as the version of the faith that emphasizes the individual, personal relationship with Jesus as the core of salvation and the natural tendency to 'witness' and proselytize for that purpose. As many students of American religion have concluded, evangelistic revivalist Christianity is the basic religious style in this country and has been perhaps from its inception. Even today, there is a distinction between evangelism (personified best in Billy Graham) and fundamentalism (personified best in Jerry Falwell), and also between both of those and Pentecostalism, emphasizing the presence of the Holy Spirit in believers and often taking the form of speaking in tongues, healing, and other trance-like behaviors. None of these movements likes the others very much.

So fundamentalism is more than evangelicalism, although it presupposes the latter. Nancy Ammerman, a leading scholar on fundamentalism, posits that it differs from other traditionalist or orthodox forms of religion "in that it is a movement in conscious, organized opposition to the disruption of those traditions and orthodoxies" (1991, 14). George Marsden, who has a way with words, calls it evangelicalism that is angry about something, or, more seriously, that a fundamentalist is "an evangelical Protestant who is militantly opposed to modern liberal theologies and to some aspects of secularism in modern culture" (1990, 22). They "must not only believe these evangelical teachings, but they must be willing to fight for them" (23).

Marty and Appleby, in their encyclopedic study of fundamentalism, insist that calling fundamentalists militants is no insult, since they proudly call themselves such. Fundamentalists see themselves as fighting against the outsider or infidel or against the insider liberal "who seeks compromise, middle ground, or a civil 'agreement to disagree' [or] who would be moderate, would negotiate with modernity, would adapt the movement"; fighting for the religious worldview they hold and which they take as entirely and exclusively true; and fighting with "the actual or imagined ideal original concept or concepts" of their religion (1991, ix–x). The fundamentalist historian George Dollar, writing under the auspices of the fundamentalist Bob Jones University, says it for himself when he claims: "Historic fundamentalism is the literal exposition of all the affirmations and attitudes of the Bible and the militant exposure of all non-Biblical affirmations and attitudes" (Marsden, 23). In his and their view, fundamentalism perceives itself as at war — at war not only with secular society but liberal religion. It sees the stakes as absolute: the very future of America is at risk. It accepts the Protestant Bible as true on all matters of faith and fact. And it understands its position as the only true one: even people who call themselves Christians but do not believe the way fundamentalism teaches are not Christians at all. There is only one way, and that is the fundamentalist way.

So Many Fundamentalisms

What we have described so far makes fundamentalism a uniquely modern, uniquely Christian, and even uniquely American phenomenon. There are even some Jewish and Muslim scholars, for example, who suggest that there is no such thing as fundamentalism in their religions, since it is an exclusively Christian thing. But this is just being obtuse: of course Jewish or Muslim or any other kind of fundamentalism is not going to take the New Testament and the claims about Jesus literally. Rather, it will cling to its own 'fundamentals' and seek to restore some other past against some other perceived threat. As such, fundamentalism is a recurrent theme in history.

To take one tangible illustration that we have discussed previously, the Protestant Reformation could well be seen as a fundamentalist movement. Martin Luther's purpose, quite explicitly, was to dispense with the accretions of time and tradition (namely, the Catholic church) and to return to a simpler, purer, and therefore more true Christianity, one without priests and sacraments, one with only the believer and the Lutheran Bible. The fact that it failed — at least in the sense of establishment of the 'one true religion' — will be the subject of a later section of this chapter. Even before that, we could comprehend such dissent movements as the Free Spirits of the twelfth century and beyond as kinds of fundamentalist groups, who took their inspiration from a literalist reading of (at least some parts of) scripture for the beliefs and lifestyles they adopted. And even further back, Unitarian and other such challenges to Catholic orthodoxy can be seen as attempts to dip directly from the source and to restore a lost original orthodoxy. In a sense, many if not all ascetic and monastic traditions are equally attempts to create an oasis of right belief and conduct in a desert of chaos and corruption.

Christianity is of course not alone in experiencing restoration or cultural resistance movements within its ranks. In fact, I think it can be said with authority that fundamentalism is not even an exclusively religious phenomenon, that other aspects of culture can be 'fundamentalized' or actively or militantly restored to some former (real or putative) glory. Within religion, there are certainly ancient and contemporary examples of non-Christian fundamentalist movements. In the Old Testament, prophets and other devotees are forever trying to bring the people back to the right worship of their god; one of the most persistent and pernicious issues among the ancient Jews was the influence of 'baals' or gods of foreign neighbors, and they are constantly admonished to abandon these false gods and return to their own god, the god who delivered them from Egypt and did other wonders in the past. When Israel came under the influence, first of the Greeks and then of the Romans, this created a new fundamentalist dynamic; now they could resist religious and cultural syncretism alike. As in every case of culture contact, some Jews adopted the culture of the outsider for prestige or as resistance to traditional authority. Some mixed old and new cultures and molded something locally unique from the mixture. But some held firmly to the old-time religion and even became champions of orthodoxy against outside and inside challenges alike.

The Essenes and the Maccabees are two examples of restorationist groups in Jewish history. When, after centuries of foreign rule, Judas Maccabeus led a Jewish revolt and temporarily established a Jewish state in the late 60s CE, this was the restoration of not just a kingdom but a religion. And the Essenes, a monastically separatist faction, sound oddly modern in their attitudes, including their denunciation of the priests of Jerusalem 'as being hopelessly corrupted by their accommodation to Gentile ways, and by collaboration with the Roman occupiers,' as well as their doctrines 'of repentance and God's coming judgment [which meant that] Jews must separate themselves from such polluting influences and return to strict observance of God's law' (Pagels 1995,18).

Another, less familiar but instructive ancient Jewish fundamentalist group was the so-called *sicarii* or knife-bearers, who leavened their convictions with violence. They were a sect of nationalist religionists who attacked enemies in broad daylight, preferably on holidays when the temple was crowded, and killed with a short sword that gives them their name. Their victims, predictably, were not exclusively or even normally the occupying foreigners but the moderates and collaborationists among their own people, again highlighting the fact that fundamentalists often target their less-adamant coreligionists as their main enemy. And their religious motivation is undeniable; the historian Josephus describes them as having 'a passion for liberty that is almost unconquerable since they are convinced that God alone is their leader and master' (quoted in Rapoport 1989, 29).

In modern times, one could perhaps call even the Zionist movement started by Theodor Herzl in the late nineteenth century a sort of fundamentalist movement, in the sense that it was an attempt, quite successfully, to 'restore' the state of Israel and the Jewish presence in Palestine. Zionism as usually understood, however, is fairly secular in nature, having as its goal certain secular ends, especially the creation of a modern nation-state. However, not all contemporary Jews see things the same way. Groups like the *haredim* and *Gush Emunim* evince most of the characteristics of fundamentalists.

The *haredim* ('those who tremble') are ultra-orthodox Jews in lifestyle and belief who, true to the fundamentalist form, consider themselves merely the 'true Jews' and not a separate sect. The *Gush Emunim* ('Bloc of the Faithful') is a self-conscious movement that sees itself as the religious aspect of Zionism, or rather sees secular Zionism as nothing more than the first stage in a greater religious restoration. Emerging after the Six-day War in Israel (which occurred in 1967), *Gush Emunim* envisions a day when all of ancient Israel and beyond — "from the Euphrates River in Iraq to the Brook of Egypt' (Aran 1991, 268) — will be returned to the Jewish people. Toward that end, they have been willing to engage in illegal settlement, vandalism, harassment of Arabs, and even a plot to destroy the Muslim Dome of the Rock believed to sit atop the old Temple of Yahweh in Jerusalem.

Islam has its share of fundamentalist spirit too. Again, if one were so bold, one might consider the very founding of Islam as a kind of fundamentalist movement — not the instigation of a new religion but the recovery and re-establishment of an original and basic monotheism (whether real or imaginary). Nevertheless, it is less disputable to identify a fundamentalist schism in the very early history of Islam, when followers split over the right succession after the prophet Muhammad himself. Many felt, upon the prophet's death in 632 CE, that his kinsman Ali should become *caliph* ('successor'), but Ali was passed over three times and, when he finally ascended to leadership, was assassinated in 660; subsequently, his son Hasan abdicated after less than six months, ending the dynasty of the 'rightly-guided' caliphs. The 'partisans of Ali,' though, or in Arabic the *Shia-i Ali* or Shi'ites, never accepted this political and secular corruption of Islam, and, although they have splintered into numerous sects, they hold some variation of a belief that Islam will someday be restored to its true leadership and spiritual path.

Throughout its history, Islam has periodically 'looked back' like other religions to its earlier and better days. The movements that have arisen since sustained contact with and colonialism by modern Europe pose the most interest for us. Wahhabism is one of the more familiar and important developments. Originated by Muhammad Ibn 'Abd al-Wahhab

(1703–92) in Arabia, it opposed both popular superstitions that had penetrated Islam as well as the political/secular practices of the Arabian monarchy, calling for "the Islamization of society and the creation of a political order which gives appropriate recognition to Islam" (Voll 1991, 351). Specifically, this entailed a return to the textual fundamentals of the Qur'an and the other main Islamic scripture, the *Hadith* or 'traditions.' In Egypt, Hasan al-Banna (1906–49) founded the Muslim Brotherhood in 1928 to oppose Westerners and their influence, including "their half-naked women ..., their liquors, their theaters, their dance halls, their amusements, their stories, their newspapers, their novels, their whims, their silly games, and their vices" as well as "schools and scientific and cultural institutes in the very heart of the Islamic domain, which cast doubt and heresy into the souls of its sons and taught them how to demean themselves, disparage their religion and their fatherland, divest themselves of their traditions and beliefs, and to regard as sacred anything Western" (Voll, 360–1). This raises the point, of course, that each fundamentalism is different: in the Islamic world, Western influences are part of the complex of vices, while in America most of these same phenomena are accepted parts of culture — although not all equally accepted even by American fundamentalists.

Without belaboring the point, I think we can fairly see the 1979 theocratic revolution in Iran, led by the Ayatollah Khomeini, as a major religious restoration, as well as the rise of the Taliban in Afghanistan a decade later. While each might have been one faction's image of religious fundamentals, they were fundamentalist all the same. And Islam even got its own modern fundamentalist text in 1985, the *Fundamentals of Islamic Thought* by Ayatollah Murtaza Mutahhari. Other religions, too numerous to describe in detail here, also developed their local fundamentalist-type movements. To mention a few very briefly, within Hindu society the *Arya Samaj* ('Society of Aryas') and the *Rashtriya Svayamsevak Sangh* ('National Union of Volunteers' or RSS) manifested various attitudes toward religion, culture, and the past. The *Arya Samaj*, founded in 1875, is, if we can say such a thing, a Vedic fundamentalist organization, observing a strict adherence to the very oldest of Hindu texts, the Vedas, and dismissing "much of later

Hindu tradition as degenerate practice that is best forgotten" (Gold 1991, 534). The RSS, on the other hand, takes a more general (but no less exclusive) cultural stance, emphasizing 'Hindu Nation' and 'Hindu-ness' as its central features; writes Madhav Sadashiv Golwalkar, the second leader of RSS: 'The non-Hindu people in Hindustan must adopt the Hindu culture and religion, must learn to respect and hold in reverence Hindu religion, and must entertain no ideas but those of glorification of the Hindu race and culture...claiming no privileges...not even citizens' rights' (quoted in Nielsen 1993, 111).

Other examples could be cited. Elsewhere (Eller 1999) I have described the mobilization and politicization of Buddhism in Sri Lanka. Prior to the open conflict in that country, important religious discussions, between Buddhists and Christians as well as Buddhists and Hindus, helped to shape the national consciousness of the society. The Buddhist monks (essentially Sinhalese) went so far as to form a political party, the *Eksat Bhiksu Peramuna* or United Monks' Front to influence elections and policy, and much of the violent conflict between Sinhalese (Buddhists) and Tamils (Hindus) has been based on interpretations of texts like the Sinhalese *Mahavamsa* that allege to tell the ancient history of the island and therefore to establish first occupation, therefore ownership, therefore contemporary political rights to it. Scholarly studies of Sikh, Confucian, Japanese, and many other religions simply demonstrate the same general processes.

What Fundamentalists Want

It should be evident by now that fundamentalism is not a uniquely American or Christian phenomenon, nor even entirely a modern one, although modern fundamentalisms will be distinct from pre-modern ones in their motivations and their goals. Therefore, returning to the situation in America, we can rightly ask, what do fundamentalists want? The answer is neither simple nor reassuring.

It has been noted that after 1925 (the year of the infamous Scopes 'monkey trial') American fundamentalism fell into disrepute, and, this being the heyday of secularization theory, it was expected that it would never rear its ugly head again. However, old movements never die, they just lie in wait until they are stirred to life again. The factors that lifted fundamentalism to attention and recently some power in America began in the 1950s, accelerated in the 1960s, and reached fever pitch in the 1970s, leading to the emergence of the Moral Majority in 1979 and related organized fundamentalist efforts.

American fundamentalism has a history through the middle of the twentieth century that has been studied elsewhere, including the schism in the 1930s between those who wanted to work within existing religious institutions and those who wanted to create their own separate institutions, and the 1957 split triggered by Billy Graham between his more liberal and inclusive evangelicals and the more strict and exclusivist fundamentalists. I mention these facts simply to show that fundamentalism did not disappear but merely inverted for a time. However, developments in American society gradually energized and politicized them, leading to their explosion into the public light in recent years. First, the civil rights movement of the 1950s rubbed some of the most conservative of Christians the wrong way, as can be seen from the anti-integration activities of the Ku Klux Klan and certain Southern politicians. However, the 1960s was the decade that really began to rankle religious and social conservatives, with the feminist, 'hippy'/antiwar, and supposedly 'Atheist' — and eventually the gay — movements, all of which seemed to trample on traditional values and conventional definitions of family and society. We should particularly stress the prayer-in-school cases of the early 1960s, which we discussed in a previous chapter, as well as the struggle for the Equal Rights Amendment. These decisions and efforts felt completely un-Christian and un-American to religious and cultural conservatives.

The straw that broke the fundamentalists' back may have been the abortion-rights *Roe v. Wade* decision of 1973. To orthodox Christians, this was tantamount to legalized murder and Satanism. From that date, it only took a few years for organized fundamentalism to crystallize. That these are precisely the issues that preoccupy fundamentalists is evidenced by the litany of complaints featured in Tim LaHaye's *The*

Battle for the Mind (1980), including the ERA, prayer in school, the permeation of Humanist ideas, abortion, gay rights, and such other matters as the limitation of corporal punishment on children, certification requirements for Christian schools, and IRS investigations into church finances. In a word, fundamentalists felt mortally assaulted by these developments — as if the very soul of America and the very future of Christianity were on the line. It is no coincidence, then, that the 1970s was the decade of fundamentalist mobilization and empowerment, not just in America but around the world, including the following:

- 1974 — *Gush Emunim* launched
- 1977 — right-wing Likud party elected in Israel, and new West Bank settlement program begun
- 1979 — Moral Majority founded
- 1979 — Islamic revolution in Iran under Ayatollah Khomeini succeeded
- 1980 — conservative Republican Ronald Reagan elected president of the United States

The odd thing is that, until the 1970s, fundamentalism had essentially forsaken political action and social reform, viewing its mission as spiritual rather than temporal. However, by this time they felt themselves so under attack that a counterattack was all but inevitable, and fairly quickly they became prepared to fight with prayer and politics. As Hal Lindsey, author of *The Late Great Planet Earth*, wrote, this readiness to fight meant "that we must actively take on the responsibility of being a citizen and a member of God's family. We need to get active, electing officials who will not only reflect the Bible's morality in government, but will shape domestic and foreign policies to protect our country and our way of life" (Armstrong, 274). And Pat Robertson knew that they had what it takes to accomplish the goal: "We have together with the Protestants and Catholics enough votes to run this country. And when the people say, 'We've had enough,' we are going to take over" (310–11).

But what exactly would they do with that power? What is their agenda? The answers should be relatively obvious.

However, whether honestly or dishonestly, Falwell maintained that fundamentalists "are not interested in controlling America; they are interested in seeing souls saved and lives changed for the glory of God. They believe that the degree to which this is accomplished will naturally influence the trend of society in America" (Pinnock, 50). And there is the key: whether or not fundamentalism is a conscious and deliberate attempt to control or change the *government* of America, it is demonstrably a conscious and deliberate attempt to control or change the *culture* of America. And once the latter change is effected, the former change is a matter of course.

Accordingly, the battleground of fundamentalism is, as LaHaye indicated, the mind and the institutions that produce the mind — predominantly schools, but also television, print and other media, courts, and ultimately government. They seek, clearly, to impose their view of values, of family, of religion, even of history on society as not only the dominant but the correct view. They aim to reshape culture in their image, which is their idealized image of the past, the roots, the origins, and the fundamentals of American society. What this means in practice varies somewhat from fundamentalist to fundamentalist, but overall it means purging American culture of non-fundamentalist influences — including feminist, gay, pro-choice, liberal, Humanist, secular, multicultural, 'pagan,' and certainly Atheist influences — and converting (or in their language, "restoring") the country to the true (meaning *their*) values, beliefs, and practices on which it was formed. It means, as is the case with all fundamentalisms, making the future of the society by remaking the (factual or fictitious) past in the present. It is a cultural war, with culture understood in the broadest possible sense.

In a way, fundamentalists want what all constituencies in America or any society want — to sway opinion, to influence practice and policy, to determine the course of society. They are a pressure group like all others. In that effort, they have the same rights as any other pressure group. However, the main and critical difference is that *they do not recognize the legitimacy of other pressure groups*. Fundamentalism, we noted, is born of refusal to compromise, and while it has made some strategic compromises (like allowing Catholics and other non-Protestants into the Moral Majority), at heart it remains exclusivistic. Imagine Pat Robertson saying the following, and then someone like him actually achieving political power in this country: "The Constitution of the United States, for instance, is a marvelous document for self-government by Christian people. But the minute you turn that document into the hands of non-Christian people they can use it to destroy the very foundations of our society. And that's what's happening" (*Washington Post*, March 23, 1981). In fact, as this statement suggests, and as Borowitz has argued, extreme and exclusivistic orthodoxies like fundamentalism 'have a principled problem with democracy' (1990, 237). Without being too alarmist, what he is saying is that liberal religion has made a truce with and even "intrinsically affirms" religious pluralism, for all the reasons that we have seen in this book — the intolerance, the persecution, the wars, and so on that flow from a rejection of this pluralism. But fundamentalism is by definition the rejection of religious pluralism, the very denial that there is or could be such a thing: there is 'true religion' (fundamentalism) and there is false religion or no religion at all (everything else). Democracy cannot help but respect diversity of belief and opinion, but then, at least some fundamentalisms have little or no use for democracy.

The Relativity of Fundamentalism

The quintessence of fundamentalism, wherever it appears and whatever it preaches, is a purity and absoluteness of thought, belief, and identity, generally captured in a golden (or at least superior) past that has been or is being lost through the confusion and corruption of external influences, whether those influences are modern, foreign, demonic, or atheistic. It takes on a combative, almost desperate quality, either inherently or strategically, as it fights for its life against the forces of corruption, which must be seen as sufficiently strong or advanced to have caused the fundamentalist response in the first place; there is no need for fundamentalism when things are going well for orthodoxy. Therefore, its practitioners tend to "think in black and white polarities, finding the intermediate shades of gray inconceivable. They do not tolerate uncertainty or ambiguity. They disparage those outside their own group" (Ostow 1990, 113).

Fundamentalism, in other words, is the very opposite and the mortal enemy of relativism. Relativism teaches, as we have shown, not that 'everything is true' and 'anything goes,' which is how fundamentalists like to characterize it, but that every judgment of value or morality is made from some particular perspective — that it is relative to some standard of value or morality. Fundamentalism denies this bitterly, or rather claims that its standard is the only standard, so that relativism withers away from lack of any other (legitimate) perspective to hold. Imagine, then, the consternation of fundamentalism if we could demonstrate that even *it* is relative. And in fact, like everything else that is completely cultural, fundamentalism is relative, and in two particular ways. One way rests on the distinction between what is often referred to as *mythos* versus *logos*, or symbol versus fact. The other way concerns precisely what is fundamental in the first place.

This primary problem, of *mythos* versus *logos*, is one that is basic to religion, or at least to the scholarly study of religion. *Mythos* is myth, not in the sense of 'false story' but in the sense of *story* — that is, of representative story, exemplary tale, 'charter,' paradigmatic act, symbol, allegory. For about a century, myth and symbol have preoccupied the study of religion and even much of philosophy, from the work of Otto to Eliade to Jung to Cassirer and Langer to Lévi-Strauss to Ricoeur to Campbell. In this mythical view of religion, or perhaps it would be better to say, in the mythical *function* of religion, two human tendencies are immanent: (1) the tendency to tell stories, to make narratives out of events or situations, and (2) the tendency to use symbols to represent or encapsulate things that either cannot be expressed concisely or cannot be expressed at all. Rudolf Otto, in his *The Idea of the Holy*, was one of the first to conceive of religion as emanating from a human experience of something — in his view, awe, wonder, and fear — that cannot be formulated any other way than through myth and symbol. Many other students of religion, including the ones above, have inherited and developed this thought.

Karen Armstrong bases her otherwise empirical book *The Battle for God* on the *mythos/logos* dynamic and describes them well. *Mythos* is not oriented toward or concerned with practicality and is not meant to be taken literally; it cannot be and does not want to be 'proven,' since it is not about fact. Its accounts, often in narrative (story) form, are not about specific historical events but are "external manifestations of constant, timeless realities" (xvi) that cannot be communicated any other way. In many versions, including hers, the actual phenomena that are being symbolized or mythologized are *psychological* realities. Joseph Campbell is then perhaps the leading modern proponent of this view. His books and lectures and television appearances are pervaded with references to myth and metaphor and the ineffable subjective realm to which they refer. In one of his many formulations of his position, he states: "A basic methodological principle, to be regarded when mythology is being interpreted in psychological terms, tells us that what is referred to in myth as 'other world' is to be understood psychologically as inner world ..., and that what is spoken of as 'future' [and past] is now" (2001, 25). At the extreme, "God is a symbol. The connotation of the symbol lies beyond all naming, beyond all numeration, beyond all categories of thought" (48).

This is a highly appealing vision for modern Americans, as indicated by the popularity of Campbell and other similar thinkers. However, it runs up against two obstacles: *logos*, or the capacity for literalness and factuality, and *the actual beliefs and practices of believers. Logos* is "the rational, pragmatic, and scientific thought that enabled men and women to function well in the world" (Armstrong, xvi). In fact, it is rationality, literalness, 'logic' (as the name suggests), 'truth-or-falseness.' As such, it is the antithesis of symbolic thought, for it follows the rule 'X does not equal not-X,' the basic logical rule of exclusion. Symbols, to be symbols, must be both X and not-X. Obviously, humans could not operate in the real world if their heads were full of nothing but symbols; sometimes, we need straightforward cause-and-effect thinking. For example, you cannot just pray or do rituals for farming; you must put some seeds in the ground. However, the symbol-sympathizers like Armstrong, Campbell, Huston Smith, and many others also posit that man cannot live by *logos* alone, which cannot soothe the human heart nor answer the big questions. Huston Smith specifies six areas that *logos* (which he erroneously calls 'science') cannot make any contributions to: values, meaning, final causes, "invisibles," quality (or subjective aspects of experience), and "our superiors" (2001, 197–9).

Notwithstanding the fact that we do not even know whether about half of these things actually exist, this is a typical and popular position in America and one that represents the *separate worlds* model of science and religion that we discussed previously. Stephen Jay Gould, for example, based his reconciliation of science and religion on the notion that science deals with facts (*logos*) and religion deals with values or meanings (*mythos*). He argued that it is important to keep the two straight and separate, and others agree; both are essential to human life, even if they are intrinsically different. While it would be dangerous to try to live without one or the other (oh, what a dismal and lonely world it would be without religion!), it is equally if not more dangerous to conflate the two — to take one's symbols and metaphors for facts and histories.

What does this all have to do with fundamentalism? Everything, as it turns out, for fundamentalism is precisely the position that takes religious narratives as fact — *mythos* as *logos*. After all, that is the whole point of fundamentalism (or at least one of its two points). The source, whatever it is — Christian Bible, Muslim Qur'an, Hindu Vedas, Jewish Torah, Sinhalese Buddhist Mahavamsa, *etc.* — is completely, absolutely true and authoritative in matters of faith and fact. In Christian fundamentalism in particular, the Bible's 'science' and 'history' are inerrantly accurate. Religion is fact, and when man-made *logos*, *i.e.*, science, disagrees with religion, then science is wrong and religion is right. This necessitates that fundamentalist religion denigrate human reason (which does often disagree with 'revealed truth'); like Tertullian, whom we quoted and criticized before, religion does not need reason because religion *is* reason.

Liberal religionists try, fairly successfully, to circumvent the problem of empirical conflict between reason and religion by converting the discredited passages of scripture into 'allegory,' what we can now call *mythos*. Thus, the moral parts and certain historical parts of the Bible, say, can be true, while the other historical and 'natural' parts (like creation in six days) are not literal but figurative: as Huston Smith opines, "That this scientific cosmology retires traditional ones with their six days of creation and the like goes without saying. Who can possibly question that when the scientific cosmology has landed people on the moon?" (13). The answer, of course, is the fundamentalists! Campbell goes even further: "God is not a fact" (17). This is precisely the corrupt, syncretistic, modernist kind of stuff that drives fundamentalists insane. If 'God' is not a fact, then why are we fundamentalists all in an uproar in the first place? Of course he is a fact!

The other thing that symbolizing religionists like Campbell and Smith and even Gould misunderstand is that their position does not represent the beliefs and aspirations of actual believers. Few believers — and no fundamentalists — say, "Oh, my belief is just a symbol, it's not really true." At least Gould appreciates this when he admits that his NOMA concept is not compatible with "popular religion" which actually believes that its claims are true. But popular religion *is* religion, and there has never been more than a small minority of religious elites who knew that their religion was just a psychological allegory. For the vast majority, religion is true, or else why bother? James Kennedy, the fundamentalist televangelist, refutes the symbolists when he argues that some parts of the Bible are figurative, like "faith of a mustard seed," but other parts are literal, like Jonah being swallowed by a whale, and that the Bible is clear as to which is which (35). For him, as for all fundamentalists, there is no interpretation, no symbolic analysis: "In living, explaining, or defending our faith, we are most likely to say, 'The Word of God says ....' As believers, that settles the matter, no matter what the matter may be" (20).

Fundamentalism is the vital contradiction of all attempts to reduce religion to symbol, allegory, psychological phenomena, and degrees of truth. For fundamentalists, religion is fact, truth, reason, and science. Symbolists try to tell fundamentalists and all other Theists that they do not really believe what they think they believe; fundamentalists answer, "Yes, we believe exactly what we say we believe." To them, symbolic analysis belongs with all the other decadent, degenerate, collaborationist, modernist and postmodernist dross that has to be flushed from the religious system to get back to the uncorrupted religion of days past. Such symbolic analysis relativizes religion, which they despise, as it misses the very point of religion — *that it tends to, that it wants to take itself seriously, even literally.* Yet the very fact that one fundamentalist chooses the Bible and another the Qur'an and another the Vedas and another the Torah and another the Mahavamsa, *ad infinitum* — in other words, that their own fundamentalism is relative — escapes them. You cannot just be a fundamentalist; you must be a Christian fundamentalist or Muslim fundamentalist, *etc.*

So fundamentalism rejects one form of religious relativism by conflating the mythical and logical aspects of religion, or better yet by denying the mythical and insisting on the logical. This, as Armstrong notes, is a particularly modern attitude toward religion, so in a way fundamentalists are modernists themselves, a realization which I am sure would lead them to pull their hair out. And as such they are relativists, because they represent not only one particular tradition but a specifically modern version of that tradition to boot. But they are relativists in one other important way as well, and this has to do with the very meaning of 'tradition.' Fundamentalism wants to look back to a pure or real state of religion. But the question lingers: how far back? Which state? And since they were not there, how can their purism constitute anything more than religion remembered — or even worse, religion reminisced, which as we stated early in this chapter also means religion forgotten, religion interpreted, and religion invented?

Fundamentalists' relation to the past is problematic and relative in two ways: they select how far back in the past they want to go, and they select which aspects of that past they want to bring forward. The most powerful example is the Christian fundamentalist fetishizing of the Bible; they want to go back to proper Bible worship and proper Bible belief. However, they forget that *there was no Bible* in Jesus' time and that the Bible as it exists today was not compiled until the fourth century and then only by a committee vote on the various available writings. The first apostles did not write anything down for decades (if ever) because they thought the world was going to end in their lifetimes; who would read it? Early Christianity was not about believing texts but following Jesus immediately. All that fundamentalists have today is texts, since Jesus is so conspicuously missing.

Admittedly there have been some attempts to recreate truly 'primitive' churches, like the gatherings at the time of the Apostles. But (1) who really knows what those times and gatherings were like, and (2) who wants to live *exactly* as they did? Few fundamentalists appear to want to give up their televisions and computers and air-conditioned homes and cars and live like first-century peasants. In fact, modern fundamentalism depends fundamentally on the tools of modernity; where would Falwell and Robertson and their ilk be without television, radio, satellites, and the Internet? Some sects that might rightly deserve the name 'fundamentalist,' like the Amish or the Mennonites, really do live in a 'present past,' but even then, they do not live in the Apostles' past. Rather, they have chosen a much more recent historical moment — say, eighteenth-century Europe — to freeze and perpetuate as a 'permanent past.' And their fundamentalism is much more authentic and complete than any televangelist's; I'm sure Falwell's planned community in Virginia will include running water and satellite television.

The point is that there is no such thing as 'real fundamentalism' or 'complete fundamentalism,' because fundamentalism itself is relative. You can be fundamentalistic about the eighteenth century, the sixteenth century, the fourth century, the first century, or the third millennium BCE. In fact, people in those lost times were sometimes fundamentalistic themselves about some yet earlier time and struggled against the modernist forces of their day. After all, every time is 'modern time' to the people who are living in it! So fundamentalists pick, without realizing it, which particular past they want to recreate, and they (usually) winnow out the unpleasant stuff. For instance, hardly any (but, incredibly, some) Christian fundamentalists want to re-institute slavery and death by stoning and other biblical injunctions.

Conclusion: The War We Did Not Choose

In the last three chapters, we explored some of the reasons why a vocal and active Atheism is desirable, not just to protect our own rights as American citizens but to serve, involuntarily I will admit, as the old canary-in-a-coal-mine to indicate the cultural health of diversity and toleration. We saw that toleration is not the natural state of monotheistic religion and that only a long and hard history has won what fragile toleration exists in this country and civilization. We discovered that dissidents, not always Atheists but almost always labeled as Atheists, were the ones who sacrificed comfort and sometimes life for the possibility of freedom (for themselves if not for others). We learned that keeping religious sects out of political power was a conclusion arrived at from this experience and that this lesson, while sometimes hard to remember or apply, keeps everyone free and equal in America. And finally, we discussed reasons why Atheists can and should organize and agitate for the right to dissent and should represent themselves as they are in public.

However, we truly encountered in the present chapter what is at stake in these circumstances. There are those anti-Atheists in our society who think that Atheists are the angry ones and have an agenda to change and control American culture and politics. In fact, there is not and never has been an Atheist agenda — perhaps until now. When the founding fathers disestablished religion at the federal and state level, that was not an Atheist agenda. When Darwin published the theory of natural selection, that was not an Atheist agenda. When physics postulated that the universe began with a big bang, that was not an Atheist agenda. When anthropologists determined that all cultures are different and man-made and equally valid from their own point of view, that was not an Atheist agenda. And when the Supreme Court banned official prayer from public schools, that was not an Atheist agenda.

It takes some creativity to perceive these things as part of an Atheist conspiracy, when they are in fact the realization of the promises of both scientific inquiry and democratic principle. Nevertheless, I can understand how the accumulated burden of these developments felt like siege to serious religionists, which is what religionists ought to be — serious about their beliefs and claims. It felt like religion was on the retreat, because it was. Each step chipped away, if not at the truth of religion, then at least at the certainty and authority of it. At some point, some religionists were bound to dig in their heels and say, "Not one more inch" — or perhaps even, "We are taking back some of the inches we lost."

Not science nor democratic politics nor even Atheism was ever really at war with religion. Each was just going about its business, finding more and more places where religion simply could not hold. I would never deny that there were not Atheists in the works, nor that Atheists took a certain pleasure in seeing religion on the run. But it is fact and reason that are the adversaries of falsehood and unreason, in whatever form they take. Regardless, at a critical moment religion refused to yield further ground and even launched its counteroffensive, and fundamentalism was born. A war was declared — a war against modernity, secularism, diversity, relativism, in fact against everything but orthodox religion (although also against all unorthodox religion as well!). And the war was not just declared but prosecuted with some force and effectiveness.

We did not ask for a war. We only asked for freedom and reason. But we find ourselves in a war that we did not choose and do not really want. We would prefer the peaceful and steady march of human reason and human rights. But that is not an option at this time. Every advance we advocate in reason and rights will be seen by them as another affront, another piece of the anti-religion Atheist agenda. But to cease to advocate advances is to relinquish the battlefield, and a unilateral surrender or refusal to play the game anymore simply leaves them to continue to carry out their campaign. Unfortunately, in the presence of radicals, we face the danger of being radicalized; that is how human affairs work. But to decline to participate in the challenge once it has been thrown down is to lose, and they are certainly not going to stop until someone stops them. Like it or not, choose it or not, we have to resist — and keep our reason and compassion in the process. We cannot turn into — let them turn us into — fundamentalist Atheists.

CHAPTER TWELVE

Living in the Disenchanted World — Toward an Atheism of the Future

Here at the end, we can look back with satisfaction at the arguments against irrational claims and at the proper identification of nonrational claims — and at the costs in human terms of mistaking irrational and nonrational claims for facts, of rejecting diversity, and of enforcing conformity — and be happy with our Atheism. We can appreciate that Atheism, or rather, the rationality that leads us naturally to Atheism, is good and right. It is not, never has been, and probably never will be easy to be an Atheist, but that does not make it any the less correct, valuable, or noble.

We Atheists have been maligned throughout history, as we have seen, as licentious and immoral, un-American (or un-whatever society we happen to live in), angry, sad, lonely, cold, and even demonic. These dishonors are all completely ridiculous and not based in any way in reality. However, two criticisms of Atheism as we see it practiced are probably valid, and these are that it is 'negative' and that it is 'merely intellectual.' By the first criticism, I mean that, while it rips through religion, it does not have much of a positive program of its own to offer; it has not, for example, attempted to envision or represent a future without religion. By the second, I mean that it typically, in its various forms — mostly writing and speaking — does not express or address much of the emotional or nonrational side of humanity. Some opponents of Atheism even suggest that it denigrates or devalues the subjective aspect of experience, only valuing objectivity, rationality, and the disembodied mind. Atheists, they say, only live from the neck up.

It is probably true that 'formal' or 'public' Atheism is negative and intellectual, but this is more methodological than essential. That is to say, since the methodology of Atheism is the essay, the logical argument, the debate, and the public speech, its argumentative and intellectual aspects will naturally be emphasized. It is also situational: Atheists find themselves, as we just noted and as we all know, under attack constantly and therefore in a permanent position of defensiveness. There is nothing inherently defensive about Atheism, any more than there is about Christianity, although the latter also found itself in a defensive posture in its early years — until it attained political power — and still today in places where it is the (often disapproved) minority. Defensiveness always distorts any position, misrepresenting or *dys*-representing what it would be if it were allowed to develop and express itself naturally.

Finally, these less endearing characteristics of Atheism are partly an artifact of psychology, of the psychology or personality of individual Atheists. There is no doubt at all that Atheists tend to be intellectual, that they tend to like to debate or argue, that they tend to be extreme individualists and to be rather restrained in their emotional expression. It would be hard to imagine an Atheist revival meeting with shouting and singing and crying and falling to the floor. Atheists are simply not given to such outbursts, and this might be a, if not *the*, distinguishing feature of Atheism as opposed to religiosity. But this personality type, while it has something to do with the appeal of Atheism to individual Atheists, has nothing to do with the message and therefore the truth of Atheism. And of course, in their private lives, there is no reason whatsoever to suppose that Atheists feel less, love less, wonder less, grieve less, or are in any way deficient emotionally compared to our more excitable and demonstrative colleagues. Atheism is not about these emotions. We have them, they are just not part of the message of Atheism.

If I could add a third item to the list of characteristics of the 'Atheist way,' it would be *disenchanted*. Often in English, when we use the term *disenchanted* we mean something like 'disappointed' or 'displeased' or 'emotionally disengaged.' However, I employ the term here in its original sense — 'free of enchantment,' enchantment meaning 'being influenced by chants, charms, and other illusory appeals.' Max Weber, the famous early sociologist, described disenchantment as the condition of modernity and particularly of bureaucracy — rational, literal, impersonal, objective, and definitely devoid of any magical or supernatural qualities. Weber, like many others since him, disparaged disenchantment, and the entire modernist project that includes it, for being barren, ugly, depersonalizing, emotionally distant, and ultimately insufficient to human needs for meaning and value.

We Atheists are necessarily and by definition disenchanted. We experience (or at least *should* experience — there may be some Atheists who reject the notion of gods but still entertain other 'spiritual' claims) no supernatural or magical aspect to the world. But we do not find the world more barren or ugly for it. We still perceive beauty and wonder, we still feel happiness and sadness and love and hate. We do not experience depersonalization (any more than anyone else does in our mass bureaucratic society); in fact, the world may be more 'personal' for us, since there is no greater intelligence or power in it than people. Nor does the world seem cold and sterile or meaningless to us. How do we do that?

On an Atheist Mythos

Despite, or more likely because of, two thousand years of Christianity and five thousand years of civilization and its religion, Atheism is very much an unfinished product. I liken this situation to the one in the unfinished communist societies of the twentieth century. I am no communist, mark my words, but it would have been interesting to learn what communist society could have become if it had been allowed to follow its course without outside interference. However, capitalist societies like our own, for reasons good and bad, would not let this happen. Among the bad reasons is what Noam Chomsky has called "the threat of the good example," wherein one dares not let one's opponent succeed for fear that others will follow the example. So, as capitalist societies have prevented communist ones from exploring the consequences of their system, religions have prevented Atheism from exploring the full expression of its philosophy.

Therefore, there has never developed in the history of mankind a complete, full-bodied version of Atheism, so we do not know what that would look like. The few Atheist societies that have arisen, like the Soviet Union and the People's

Republic of China, were perversions of Atheism for the sake of other ideological causes including state control, total conformity of thought, and the fanatical cult of personality of certain leaders. Perhaps the only even approximately successful attempt to imagine an Atheist reality comes from the greatest modern Atheist, Nietzsche, who curiously put his atheistic vision in mythological form in his *Thus Spake Zarathustra*, complete with a prophet of Atheism. I would like to quote a whole section from early in that work, on what he calls the "three metamorphoses," partly because it represents the style of his mythological Atheism and partly because it captures so poignantly and poetically the current condition of Atheism, in his day (late 1800s) and ours.

Three metamorphoses of the spirit do I designate to you: how the spirit becometh a camel, the camel a lion, and the lion at last a child.

Many heavy things are there for the spirit, the strong load-bearing spirit in which reverence dwelleth: for the heavy and the heaviest longeth its strength. What is heavy? so asketh the load-bearing spirit; then kneeleth it down like the camel, and wanteth to be well laden. What is the heaviest thing, ye heroes? asketh the load-bearing spirit, that I may take it upon me and rejoice in my strength.

Is it not this: To humiliate oneself in order to mortify one's pride? To exhibit one's folly in order to mock at one's wisdom? Or is it this: To desert our cause when it celebrateth its triumph? To ascend high mountains to tempt the tempter? Or is it this: To feed on the acorns and grass of knowledge, and for the sake of truth to suffer hunger of soul? Or is it this: To be sick and dismiss comforters, and make friends of the deaf, who never hear thy requests? Or is it this: To go into foul water when it is the water of truth, and not disclaim cold frogs and hot toads? Or is it this: To love those who despise us, and give one's hand to the phantom when it is going to frighten us?

All these heaviest things the load-bearing spirit taketh upon itself: and like the camel, which, when laden, hasteneth into the wilderness, so hasteneth the spirit into its wilderness.

But in the loneliest wilderness happeneth the second metamorphosis: here the spirit becometh a lion; freedom will it capture, and lordship in its own wilderness. Its last Lord it here seeketh: hostile will it be to him, and to its last God; for victory will it struggle with the great dragon.

What is the great dragon which the spirit is no longer inclined to call Lord and God? "Thou-shalt," is the great dragon called. But the spirit of the lion saith, "I will." "Thou-shalt," lieth in its path, sparkling with gold — a scale-covered beast; and on every scale glittereth golden, "Thou shalt!"

The values of a thousand years glitter on those scales, and thus speaketh the mightiest of all dragons: "All the values of things glitter on me. All values have already been created, and all created values do I represent. Verily, there shall be no 'I will' any more." Thus speaketh the dragon.

My brethren, wherefore is there need of the lion in the spirit? Why sufficeth not the beast of burden, which renounceth and is reverent? To create new values — that, even the lion cannot yet accomplish: but to create itself freedom for new creating — that can the might of the lion do. To create itself freedom, and give a holy Nay even unto duty: for that, my brethren, there is need of the lion.

To assume the right to new values — that is the most formidable assumption for a load-bearing and reverent spirit. Verily, unto such a spirit it is preying, and the work of a beast of prey. As its holiest, it once loved "Thou-shalt": now is it forced to find illusion and arbitrariness even in the holiest things, that it may capture freedom from its love: the lion is needed for this capture.

But tell me, my brethren, what the child can do, which even the lion could not do? Why hath the preying lion still to become a child? Innocence is the child, and forgetfulness, a new beginning, a game, a self-rolling wheel, a first movement, a holy Yea. Aye, for the game of creating, my brethren, there is needed a holy Yea unto life: its own will, willeth now the spirit; his own world winneth the world's outcast.

Three metamorphoses of the spirit have I designated to you: how the spirit became a camel, the camel a lion, and the lion at last a child.

Nietzsche's tale is an allegory, a form of writing that Atheists usually do not attempt, if they even respect it. He is speaking allegorically of religion and Atheism and something yet beyond Atheism, some reality of the future. It should not be hard to recognize each. The camel is the long-suffering Theist, and her religion is the dragon — the realm of authority, of command and commandment, of the past and tradition, of pre-existing values that one must not question. The lion is Atheism, the resisting spirit, the great 'No,' the denier and destroyer of old authorities and commandments. In this sense, Atheism is in fact negative, but this negation is a liberation: one cannot be free until one has shed old burdens, which takes strength and courage and will be perceived by the dragon-lovers or the merely dazed camels as wanton, even demonic, destructiveness. But notice, with Nietzsche, that the job is not done with the lion's forceful nay-saying, its purely (if liberatingly) negative action. Something positive must follow — something innocent (of the destruction from which it was born), something forgetful and unmindful (of the traditions and 'truths' left behind and of the negative escape-process itself), something creative (of new values and meanings), something 'yes-saying.' This is Nietzsche's transcendent man and society and the future that contemporary Atheism has not formulated and offered as an alternative to the theistic past and present.

I am not prophetic enough to envision and describe this post-theistic future, but I know that contemporary Atheism is not it. It cannot be, for it plays the lion's role in the history of thought and belief. The really creative, affirmative movement comes after, when one does not have to be destructive or negative anymore. However, elsewhere Nietzsche reminds us that we must forever or recurrently return to the lion, lest our new values become as old and ossified as our current values — lest we become prisoners of the systems we have created.

This, I think, is the great challenge for a future Atheism, which I will simply refer to as the 'natural' or 'disenchanted' future. (I change terms here because a natural or disenchanted future would not be combative or argumentative or 'negative' any longer, since the counter-argument — Theism — would cease to exist.) Atheism today, it seems to me, eschews symbols and allegories and myths, not just out of personal taste but out of a well-justified fear: the fear that those objects will become hardened into tomorrow's 'truth' and Theism. We have seen how the likes of Armstrong and Campbell and Smith and many before and since them have descried the myth-less condition. From anthropologists like Mary Douglas to philosophers like Karl Jaspers, sensitive scholars have bemoaned a human world without the depth of symbol and allegory. Jaspers wrote, in almost ecstatic words: "How wretched, how lacking in expressiveness our life would be, if the language of myth were no longer valid! To fill myth with banal content is to commit an unpardonable error. The splendor and wonder of the mythical vision is to be purified, but must not be abolished" (Nielsen, 58). Theodoor Marius van Leeuwen also wants to preserve the majesty of myth, although (significantly) not quite in its present form:

> *Demythologizing* is an urgent necessity of modern thought, but *demythizing* would cause a deplorable impoverishment. In fact modern man has been the first to discover the proper *symbolic dimension of myth*. Our modernity is born out of the distinction of history and myth, and out of the desacralization of nature. It is after this "crisis" that man recognizes myth as myth .... Myth as *explanation* must be dissolved. Its logos, its pretension to be an account of history or an explanation of nature, is pseudo-logos. But the demytho-*log*-ization of myth is the condition for a rediscovery of myth as symbolic narration. The "greatness of myth" ... is that it has more meaning than a history which is objectively true. This meaning is not etiological but *explorative*. Myth explores the possibilities of man and his place within being. It is "an opening up and a disclosure" ... of a field of human experience' (Nielsen, 64).

Herein lies the problem. Atheism as demythologizing and remythologizing walks a fine line between two hostile or corrosive alternatives. On the one side is fundamentalism and on the other side is relativism. Fundamentalism is the easier enemy to understand. If we create our own symbols and allegories and myths — and all the attendant trappings of the human experience of the ineffable, including repetitive behaviors (rituals) and special days (holidays) and special places (sacred sites) and exemplary persons (saints or officiates), *etc.* — we risk having all those things taken *seriously*. Literalism, fundamentalism, is a perennial danger, especially to every generation after the generation that invented the symbols. Atheists are, granted, not prone to fundamentalism, but then they are probably not prone to mythologizing at all. However, as we learned in our discussion of anthropology, humans have an understandable tendency to take their 'artificial' (man-made, that is, cultural) environment for granted, to take it as 'real' rather than merely conventional. And any man-made system that has been taken for real is just a short step from fundamentalism. Then we start arguing about the correct symbols and rituals and persons, *ad absurdum*, and we have committed the error of mistaking *mythos* for *logos*. We have created our own new dragon.

The danger on the other side is relativism, which is not a bad thing in itself — it is just a fact, that all judgments and values come from some particular point of view. The problem is that this awareness is inimical to believing in your own man-made environment: if we know that we just made it up ourselves, it has no special or exclusive claim to our credulity or affection. 'Why this and not that?' is the perpetual response of relativism to any specific nonrational appeal to our attention and commitment. As Atheists, rationalists, and relativists, we would never want to lose our relativistic perspective, and as citizens in a diverse world it is virtually impossible that we ever would. But then, we would also always know that we created our symbolic mythical world for ourselves and that we — or anyone else — could create another just as valid at any time. The believer cannot and does not live in this state; believing depends centrally on forgetting the human authorship of the mythical reality in which we exist.

A final and fateful question is whether rationalists like ourselves even *want* to create a mythology. This question comes down to two issues: (1) is it truly necessary, as all poets and philosophers say, to have a mythology in order to live a full and deep human life, and (2) are we the kind of people who can do it, or is mythology a closed option to us? In other words, perhaps mythology, in whatever form it takes, is a religious/enchanted enterprise at heart, and the natural/disenchanted future has a different form altogether.

I would like to think that mythology is not a necessary part of human experience. But do I think that simply because I, because we, are incapable of it? I don't know. Humans are story-telling creatures. We are meaning-making creatures. Atheists tell stories and make meanings too. We are certainly aware of the great archetypal moments of existence like birth and death, of the beauties and wonders of the universe, sometimes even of the transcendent or mystical experiences that are possible for humans. But is it really obligatory in the end to mythologize these phenomena, to make them something that they are not, to impose human meanings and motivations on them? I am inclined to say no. Does this make the world a thinner, shallower, less human place? No, no, and maybe yes. The world is what it is; whether or not it is 'human' is irrelevant and actually a little funny. It is precious to think that the world — be it paramecia or puppies, plants or planets — are 'people' in some way, which is intrinsic to the mythological imagination, but they are not. In fact, as our old friend Xenophanes observed, puppies would probably impute puppy meanings and motivations to plants and people and planets, and plants would probably impute plant meanings and motivations to puppies and people and planets, *etc. etc. etc.*

The conclusion is that if Atheism ever is allowed to evolve from the lion stage to the child stage (a dubious proposition in itself, since vibrant forces seek to prevent exactly that), it will pass into a creative phase the likes of which we have never seen in the history of humankind. Does this mean that all Atheists will suddenly become artists and painters, poets and philosophers? No. Does this mean that we even need an Atheist art or poetics or philosophy? Not necessarily. *The question is not what Atheists would create but what a creative Atheism would be.* The one thing perhaps that it will not be is religion. There is no reason why we must tear down the myths only to establish myths of our own; there is no reason why we must embrace the language of the old in the new. It might be that mythical, symbolic, allegorical language is the language of religion, not of humanity, since humanity has never had the chance to learn and speak any other language. The disenchanted world may speak and experience entirely differently. I kind of hope that it does. That might be why it will never happen.

On Atheist Morality

Another issue for the disenchanted future is morality, or — since I hate that word, smacking as it does of religion and commandment — proper or ethical behavior. One of the litanies against Atheists is that we cannot possibly have morality, since we do not have a 'code' such as a sacred text, nor do we have a spiritual policeman giving that code teeth. In fact, some anti-Atheists actually maintain that Atheists are closet Theists, since we might bad-mouth god(s) but we ultimately and surreptitiously derive our code of conduct from religion.

This is less of a problem for Atheism than some think, while morality is more of a problem for Theism than it thinks. As we have stated again and again, there is no demonstrable evidence that, by whatever standard, Atheists are more immoral than Theists, that we do more 'bad stuff' than they. Notwithstanding the relativity of morality, Atheist and Theist behavior is roughly comparable. This may be because, to the consternation of Theists, *religion is not the sole or maybe even major basis of their morality either*. Morality, in actuality, has four bases: religion, culture, nature, and reason. Even worse, religion is just a domain of culture, so in the final analysis there are three fundamental bases of morality, and religion is not one of them.

Culture, as anthropology instructs us, is all that humans learn and share by being members of a society. Culture includes knowledge and skills, beliefs, norms, values, morals, and much more. It has also been analyzed as containing four distinct domains, including economics, kinship/family, politics, and religion, and generally economics — the practical aspects of living in a particular environment with a particular technology — is deemed to be the core or base of culture. Therefore, other aspects of culture, including religion, are derivative from and dependent upon the more mundane economic realities of a society.

We know with certainty that different societies hold different moral standards. Morality is culturally relative. *This is a fact.* So members of a society learn the appropriate standards of conduct of their culture, and many of these standards have nothing whatsoever to do with religion. Furthermore, insofar as standards of conduct do have to do with religion, they are learned too; no child is born with a 'genetic morality.' Religions (at least the kinds of religions with which we are most familiar) tend to have the most formal moralities, often with specific lists of expected conduct and sometimes associated punishments. It is well to note, though, that not all religions (in the largest sense, as 'supernatural belief-and-behavior systems,' not just as theologies) have moral codes and not all are even particularly preoccupied with morality. Christianity in particular is more about (orthodox) belief and faith than about works and morality; how many real moral injunctions actually exist in the New Testament — and how many of those are really useful? Also, sometimes culture outside the domain of religion has an extensive and explicit set of moral/behavioral injunctions, often captured in the form of sayings and proverbs and folk wisdom. Finally, even when religion does provide a moral code, *that code is always and necessarily deficient*, since it is sometimes too general ('you should not kill') and sometimes too specific (Jesus did thus-and-so in a particular situation) to be much use and must be and is interpreted and applied in specific situations. Obviously, even for Christians, sometimes you can or should kill. And of course many areas of behavior (like jaywalking or spitting on the sidewalk or computer hacking) are conspicuously left out of these codes. And the mere possession of a moral code is a far cry from actual morality, as is evident from the high rate of crime, deviance, and antisocial behavior committed by Theists.

Some, going back as far as Kant, have marveled at the very presence of a moral sense in humans and located the seat of religion in this god-given moral awareness. But a moral sense is not really all that marvelous, and there is no need at all to conclude that it is god-given. In fact, we see recognizably 'moral' behavior in many if not most living mammalian species; it might even be argued that humans are *less moral* than many species, since we do more harm to each other and to the world than they. Morality, in the sense of standardized and restrained (that is, pro-social) behavior, is actually a natural, evolution-based phenomenon. All social animals and many non-social animals have standardized behaviors and 'rituals' or gestures that trigger things like aggression or the cessation of aggression. Many species show 'altruistic' behaviors like sharing and self-sacrifice. And the more that species are capable of learning, the more they demonstrate moral-like behavior. The higher primates, closely related to humans, have 'moral' awarenesses so similar to ours that it is impossible not to see the origins of our own in them. Morality, in other words, is a completely reasonable adaptation of social and behavior-acquiring (that is, not entirely instinct-driven) beings.

Some observers remark on the fact that all humans have morality, whatever that exact morality might be, as evidence that it must have a 'source' or a 'designer.' Instead, the ubiquity of morality, like the ubiquity of language or of culture itself, is clearer testimony to the evolutionary and genetic oneness of humanity. Just as humans exhibit many languages which shows that there is some powerful propensity to acquire language (which propensity must be fed with social experience to develop), so the exhibition of many moralities shows that there is a powerful inborn propensity to acquire morality that must also be supplied with experience and that also develops. Psychologists like Lawrence Kohlberg have studied the development of morality in children and found, strikingly, that the kind of morality that religion tends to reflect — reward and punishment morality — is the lowest stage in moral development, surpassed even in young children by principled and intersubjective morality.

Let us now consider the realm of reason. Even if there were no religion, even if there were no genetic predisposition to acquire morality, reason itself would still lead us to standardized and socially beneficial behavior on the basis of principle and intersubjectivity (that is, the awareness of the feelings of others). I need no religion to tell me that killing is generally destructive to other people, to myself, and to social order. Reason can and does arrive at most of the moral principles of the great religions without any appeal to god(s) or spiritual rewards and punishments. Why, one of the great moralists of all times, Socrates, argued that virtue was its own reward. We require no gods to order us nor prizes to induce us. In fact, since morality always involves the voluntary choice of actions from possible alternatives, it can be and has been argued that Atheists are *more moral* than Theists, since Atheists, when they behave well (and they usually do), do so purely on the basis of ethical principle and without any regard for self-reward or self-punishment, of which there is none. I do not want to press the claim that Atheists are better people than Theists; we are all just people, trying to figure our way through this big world. But the fact that Atheists do pretty well without an invisible omnipotent friend and enforcer testifies that this friend/enforcer is really secondary to the basic moral fact that social animals — humans included — tend and need to act responsibly toward one another. I can go one step beyond this, as Plato did in *Euthyphro*: the moral code that some god has given has one of two grounds. It is either arbitrary (the god just made it up, and it is only 'good' because he/she/it ordains it) or it is 'natural' or 'logical' (the god ordained it because it is good in itself). If the morality is arbitrary, then killing, for example, is neither good nor bad in itself but only because the god says so, and it is hard to see what is 'moral' about that. If, on the other hand, it is natural or logical, then human reason could arrive at it just as dependably without the god — in fact, the god him/her/itself is bound by nature and logic too — so the god is unnecessary to morality.

On Atheist 'Spirituality'

If there is one thing that Atheists agree on (and there may only be one thing), it is that there is no good reason to believe in god(s). It is not impossible, however, that one can be an Atheist and still believe in other 'spiritual' things; in fact, we know that there are people who call themselves 'spiritual Atheists.' And indeed, it is possible that, even if there is no such thing as god(s), there might still be other lesser spiritual beings or forces — angels, souls, nymphs, fairies, and genies, or karma, mana, auras, and so on. Atheism, in the strict interpretation, refers only to 'no god(s),' not to 'no spiritual/nonmaterial things.' So, when Atheists or other Humanists talk about spirit and spiritual experiences, they might literally mean that they believe in and experience non-god spiritual beings or forces.

I certainly think and hope that this is not so. Atheism is not identical to thorough materialism and rationalism, but rationalism is definitely the firmest philosophical underpinning for Atheism, and materialism is surely the most compatible view of the universe. There is no more evidence for other nonmaterial and spiritual beings or forces than there is for gods, so there is no more reason to accept their existence than that of gods. But likelier than this interpretation is the chance that 'spiritual' Atheists mean something different when they use the word *spirit* or *spiritual*. I assert that such talk is false, and even more than false, it is antihuman talk — the kind of talk that degrades and diminishes humans and the natural world.

Obviously enough, spiritual means 'of or pertaining to spirit.' When one is having a spiritual experience, one is experiencing spirit in some way. Ordinarily, we use spirit in two different senses. The first is as a general name for a class of allegedly real beings that have specific qualities unique to the class; in particular, they are usually invisible, immaterial, and often powerful. Gods are spirits, as are lower (but higher-than-human) beings like angels and cherubs and ascended masters, *etc.* The second is a name for a disposition or feeling or essence, such as 'the spirit of '76' or 'the spirit of the law.' Whether these latter spirits exist independently of 1776 or the law is dubious and probably not even claimed. We can have the spirit of '76 in us today, but we do not (I think) believe that this spirit resides in some spirit-world waiting to possess us.

But, at a deeper level, both of these usages of spirit share a common root. The derivation of the word is the Latin *spiritus*, which literally means 'breath,' and further *spirare* for 'to blow' or 'to breathe.' We can see this in other familiar English words that share the same root as 'spirit':

- Expire — *ex* 'out' + *-spire* 'breathe,' to breathe out, sometimes for the last time
- Conspire — *con* 'with' + *-spire* 'breathe,' to breathe with or close to (as in secrecy)
- Perspire — *per* 'through' + *-spire* 'breathe,' to breathe through, as when your body breathes through your pores
- Inspire — *in* 'in' + *-spire* 'breathe,' to breathe in or take in more breath
- Aspire — *ad* 'at' or 'upon' + *-spire* 'breathe,' to breathe at or upon, to focus your breath on
- Respire/respiration — *re* 'again' + *-spire* 'breathe,' to breathe again, to repeatedly breathe in and out
- Dispirit — *dis* 'from' or 'apart' + *-spire* 'breathe,' to deprive of breath
- Spirited — full of breath

All of these words have something to do with breath, quite obviously, but breath not in the literal sense: when we 'aspire' toward something or are 'inspired' by something, we are not literally breathing toward it or being breathed into by it. Rather, breath is here metaphorical, an image or representation of something other than our actual breathing process. *Webster's* first entry under *spirit*, in fact, gives the meaning "an animating or vital principle held to give life to physical organisms." Let us look at the same words again, in their metaphorical and everyday meanings.

- Expire — to lose or end one's energy or vitality, sometimes even to die
- Conspire — to ally one's energy or vitality with another, as in a conspiracy
- Perspire — to give off one's energy or vitality through the skin
- Inspire — to take in more energy or vitality from some external source
- Aspire — to focus or direct one's energy or vitality on some goal
- Respire/respiration — to continue to get and lose energy or vitality, in other words, to stay alive
- Dispirit — to take away the energy or vitality of another
- Spirited — full of energy or vitality

Breath in all of these words is a metaphor or analogy for energy, vitality, or what we might call life-force or even life itself; having a lot of it means lots of energy and vitality, and having little of it means being relatively — or absolutely — lifeless.

Breath, in many languages and cultures, is the manifestation or the representation of the force that animates (literally, makes us move) and gives us life. After all, when a body is alive, you can see it breathing, and when it dies, it stops breathing. Breath is motion and life. In ancient Greek, *pneuma* is the word for air or breath, from *pnein* 'to breathe.' It gives us words like *pneumatic* (full of air) and *pneumonia* (a disease of our air/lung organs). In ancient Hebrew *ruah* also means both breath and spirit, and it is commonly used in the

Old Testament to refer to the godly power that brings life out of matter and order out of chaos. Recall that, in Judeo-Christian theology, the universe was created by the speech of a god (the out-rush of air in verbal form) and that Adam was vivified by that god's breathing into earth.

Most if not all religious traditions recognize some life-force like this, whether or not they represent it as breath. Blood is another possible and potent metaphor for life; when we get agitated our blood boils, and when we have no feeling we are bloodless. Heart is still another common metaphor; someone with a lot of heart has great courage and strength, and someone who is heartless lacks either fortitude or compassion. Finally, movement itself is a sign and metaphor of life and life-force; if something packs a lot of emotional punch we call it 'moving,' but if it does not change our life we are unmoved. Most if not all traditions also distinguish between the life-force and the substrate that carries it, at least for a time. When or while a body 'has' this life-force it is active, vibrant, *alive*. When that force departs, a body is dead.

This can and almost necessarily does lead to a profound dualism — live force or spirit, non-live matter. Philosophers from Socrates and Plato to Descartes to modern-day mind-body dualists repeat the same distinction, and Christianity and Judaism certainly depend on it as well. Matter is inert, passive, dead on its own; only when it is infused with spirit is it mobile, active, and most importantly alive. But then, in a way, it never is alive, since it is only the 'ghost in the machine' that makes the machine — dead matter — jump and dance for a time. Matter, including the human body, is only (and this attitude is quite explicit in many traditions) a shell, a suit of clothing that the living aspect wears for a time. There is no natural or necessary connection between life and its clothing; reincarnation or soul-immortality equally attest to this fact.

What do people mean when they say they are 'spiritual'? What kinds of things do people, including some Atheists, point to when they describe a spiritual experience? More critically, what do these experiences have in common? Most often, people describe a sunset, a work of art, a great love, or some similar experience as an instance of the spiritual. Scholars too have studied the spiritual and (as many lay people have learned and say themselves) related it to feelings of awe and wonder. It is the majestic things (like mountains and sunsets), the immense things (distant galaxies or the universe itself), the exquisite things (like music), the precious things (like love and babies) that present us with the spiritual. These are the things that give us that feeling of rapture (a term that Christianity has hijacked), of being *rapt*, from the Latin *rapere*, 'to seize' or 'to sweep away.' We are literally seized by the power of the experience or the view.

And therein lies the clue. What spiritual experiences — whether they are religious or artistic or whatever — have in common is their power, their capacity to grab us and sweep us away emotionally in ways that ordinary life cannot or does not. They are *vibrant* (from the Latin *vibrare* 'to shake'), *vital* (from the Latin *vita* 'life'), *lively* (from the Old English *lif* 'life'), *vivacious* (from the Latin *vivere* 'to live'). These are the moments of *ecstasy*, from the Greek *ex-histanai*, 'to cause to stand out of itself or oneself.' They feel like *more than life*, like extra life — more energetic, vibrant, and alive than normal life — and they feel like *they come from outside of us*.

Spiritual experiences are those that seem to have more of that animating or vital stuff or force than mundane experiences do. They are a higher dose of life-force — one that we do not routinely encounter and one that we could not perhaps sustain for long without damaging ourselves. They speed up our breath, make it more *rapid* (also from the Latin *rapere*), and that is one overt sign of the enhancement of our life-force.

The problem is that, within the dualistic view, this life-force is 'other' than us, outside of us, foreign to us. Where then could such a spiritual experience, such spiritual power, originate from? It cannot be from us, because we are just inert matter. It must be from wherever that first spirit originated, the one that gave us life in the first place. It must be from heaven, from the spirits, from god(s).

That is the great mistake. It is the confusion of *more life* with *other life*. It is the attribution of life itself to another reality, another dimension, than the one in which we live every day — and, even more crucially, to a reality or dimension to which we do not have access. These profound, rapturous experiences depend on some other force coming and carrying us away. We are passive in the process. Funny, though, how it is nature and humanity that give us most of our supernatural experiences.

Spiritual experiences are those that make us feel more alive. It is as though we tap into an additional fountain of life or energy, one that could only arise from the source of all life or energy — outside of ourselves. It is a 'gift' in the true sense of the word: something given, something not truly our own.

Yet it is *we* — weak puny material beings that we are — who have these experiences. They are merely experiences that are livelier, more forceful, more animated and animating than our run-of-the-mill experiences. It is *our* emotions that are moved, *our* awe and wonder that are peaked, *our* life that is enhanced. It might be an external object — a mountain or a Mozart — that inspires us to this feeling, but it is our feeling. What is usually described as spiritual is really *life*, really *human*.

This talk of 'spiritual' and 'spirituality' perpetuates a profound mistake and constitutes a profound betrayal — perhaps the most profound that humans have ever committed against themselves. The mistake is the prejudice or belief or faith that life and its finer aspects, and our ability to appreciate those aspects, are not natural but must be supernatural — that beauty, awe, wonder, and love are not things of this world. No, they must belong to a better world, a higher world, and they are only revealed to us for a brief time. These finer, more powerful aspects of life are seen as separate from us, other than us, better than us, outside of us. Surely we — weak puny material beings — could not be capable of them on our own.

But the things that we call spiritual are precisely of this world. They are natural, and they are social. They are not *other life* but *simply more life*. They are not *other than human*, they are *more human*. They are the best of human. The spiritual is experienced as getting 'extra life' from somewhere outside of ourselves. In reality, it is discovering deeper or better levels inside of ourselves. It is encountering human-ness at its fullest.

Hence, spirituality is the greatest possible betrayal of humanity. Talk of spirit and the spiritual *alienates* the very best part of human-ness — literally, in the sense of making it alien to or other than our own selves. It says, 'This is the very best, the very most, that I can feel and be — and it is not me.' Therefore, it minimizes or denigrates the human or the natural (as all dualism does) and gives away the greatest things of which we are capable to some other realm or reality. It deprives us of not only part of our humanity but the best part of our humanity and ascribes it to some supernatural — and therefore nonnatural — world. In the process, we are lessened. We are alienated from ourselves and made to believe that no mere human could be the source of such wonder.

But we *are* the source. Spiritual experiences are in fact *human* experiences — the best, the strongest, the most profound human experiences, but human nonetheless. They are not a kind of non-human-ness but a kind of ultra-human-ness. We are richer by and for them, but we impoverish ourselves when we deny — or allow ourselves to be denied — our own finest nature and assign those feelings and capacities to the nonhuman, the unknown, and almost certainly the imaginary and unreal. There are, of course, religious traditions that do not want humans to feel that good, that powerful, that wonderful. Some, like Christianity, depend on the worthlessness of humanity; why else would we need salvation and a religious structure to provide it? The biggest fear of such traditions is the possibility that we will discover that we are just fine — not perfect, but pretty good — and that all of the best things in life are ... human. Thus, by rejecting spirit and the spiritual, we reclaim the wholeness of human experience and human being.

Critics often condemn Atheism for having nothing positive to offer. Sometimes they are correct, in terms of how Atheists represent Atheism. It is the rejection of god(s) — and I would add, the rejection of all nonmaterial beings and forces for which there is no evidence — and that is a negative message. But it is a negative message that makes way for a positive message. Sometimes, as Nietzsche stated, one must say no before one can say yes.

Over 150 years ago, Ludwig Feuerbach described Christianity in roughly the terms that I am suggesting here. He argued that the "essence of Christianity" is humanity's awareness of our own traits and our own greatness. This is not hubris, not sheer pride and arrogance. As he said,

> religion is the consciousness of the infinite; thus it is and can be nothing else than the consciousness which man has of his own — not finite or limited, but infinite nature. A really finite being has not even the faintest adumbration, still less consciousness, of an infinite being, for the limit of the nature is also the limit of the consciousness .... It follows that if thou thinkest the infinite, thou perceivest the infinitude of the power of thought; if thou feelest the infinite, thou feelest and affirmest the infinitude of the power of feeling. The object of the intellect is intellect objective to itself; the object of feeling is feeling objective to itself (1957 [1841], 2–9).

In other words, humans could not know or feel anything as great as what we ordinarily call "the spiritual" unless humanity was itself equally great. In fact, as I have tried to express above, what we ordinarily call the spiritual is nothing more than a misnamed part of ourselves, and the best part at that.

So the positive message of Atheism — after the air is cleared of god(s) and spirits and the spiritual — becomes a message of anthropology. By this I do not mean the academic discipline of anthropology but rather, as its roots suggest, the 'study or knowledge of humanity.' Spirituality is the opposite of humanity, but it is at once the same thing. It is humanity objectified and alienated, and as such perhaps more easily knowable. However, now we know something else — that what we once called spiritual we should now call human. Spirituality is the human expressed in terms of the non-human. That is unacceptable and self-deprecating. I urgently recommend, therefore, that we stop using the term *spiritual* altogether and replace it with the term that means what we really mean. Atheists are not spiritual and do not have spiritual experiences. Never again should we say, "I had a spiritual experience." Instead, the next time you see a particularly beautiful sunset or cute baby, simply say, "I had a life experience" — or better yet, "I had a *human* experience" — and encourage others to do the same.

On the Incompleteness of Atheism

As we discussed in the introduction to this book, it is commonly (and maliciously) claimed that Atheism is a belief system; we also explained how this is false. Atheism is, in principle and often in practice, one thing and one thing only — the lack of belief in any god(s). I know some Atheists who are still 'spiritual' (whatever they mean) or who still 'believe in' other irrational things like astrology or nontraditional medicine or what have you. In practice, Atheism tends to be associated with a constellation of other positions and values, usually liberal and humanistic, but there is no logical or necessary connection between them. It is simply that Atheists, if they are rational, arrive at certain other positions also supported by reason.

Atheism as a *lifestyle*, as a *thought system*, is therefore incomplete. This is both good and bad. Atheism has never claimed or attempted to be a whole way of life, a complete prescription for living. That is the grandiose claim of religion. I would specify two ways in which Atheism is incomplete. First, it does not come with a code of rules and regulations or concomitant positions and policies. Second, it does not give answers to, or even give place to, questions and concerns other than religious ones and then only in a rational, logical, and discursive way. The first I consider not a problem; the second might be a little different.

Theists will often accost Atheists with the question, "What is your morality?" or even worse "What is your moral code?" We don't have a good response to this tactic, which is generally intended either to discredit us ("Well, they do not have a moral code!") or to get us to admit that we share religion's morality ("Then you agree with the Ten Commandments!"). But there is no discredit, because we never claimed to be a life system, and what little pleasure Theists get out of such an admission is another example of the fallacy of composition ("You believe in Christian morality, so you must believe in all of Christianity").

I have observed Atheists, with some interest, attempting to remedy this deficiency by composing deliberate moral codes, often (sadly) with ten items in them. Sometimes these codes even take the form of 'thou shalts.' This activity, while interesting, is doomed to failure and is tangential to Atheism anyhow. If Theists cannot even agree on what is good and bad, then how are a bunch of contentious and freethinking Atheists supposed to agree? Even within a single religion, Christianity, people cannot agree; they cannot even agree on what their god is like, which is absolutely foundational to their belief. So I am untroubled by the fact that Atheists do not have an 'Atheist code.' But more to the point, Atheism is not about codes; Atheism is about the nonexistence of god(s). If the reality of god(s) is rejected, then all of the religious codes become moot, but we are not thrown thereby into intellectual and moral chaos. We still have culture, nature, and reason to guide us — which is all we ever had.

So, there is no reason why we are required to rise to the bait of the 'moral code' attack. Atheists have to limp their way through the social world just like Theists do. We have to balance individual good against social good, cost against benefit, help against harm. Atheists have to interpret and apply behavioral standards to specific situations just like Theists, although the latter object that their standards are not situational (despite the fact that conservative Christians, commandment followers that they are, tend to be hawkish about war and pro–capital punishment).

Furthermore, as we discussed earlier, Atheism does not entail any necessary political, philosophical, or other commitments. Admittedly, Atheists tend to be liberal on most issues, but to the extent that there is an Atheist orthodoxy, it is an artifact of individual Atheists and not a quality of Atheism as such. There is no 'Atheist platform' on all of the issues of the day; in fact, as freethinkers, it is unlikely there could be, since we think and choose for ourselves. There might be a certain convergence of opinion among informed rational people, but Atheism is not, does not claim to be, and does not aspire to be — and perhaps does not need to be — a total life solution.

The second incompleteness of Atheism — that it speaks to only one part of the complex human whole which includes a subjective or emotional component — is a bigger problem but still an ambivalent one. Atheism is in the end a one-issue affair, that issue being the existence or not of god(s), and that is why it is difficult to ascribe a category to Atheism at all. Is it a philosophy? A worldview? A position? I think I have shown in this book, especially in the chapters on reason and knowledge, that Atheism is really not an independent thing at all but, in the language of science, a 'dependent variable.' *It is a conclusion from evidence and logic*, like 'the earth revolves around the sun' or 'the acceleration of gravity is thirty-two feet per second per second.' As such, it is not being asked to be a whole philosophy or worldview. It is a rational conclusion on one (but a very major) matter. Why does it have to be more than it is?

The answer to this question, unfortunately, is because this one matter unsettles many other subsequent matters and forces a rethinking of some absolutely fundamental principles and truths. Nietzsche once again, the arch-Atheist, knew that the removal of god from the human horizon was no trivial thing; in his famous section, aptly entitled "The Madman," he understands the profundity of the 'death of god(s)':

What were we doing when we unchained this earth from its sun? Whither is it moving now? Whither are we moving? Away from all suns? Are we not plunging continually? Backward, sideward, forward, in all directions? Is there still any up or down? Are we not straying as through an infinite nothing? Do we not feel the breath of empty space? Has it not become colder? Is not night continually closing in on us? Do we not need to light lanterns in the morning? Do we not hear nothing as yet of the noise of the gravediggers who are burying God? Do we smell nothing as yet of the divine decomposition? Gods, too, decompose. God is dead. God remains dead. And we have killed him.

How shall we comfort ourselves, the murderers of all murderers? What was holiest and mightiest of all that the world has yet owned has bled to death under our knives: who will wipe this blood off us? What water is there for us to clean ourselves? What festivals of atonement, what sacred games shall we have to invent? Is not the greatness of this deed too great for us? Must we ourselves not become gods simply to appear worthy of it? There has never been a greater deed; and whoever is born after us — for the sake of this deed he will belong to a higher history than all history hitherto. (1974 [1887], 181)

Virtually all of human history and thought has been grounded on the premise of gods. Atheism alone has not been responsible for the gradual disintegration of this ground; rather, Atheism is the finished product, not the process. Reason, natural investigation (*i.e.* science), cultural comparison (*i.e.* anthropology), religious diversity, and other world-shaking and world-dissolving forces and discoveries have slowly but inexorably chipped away at the ground of god(s). Einstein's relativity theory, for instance, while hardly atheistic, poses the question 'Whither are we moving? Is there still any up and down?' As our *logos* has expanded, our *mythos* has become more unsustainable. We find all of our previous beliefs — which were not beliefs but *certainties* — failing us. No wonder Nietzsche spoke so often of vertigo, of nausea, of the experience of peering over into the abyss.

Ridding the world of gods is truly a heroic doing. There has never been a greater deed. But, as Nietzsche knows, there is a burden and an obligation that comes with it. We cannot sit back and say, "Oops, no more god(s)" and expect the world to welcome the news. Nietzsche's madman discovered he had come too soon, and perhaps even after two thousand years of Christianity and five thousand years of recorded religious history we come too soon. Perhaps we have to ask ourselves, what do we have to offer in its place?

The answer, I hope, is not another religion, or even another *mythos*, as we considered above. I do not want to advocate a Marxist reduction of religion to 'the heart of a heartless world,' because religion has always been, *contra* Campbell and Gould and Smith and all the similar separate-worlders, more than heart. It has also been mind and conscience and action and artifact. That has been the challenge to religion — to hold on to its heart while it lost its mind, to keep hope and value and morality alive while it was being deprived of the factual and empirical grounds that made those heartful elements real and worthy. It has succeeded, to a degree, by a variety of strategies: detaching the heart from the mind by separating value from fact; moderating the scope of its claims by retreating before the advances of science and reason; or making a last stand for the failing factuality of religion by embracing fundamentalism.

But there is a challenge in this for Atheism too, which has been, so far, predominantly an affair of the mind. Humans are not solely or perhaps even mostly rational creatures but also emotional and social ones. Some of us can and do live quite comfortably 'from the neck up,' in the mental world of debate and logic. Of course, in our private lives we love and laugh like anyone. But the Atheism that we offer to the world is noticeably lacking in love and (beneficent) laughter. Sure, we laugh at religion, often in ridicule, but non-Atheists and even some Atheists just find this offensive and off-putting. This is where religion has shined, if nowhere else — in giving humans a whole-body experience, in engaging all of our capacities (sometimes even the brain), in allowing us to sing and dance and wax poetic and bond. Nietzsche, who was a wise man, once wrote that evil men have no songs. I doubt that many Theists have read Nietzsche, but they might viscerally distrust Atheism for having no songs of its own.

Because my Atheist companions are literalists like me, let me affirm that I am not talking about actually writing songs or choreographing dances or making other works of art. *The question is not what kind of art Atheists would make but rather what kind of Atheism artists would make.* What if we Atheists were not just debaters but creators? I do not know what this complete, creative, affirmative, 'holistic' Atheism would look like — or even whether it is really feasible — but I do know that purely rational philosophies appeal only to the rational few. If we want a truly 'popular' Atheism, an Atheism 'of the people,' it will have to convey the value, even the beauty and wonder, of disenchantment. I entreat my fellow Atheists to spend some time trying to craft a vision of the future world and life of Atheism — that is, as much as is possible, and desirable, to begin the work of Nietzsche's child in imagining a more complete, human, and natural Atheism to which we can some day say "Yes!"

BIBLIOGRAPHY

Alley, Robert S., ed. 1985. *James Madison on Religious Liberty*. Amherst, New York: Prometheus Books.

———. 1999. *The Constitution and Religion: Leading Supreme Court Cases on Church and State*. Amherst, New York: Prometheus Books.

Ammerman, Nancy T. 1991. "North American Protestant Fundamentalism." *In* Marty, Martin, and R. Scott Appleby, eds. *Fundamentalisms Observed*. Chicago: The University of Chicago Press, 1–65.

Anderson, Benedict. 1983. *Imagined Communities: Reflections of the Origin and Spread of Nationalism*. London: Verso.

Aran, Gideon. 1991. "Jewish Zionist Fundamentalism: The Bloc of the Faithful in Israel (Gush Emunim)." *In* Marty, Martin, and R. Scott Appleby, eds. *Fundamentalisms Observed*. Chicago: The University of Chicago Press, 265–344.

Armstrong, Karen. 2000. *The Battle for God*. New York: Ballantine Books.

Barbour, Ian G. 1997. *Religion and Science: Historical and Contemporary Issues*. New York: HarperCollins Publishers.

Barker, Dan. 1993. "Evangelistic Atheism: Leading Believers Astray." Http://www.ffrf.org/fttoday/Back/evangel.html.

Barrow, John, and Frank Tipler. 1988. *The Anthropic Cosmological Principle*. New York: Oxford University Press.

Behe, Michael. 1996. *Darwin's Black Box*. New York: Free Press.

Borowitz, Eugene B. 1990. "The Enduring Truth of Religious Liberalism." *In* Cohen, Norman J., ed. *The Fundamentalist Phenomenon: A View from Within, A Response from Without*. Grand Rapids: William B. Eerdmans Publishing Company, 230–47.

Campbell, Joseph. 2001. *Thou Art That: Transforming Religious Metaphor*. Novato, California: New World Library.

Capra, Fritjof. 1991. *The Tao of Physics: An Exploration of the Parallels Between Modern Physics and Eastern Mysticism.* Boston: Shambhala Publications.

Davies, Paul. 1993. *The Mind of God.* New York: Simon and Schuster.

Dawkins, Richard. 1986. *The Blind Watchmaker: Why the Evidence of Evolution Reveals a Universe without Design.* New York: W.W. Norton & Company.

———. 1996. *Climbing Mount Improbable.* New York: W.W. Norton & Company.

Dunn, Richard S. 1970. *The Age of Religious Wars, 1559–1689.* New York: W.W. Norton & Company.

Edis, Taner. 2002. *The Ghost in the Universe: God in the Light of Modern Science.* Amherst, New York: Prometheus Books.

Eller, Jack David. 1999. *From Culture to Ethnicity to Conflict: An Anthropological Perspective on International Ethnic Conflict.* Ann Arbor: University of Michigan Press.

Feldman, Stephen M. 1997. *Please Don't Wish Me a Merry Christmas: A Critical History of the Separation of Church and State.* New York: New York University Press.

Feuerbach, Ludwig. 1957 [1841]. *The Essence of Christianity.* George Eliot, trans. New York: Harper & Row, Publishers.

Flew, Antony. 1984. *God, Freedom, and Immortality: A Critical Analysis.* Buffalo, New York: Prometheus Books.

Freke, Timothy, and Peter Gandy. 1999. *The Jesus Mysteries: Was the 'Original Jesus' a Pagan God?* New York: Harmony Books.

Friedman, John Block. 2000. *The Monstrous Races in Medieval Art and Thought.* Syracuse: Syracuse University Press.

Gaustad, Edwin S. 1999. *Church and State in America.* New York: Oxford University Press.

Geertz, Clifford. 1973. *The Interpretation of Cultures.* New York: Basic Books.

Gold, Daniel. 1991. "Organized Hinduisms: From Vedic Truth to Hindu Nation." *In* Marty, Martin, and R. Scott Appleby, eds. *Fundamentalisms Observed*. Chicago: The University of Chicago Press, 531–93.

Goodwin, Judge Alfred T. 2002. Ninth Circuit Court Decision on *Michael Newdow v. US Congress; United States of America; George W. Bush, President of the United States; State of California; Elk Grove Unified School District; David W. Gordon, Superintendent EGUSD; Sacramento City Unified School District; Jim Sweeney, Superintendent SCUSD*. 9105–92136.

Gould, Stephen Jay. 1999. *Rock of Ages: Science and Religion in the Fullness of Life*. New York: The Ballantine Publishing Group.

Green, Ruth Hurmence. 1982. *The Born Again Skeptic's Guide to the Bible*. Madison, Wisconsin: Freedom from Religion Foundation.

Hatch, Nathan O. 1989. *The Democratization of American Christianity*. New Haven: Yale University Press.

Horgan, John. 2003. *Rational Mysticism: Dispatches from the Border Between Science and Spirituality*. Boston: Houghton Mifflin Company.

Jastrow, Robert C. 1992. *God and the Astronomers*. New York: W.W. Norton & Company.

John Paul II. 1996. "Truth Cannot Contradict Truth." Http://www.newadvent.org/docs/jp2tc.htm.

Jordan, Michael. 1993. *Encyclopedia of Gods: Over 2,500 Deities of the World*. New York: Facts on File, Inc.

Just, Bob. 2002. "Amendment: Separation of Atheism and State." Http://www.worldnetdaily.com/news/article.asp? ARTICLE_ID=28288.

Kennedy, James. 1997. *Skeptics Answered: Handling Tough Questions About the Christian Faith*. Sisters, Oregon: Multnomah Publishers, Inc.

Lederman, Leon, and Dick Teresi. 1994. *The God Particle: If the Universe is the Answer, What is the Question?* New York: Dell Publishing.

Lett, James. 2001. "A Field Guide to Critical Thinking." Http://www.csicop.org/si/9012/critical-thinking.html. July 27, 2001.

Levy, Leonard W. 1993. *Blasphemy: Verbal Offense against the Sacred, from Moses to Salman Rushdie.* New York: Alfred A. Knopf.

Mackie, John L. 1982. *The Miracle of Theism: Arguments for and against the Existence of God.* Oxford: Clarendon Press.

Maloney, H. Newton. 1988. "The Psychology of Proselytism." *In* Marty, Martin, and Frederick Greenspahn, eds. *Pushing the Faith: Proselytism and Civility in a Pluralistic World.* New York: Crossroad, 125–42.

Marsden, George M. 1990. "Defining American Fundamentalism." *In* Cohen, Norman J., ed. *The Fundamentalist Phenomenon: A View from Within, A Response from Without.* Grand Rapids: William B. Eerdmans Publishing Company, 22–37.

Martin, Michael. 1990. *Atheism: A Philosophical Justification.* Philadelphia: Temple University Press.

Marty, Martin, and R. Scott Appleby, eds. 1991. *Fundamentalisms Observed.* Chicago: The University of Chicago Press.

Marty, Martin, and Frederick Greenspahn, eds. 1988. *Pushing the Faith: Proselytism and Civility in a Pluralistic World.* New York: Crossroad.

McKinsey, C. Dennis. 1995. *The Encyclopedia of Biblical Errancy.* Amherst, New York: Prometheus Books.

Miller, Ed. L., ed. 1970. *Classical Statements on Faith and Reason.* New York: Random House.

Miller, Kenneth. 1999. *Finding Darwin's God: A Scientist's Search for Common Ground Between God and Evolution.* New York: Cliff Street Books.

Newberg, Andrew, Eugene d'Aquili, and Vince Rause. 2002. *Why God Won't Go Away: Brain Science and the Biology of Belief.* New York: Ballantine Books.

Nielsen, Niels C., Jr. 1993. *Fundamentalism, Mythos, and World Religions*. Albany: State University of New York Press.

Nietzsche, Friedrich. 1974 [1887]. *The Gay Science*. Walter Kaufman, trans. New York: Vintage Books.

Novak, Michael. 2002. "The Atheist Civil-Liberty Union?" Http://www.nationalreview.com/novak/novak071202.asp.

Ostow, Mortimer. 1990. "The Fundamentalist Phenomenon: A Psychological Perspective." *In* Cohen, Norman J., ed. *The Fundamentalist Phenomenon: A View from Within, A Response from Without*. Grand Rapids: William B. Eerdmans Publishing Company, 99–125.

Pagels, Elaine. 1995. *The Origin of Satan*. New York: Random House.

Persinger, Michael. 1987. *Neuropsychological Bases of God Beliefs*. Westport, Connecticut: Praeger Publications.

Pigliucci, Massimo. 2000. "Personal Gods, Deism, and the Limits of Skepticism." *Skeptic*, v8, n2, 38–45.

Pinnock, Clark H. 1990. "Defining American Fundamentalism: A Response." *In* Cohen, Norman J., ed. *The Fundamentalist Phenomenon: A View from Within, A Response from Without*. Grand Rapids: William B. Eerdmans Publishing Company, 38–55.

Porteus, Skip. 1991. *Jesus Doesn't Live Here Anymore: From Fundamentalist to Freedom Writer*. Buffalo, New York: Prometheus Books.

Rapoport, David C. 1989. "Terrorism and the Messiah: An Ancient Experience and Some Modern Parallels." *In* Rapoport, David C., and Yonah Alexander, eds. *The Morality of Terrorism: Religious and Secular Justifications*. New York: Columbia University Press, 13–42.

Shermer, Michael. 2000. *How We Believe: The Search for God in an Age of Science*. New York: W.H. Freeman and Company.

Slotkin, James S., ed. 1965. *Readings in Early Anthropology*. London: Methuen & Co. Ltd.

Smith, George. 1989. *Atheism: The Case Against God*. Amherst, New York: Prometheus Books.

Smith, Huston. 2001. *Why Religion Matters: The Fate of the Human Spirit in an Age of Disbelief*. New York: HarperCollins Publishers.

Smith, Ken. 1995. *Ken's Guide to the Bible*. New York: Blast Books.

Stanner, W. E. H. 1979. *White Man Got No Dreaming: Essays 1938–1973*. Canberra: Australian National University Press.

Stenger, Victor. 1988. *Not by Design: The Origin of the Universe*. Buffalo, New York: Prometheus Books.

———. 1995. *The Unconscious Quantum: Metaphysics in Modern Physics and Cosmology*. Amherst, New York: Prometheus Books.

Swinburne, Richard. 1998. *Providence and the Problem of Evil*. Oxford: Oxford University Press.

Tipler, Frank. 1995. *The Physics of Immortality: Modern Cosmology, God and the Resurrection of the Dead*. New York: Doubleday.

Versluys, Jim. 2001. "Why Most Atheists Will Never Join an Atheist Organization." *Positive Atheism*, v3, n7, July, 4.

Voll, John O. 1991. "Fundamentalism in the Sunni Arab World: Egypt and the Sudan." *In* Marty, Martin, and R. Scott Appleby, eds. *Fundamentalisms Observed*. Chicago: The University of Chicago Press, 345–402.

Walker, Cliff. 2000, "Why Advocate for Individual Atheists?" http://www.positiveatheism.org/mail/eml8800.htm.

———. 2003. "Introduction to Activist Atheism." Http://www. positiveatheism.org/faq/faq1111.htm.

Wheelwright, Philip, ed. 1966. *The Presocratics*. New York: The Odyssey Press, Inc.